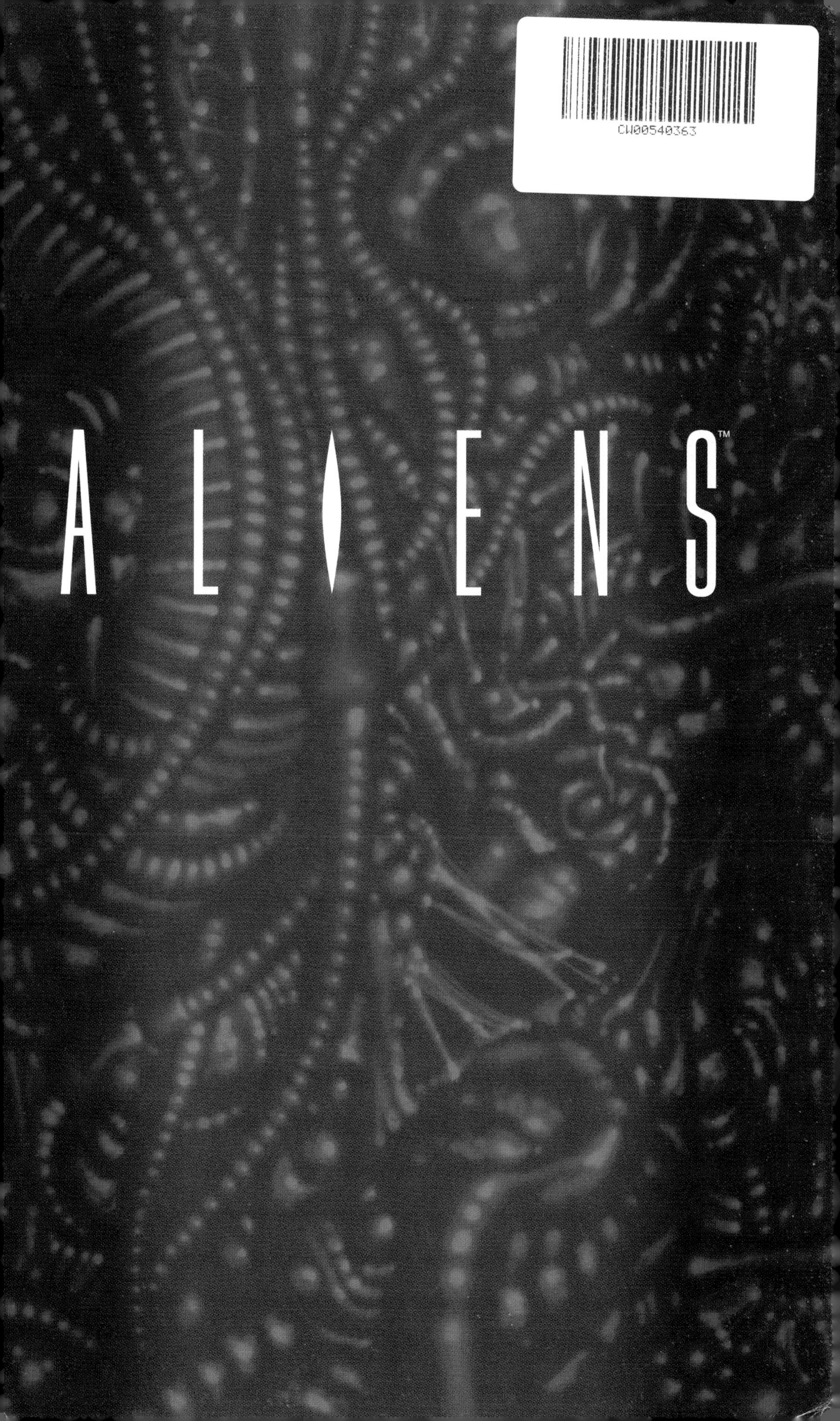
ALIENS™

publisher**Mike Richardson**

series editor**Diana Schutz**
collection editor**Lynn Adair**
collection designer**Teena Gores**
book design manager**Brian Gogolin**

special thanks to**Cindy Irwin at Twentieth Century Fox** +
Steve Perry + **Den Beauvais** + **Jamie S. Rich** + **Monty Sheldon**
+ **Rich Powers** + **Art Knight** + **Dave Nestelle** + **Cary Porter** +
Chris Chalenor + **Perry McNamee** + **Lisa Stamp** + **Jason Hvam**
+ **Stuart Hiner** and **Margaret Froese**

inspired by**The original Alien designs of H.R. Giger**

This book collects issues one through four of the Dark Horse
comic-book series **Aliens™: Earth War** and was formerly
collected as **Aliens™: Earth War**.

Published by
Dark Horse Comics, Inc.
10956 SE Main Street
Milwaukie, OR 97222

First edition: December 1996
ISBN: 1-56971-190-9

1	2	3	4	5	6	7	8	9	10

Printed in Canada

ALIENS™

FEMALE WAR

story Mark Verheiden

art Sam Kieth

cover John Bolton

lettering Pat Brosseau

DARK HORSE COMICS®

Interview with John Bolton

When John Bolton was approached to do the introduction for this trade paperback, he wasn't convinced about committing his thoughts to paper. As a compromise, he agreed to this interview, conducted over the telephone with Jamie S. Rich, one of the assistants on this collection.

John Bolton: In an effort to make this introduction more interesting, I am going to conduct the interview on the side of a building, twenty stories up. If it fails to be interesting, I'm going to jump.

Jamie S. Rich: That's because you've never done an introduction before. That's why they've never been interesting.

JB: Mind you, having said that, maybe you'll say it's not interesting just so I *will* jump, so you won't have to pay me the money you promised me.

JSR: I'd want you to finish the covers you have left first.

JB: Okay, so it's a question of priorities . . . Where should we start?

JSR: Well, wasn't doing the covers for the *Aliens: Earth War* [re-titled *Female War* for this edition] series your first professional *Aliens* job?

JB: Oh, you're going to be really boring then, Jamie.

JSR: Just to get started.

JB: Yes, that was my first Aliens painting, which is pretty scary if you go way back to the point where I saw *Alien* in 1979. It was a really good movie, and I was inspired by both Ridley Scott's direction and Giger's Alien designs.

JSR: What elements of the film do you feel you took with you into your other work?

JB: It's difficult to say. It touched on some things I was already dabbling in. Just the idea of an amalgam of flesh and metal but in my case, a more steam-pumped version. I was using less of a highly finished technique than Giger was using. It tapped into something that already interested me, and at that point, when *Alien* first came out, there wasn't much chance to explore these things. I did sketches and drawings for myself that were never published.

JSR: So when the *Aliens* comics came out, did you pursue the *Earth War* job, or did Dark Horse approach you?

JB: Dark Horse came to me. I met Mike Richardson . . . actually, I *didn't* meet Mike Richardson at a convention. I went to his table, and he wasn't there. I spoke to Randy Stradley. Mike rang me a couple of weeks later. He knew of my work and was sorry he had missed me. We talked about maybe doing some stuff for Dark Horse, and we touched on the fact that he was going to be doing *Aliens* comics. He asked me if I wanted to do covers, and that was it. I couldn't

wait. I had been greatly inspired by Giger's Alien. You can go see a horror/science-fiction movie, and you don't necessarily come away inspired. I didn't feel like drawing Robbie the Robot, for instance, after seeing *Forbidden Planet*. Dark Horse gave me a perfect opportunity for me to do what I wanted to do.

JSR: This was in 1990, at least eleven years since you had first seen *Alien*.

JB: That's right. As I said, I had done some paintings for myself, but at that point, there was not the opportunity to do it elsewhere. Everything was in its infancy, certainly as far as painting and comics were concerned . . . I think I'm going to jump anyway, Jamie [*laughs*].

JSR: Now, now. It's been six years since that *Earth War* series, and you're back with the creatures again. What keeps you going while doing these covers? What continues to intrigue you about Aliens?

JB: I guess there's something about the purity of the design that I still find inspiring. I think the films are still strong enough to maintain that interest. The second film, *Aliens*, was clever because it was so different from the first, but had I seen the second one before the first, I don't think I would have been as inspired; the Aliens were merely cannon fodder. It was an all-action, shoot-'em-up movie.

JSR: *Aliens* didn't have the mystery surrounding it. We'd seen the Alien.

JB: Yes, I agree. What I enjoyed about the film was that everything was equal — the Alien was as good as the story, the characters were as good as the Alien, and so on, and so forth. I liked the fact that the characters seemed to be equal at first, and then they all developed in their own ways, especially Sigourney Weaver [Ripley] at the end. I didn't particularly notice her as an exceptional character in the beginning. It's only as the story progressed, particularly toward the end, that she really dominated the film as much as the Alien.

JSR: You mentioned earlier that you were inspired by the direction of Ridley Scott. Didn't you meet him at some point?

JB: Blimey, that was clever, Jamie [*laughs*]. Wow, you read your notes. I'm impressed. Yeah, there was somebody who was promoting the film whom I happened to meet and who also knew Ridley Scott. At that point, Ridley was going to direct *Dune*. I met up with him, and I remember it being an incredibly cold afternoon and wearing a thick jumper. I walked into a hot office, so I spent most of the afternoon perspiring, and I'm sure he thought it was because I was in awe.

JSR: Wasn't it? [*Laughs*].

JB: No, I was dressed appropriately for the exterior but not for the interior. Anyway, we talked about *Dune* and what his plan for it was, how he saw it. There was a chance I was going to do storyboards and maybe develop something more than that, but for whatever reason, he pulled out at the last minute. I think it was because he thought the film was too complicated, but that's putting words in his mouth, and I'm not quite sure if that's true or not. What's ironic is that previous to him, it was Alexandro Jodorowsky and Giger who were going to do *Dune*, and I am now going to be doing a graphic novel with Jodorowsky.

JSR: Were you aware of Giger's connection to Dune at that point?

JB: It was only when I saw the Giger collection, *The Necronomicon*, that I saw the *Dune* conceptual work. Jodorowsky and I met earlier this year, in about March or April '96, and we talked about *Dune*. But I hadn't seen any of his work. It's ironic because I'd had a videotape of his film, *Santa Sangre*, which I lent to a friend. I hadn't even seen it. Then someone walked off with it, so I *still* haven't seen it, and I'm having a hard time finding it.

JSR: Have you had any contact with Giger?

JB: No. Although, this is an introduction, and when anyone does an introduction, they tend to use the opportunity to promote their other work . . . I have a fan club and a fan-club magazine. The third issue comes out in January. I just think it's so weird the way things connect. It's some sort of strange family tree or something. Robert Birnbock, who runs the fan club, is in contact with Giger, and he's giving an interview for the third issue of the fan-club magazine.

JSR: Hopefully he won't trash you or anything.

JB: Who cares? I've been trashed by Giger. We can put that on the cover: "John Bolton Trashed by Giger!" So, anyway, that's an incredible coincidence . . . and while I didn't get to work with Ridley Scott, I actually feel at some point I'm going to. I don't know why. I just have a feeling.

JSR: What's your hope for the future of *Aliens*, either as a concept or something you work on?

JB: I just hope the fourth film is good . . . I think the only thing that really interests me is the freedom I get in working for Dark Horse, especially in developing these trade-paperback covers. I don't particularly like working for the movie industry. I don't find it that satisfying. Maybe for two or three weeks a year as a storyboard artist, but that's it. What I liked about doing the covers for the trade paperbacks, the "remastered" series, was coming up with a design element that I tried to maintain through all of them.

JSR: They certainly seem to be your most inspired Aliens pieces. Is there anything else your readers should know?

JB: I don't do drugs [*laughs*]. Sorry, about that, kids. I have no idea. I've stopped listening to rap [*laughs*]. It's just repeating itself . . . Jamie, shall I jump, or shall I stay?

JSR: It was relatively interesting. It was dangerous and on the edge.

JB: In keeping with the theme of this interview.

JSR: You're really just a boring guy who sits in his room and paints.

JB: Thank you, Jamie. I appreciate that.

Bolton's *Aliens: Earth War*
first-edition cover art

ALIENS

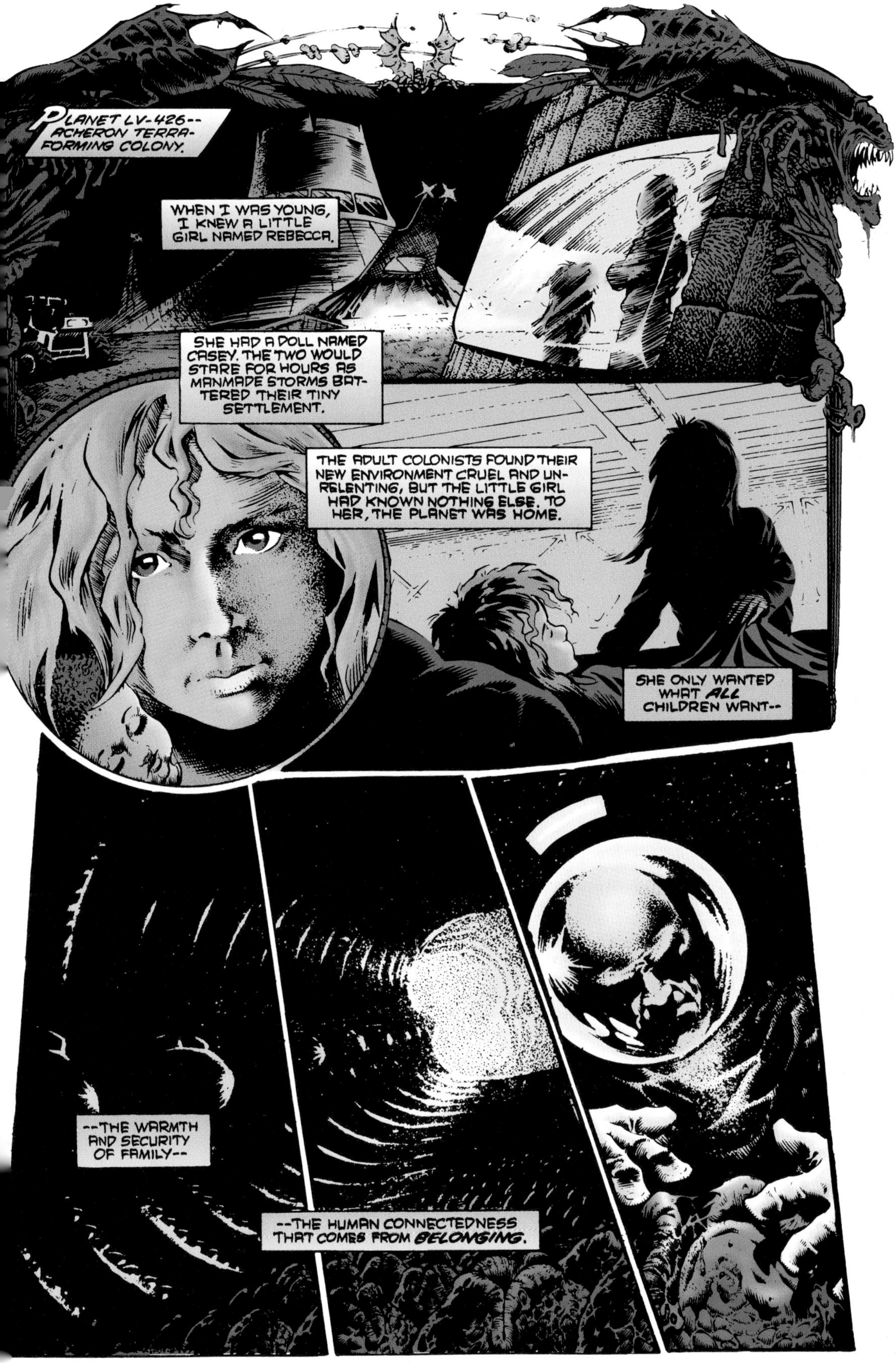
PLANET LV-426-- ACHERON TERRA-FORMING COLONY.
WHEN I WAS YOUNG, I KNEW A LITTLE GIRL NAMED REBECCA.
SHE HAD A DOLL NAMED CASEY. THE TWO WOULD STARE FOR HOURS AS MANMADE STORMS BATTERED THEIR TINY SETTLEMENT.
THE ADULT COLONISTS FOUND THEIR NEW ENVIRONMENT CRUEL AND UNRELENTING, BUT THE LITTLE GIRL HAD KNOWN NOTHING ELSE. TO HER, THE PLANET WAS HOME.
SHE ONLY WANTED WHAT ALL CHILDREN WANT--
--THE WARMTH AND SECURITY OF FAMILY--
--THE HUMAN CONNECTEDNESS THAT COMES FROM BELONGING.

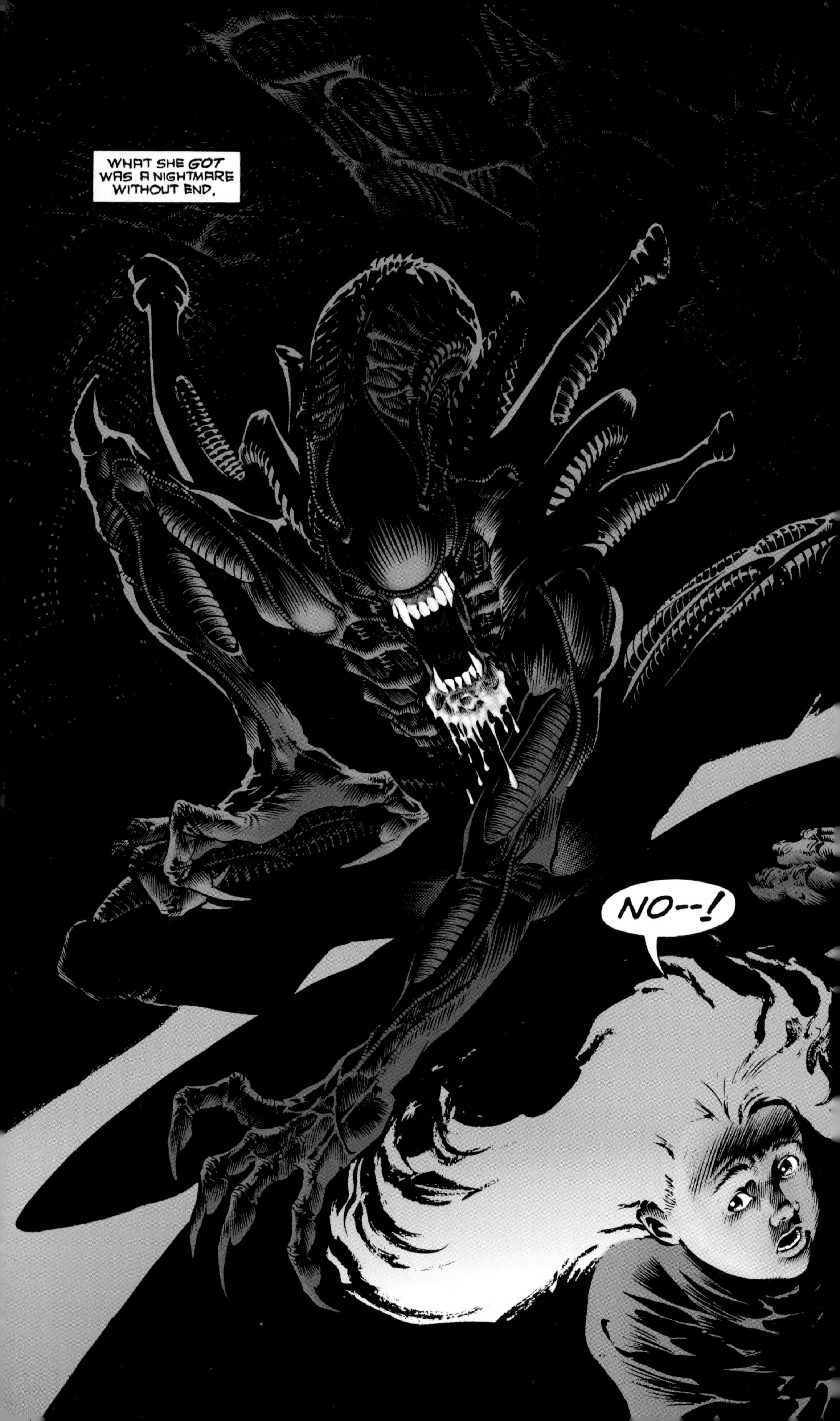
WHAT SHE GOT WAS A NIGHTMARE WITHOUT END.
NO--!

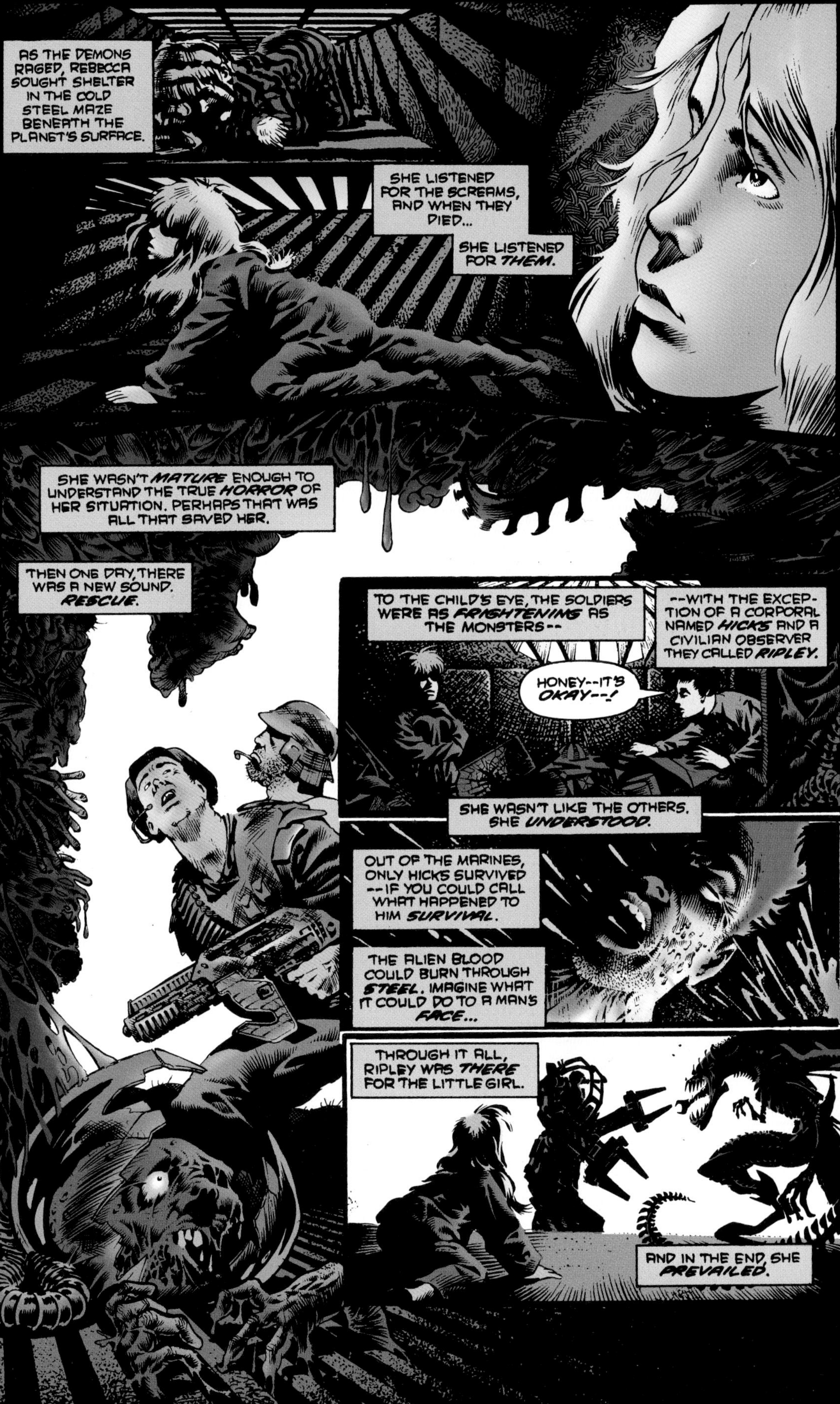
AS THE DEMONS RAGED, REBECCA SOUGHT SHELTER IN THE COLD STEEL MAZE BENEATH THE PLANET'S SURFACE.
SHE LISTENED FOR THE SCREAMS, AND WHEN THEY DIED...
SHE LISTENED FOR THEM.
SHE WASN'T MATURE ENOUGH TO UNDERSTAND THE TRUE HORROR OF HER SITUATION. PERHAPS THAT WAS ALL THAT SAVED HER.
THEN ONE DAY, THERE WAS A NEW SOUND. RESCUE.
TO THE CHILD'S EYE, THE SOLDIERS WERE AS FRIGHTENING AS THE MONSTERS--
--WITH THE EXCEPTION OF A CORPORAL NAMED HICKS AND A CIVILIAN OBSERVER THEY CALLED RIPLEY.
HONEY--IT'S OKAY--!
SHE WASN'T LIKE THE OTHERS. SHE UNDERSTOOD.
OUT OF THE MARINES, ONLY HICKS SURVIVED --IF YOU COULD CALL WHAT HAPPENED TO HIM SURVIVAL.
THE ALIEN BLOOD COULD BURN THROUGH STEEL. IMAGINE WHAT IT COULD DO TO A MAN'S FACE...
THROUGH IT ALL, RIPLEY WAS THERE FOR THE LITTLE GIRL.
AND IN THE END, SHE PREVAILED.

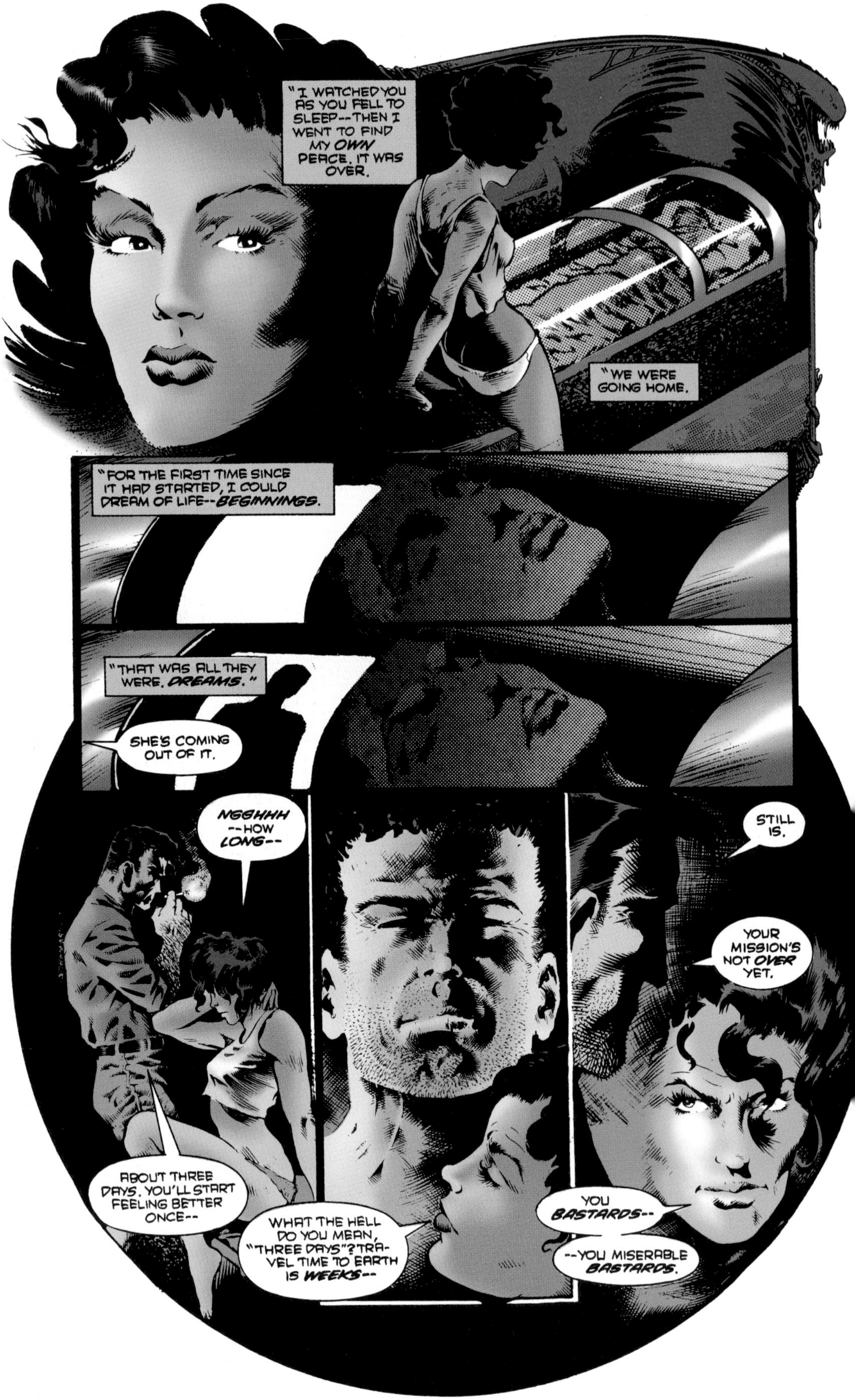
"I WATCHED YOU AS YOU FELL TO SLEEP--THEN I WENT TO FIND MY OWN PEACE. IT WAS OVER.
"WE WERE GOING HOME.
"FOR THE FIRST TIME SINCE IT HAD STARTED, I COULD DREAM OF LIFE--BEGINNINGS.
"THAT WAS ALL THEY WERE. DREAMS."
SHE'S COMING OUT OF IT.
NGGHHH --HOW LONG--
ABOUT THREE DAYS. YOU'LL START FEELING BETTER ONCE--
WHAT THE HELL DO YOU MEAN, "THREE DAYS"? TRAVEL TIME TO EARTH IS WEEKS--
STILL IS.
YOUR MISSION'S NOT OVER YET.
YOU BASTARDS--
--YOU MISERABLE BASTARDS.

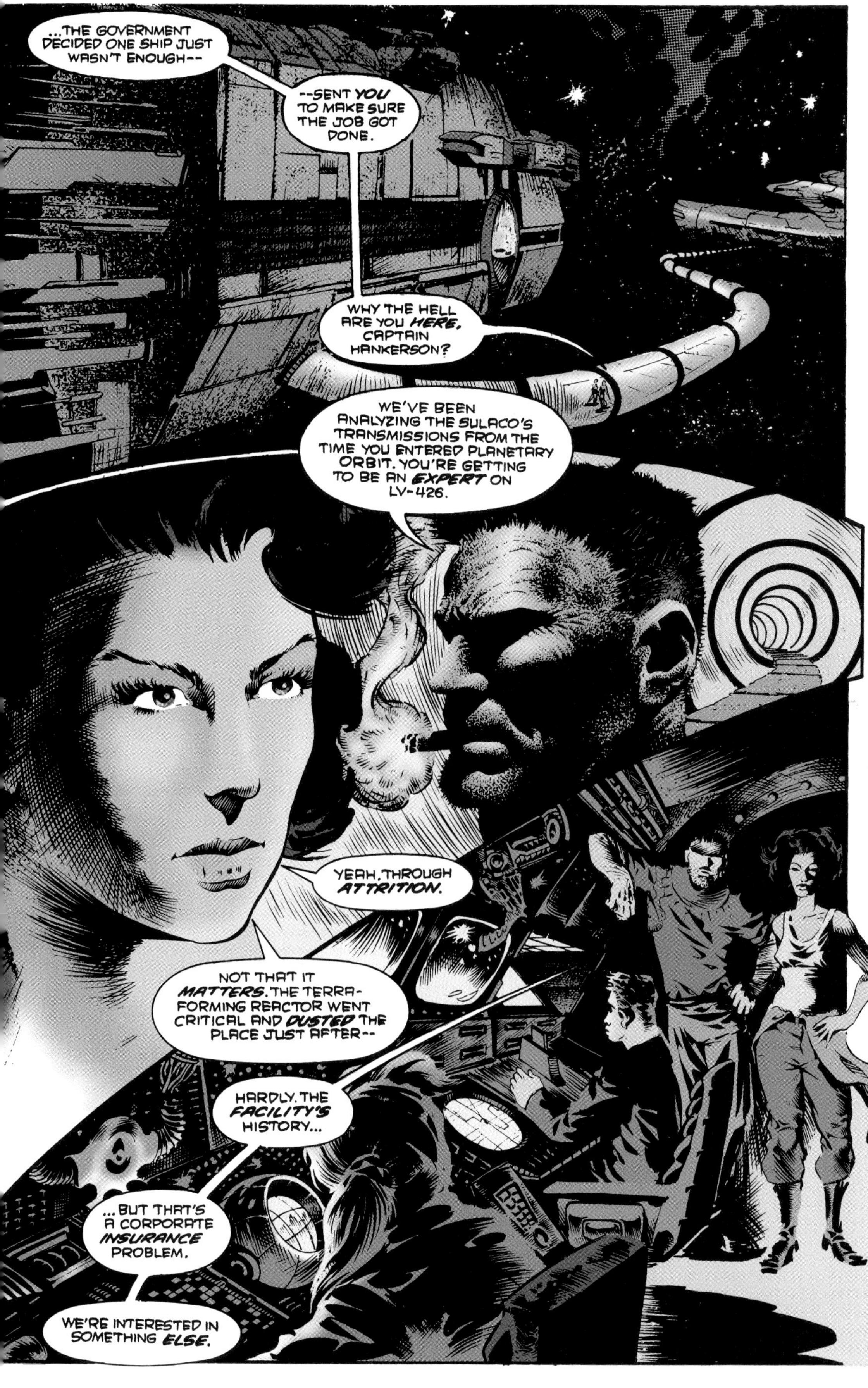
...THE GOVERNMENT DECIDED ONE SHIP JUST WASN'T ENOUGH--
--SENT *YOU* TO MAKE SURE THE JOB GOT DONE.
WHY THE HELL ARE YOU *HERE,* CAPTAIN HANKERSON?
WE'VE BEEN ANALYZING THE SULACO'S TRANSMISSIONS FROM THE TIME YOU ENTERED PLANETARY ORBIT. YOU'RE GETTING TO BE AN *EXPERT* ON LV-426.
YEAH, THROUGH *ATTRITION.*
NOT THAT IT *MATTERS.* THE TERRA-FORMING REACTOR WENT CRITICAL AND *DUSTED* THE PLACE JUST AFTER--
HARDLY. THE *FACILITY'S* HISTORY...
...BUT THAT'S A CORPORATE *INSURANCE* PROBLEM.
WE'RE INTERESTED IN SOMETHING *ELSE.*

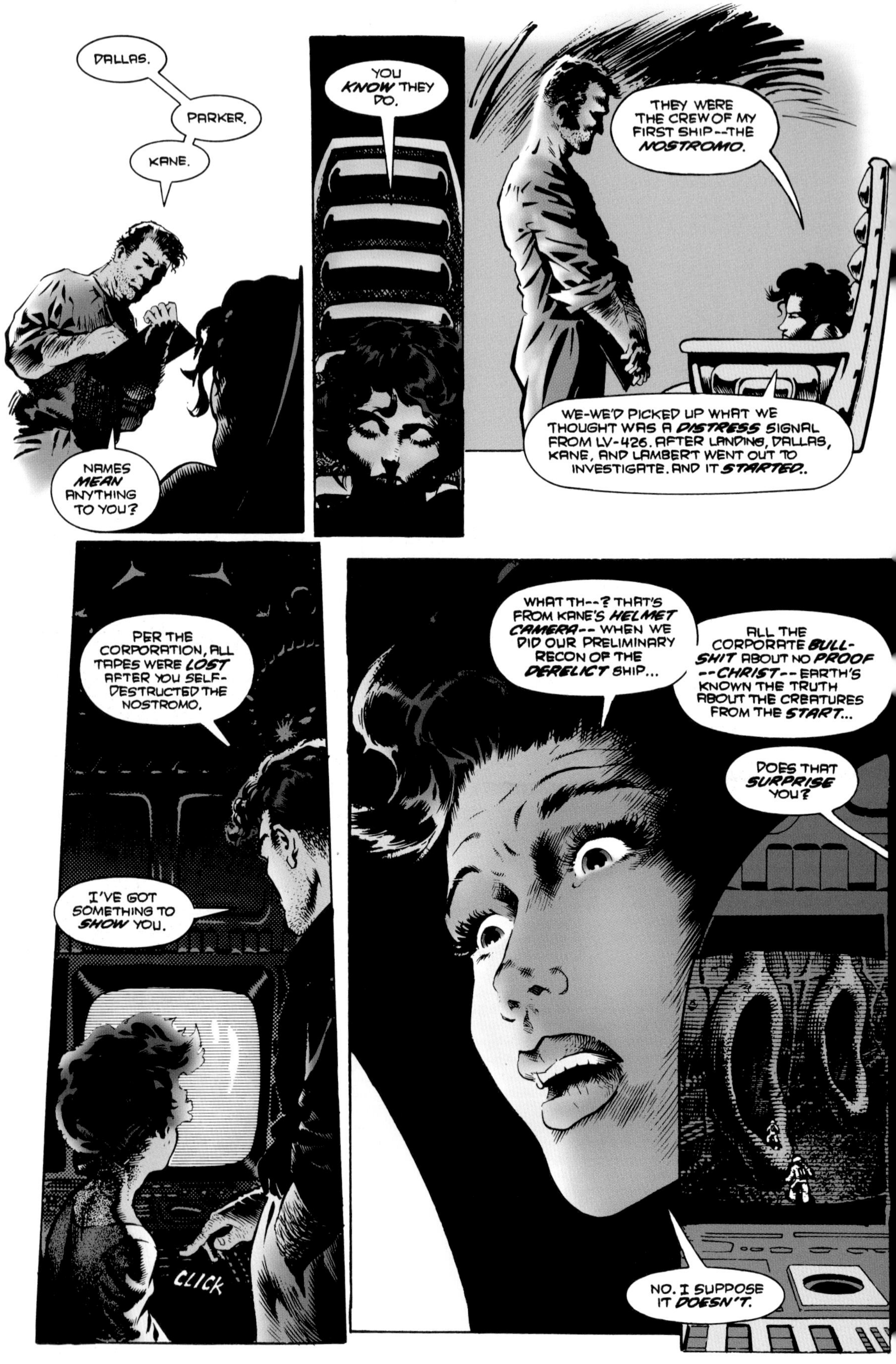
DALLAS.
PARKER.
KANE.
NAMES MEAN ANYTHING TO YOU?
YOU KNOW THEY DO.
THEY WERE THE CREW OF MY FIRST SHIP--THE NOSTROMO.
WE-WE'D PICKED UP WHAT WE THOUGHT WAS A DISTRESS SIGNAL FROM LV-426. AFTER LANDING, DALLAS, KANE, AND LAMBERT WENT OUT TO INVESTIGATE. AND IT STARTED.
PER THE CORPORATION, ALL TAPES WERE LOST AFTER YOU SELF-DESTRUCTED THE NOSTROMO.
I'VE GOT SOMETHING TO SHOW YOU.
CLICK
WHAT TH--? THAT'S FROM KANE'S HELMET CAMERA-- WHEN WE DID OUR PRELIMINARY RECON OF THE DERELICT SHIP...
ALL THE CORPORATE BULL-SHIT ABOUT NO PROOF --CHRIST-- EARTH'S KNOWN THE TRUTH ABOUT THE CREATURES FROM THE START...
DOES THAT SURPRISE YOU?
NO. I SUPPOSE IT DOESN'T.

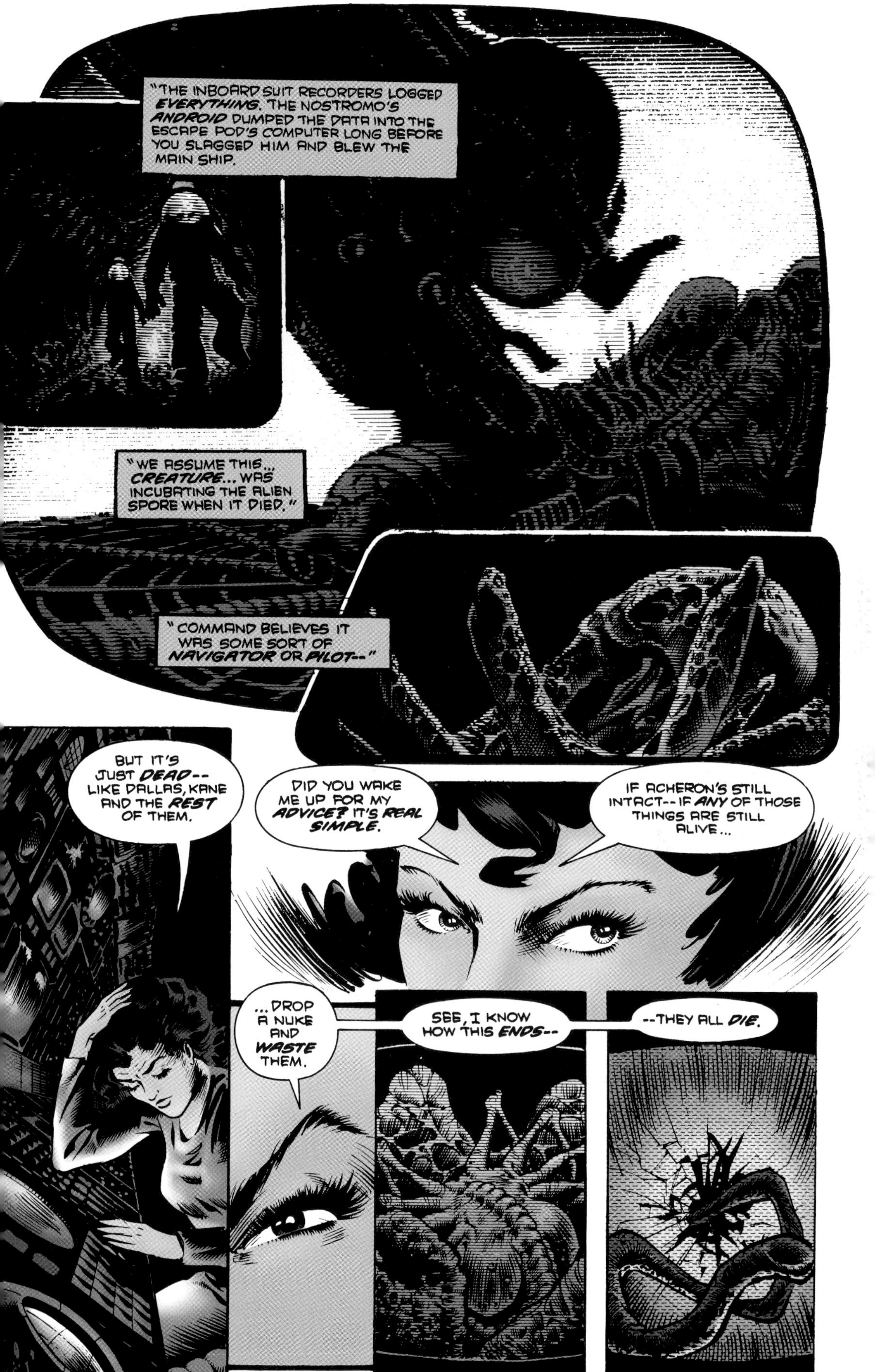
"THE INBOARD SUIT RECORDERS LOGGED EVERYTHING. THE NOSTROMO'S ANDROID DUMPED THE DATA INTO THE ESCAPE POD'S COMPUTER LONG BEFORE YOU SLAGGED HIM AND BLEW THE MAIN SHIP.
"WE ASSUME THIS... CREATURE... WAS INCUBATING THE ALIEN SPORE WHEN IT DIED."
"COMMAND BELIEVES IT WAS SOME SORT OF NAVIGATOR OR PILOT--"
BUT IT'S JUST DEAD-- LIKE DALLAS, KANE AND THE REST OF THEM.
DID YOU WAKE ME UP FOR MY ADVICE? IT'S REAL SIMPLE.
IF ACHERON'S STILL INTACT-- IF ANY OF THOSE THINGS ARE STILL ALIVE...
...DROP A NUKE AND WASTE THEM.
SEE, I KNOW HOW THIS ENDS--
--THEY ALL DIE.

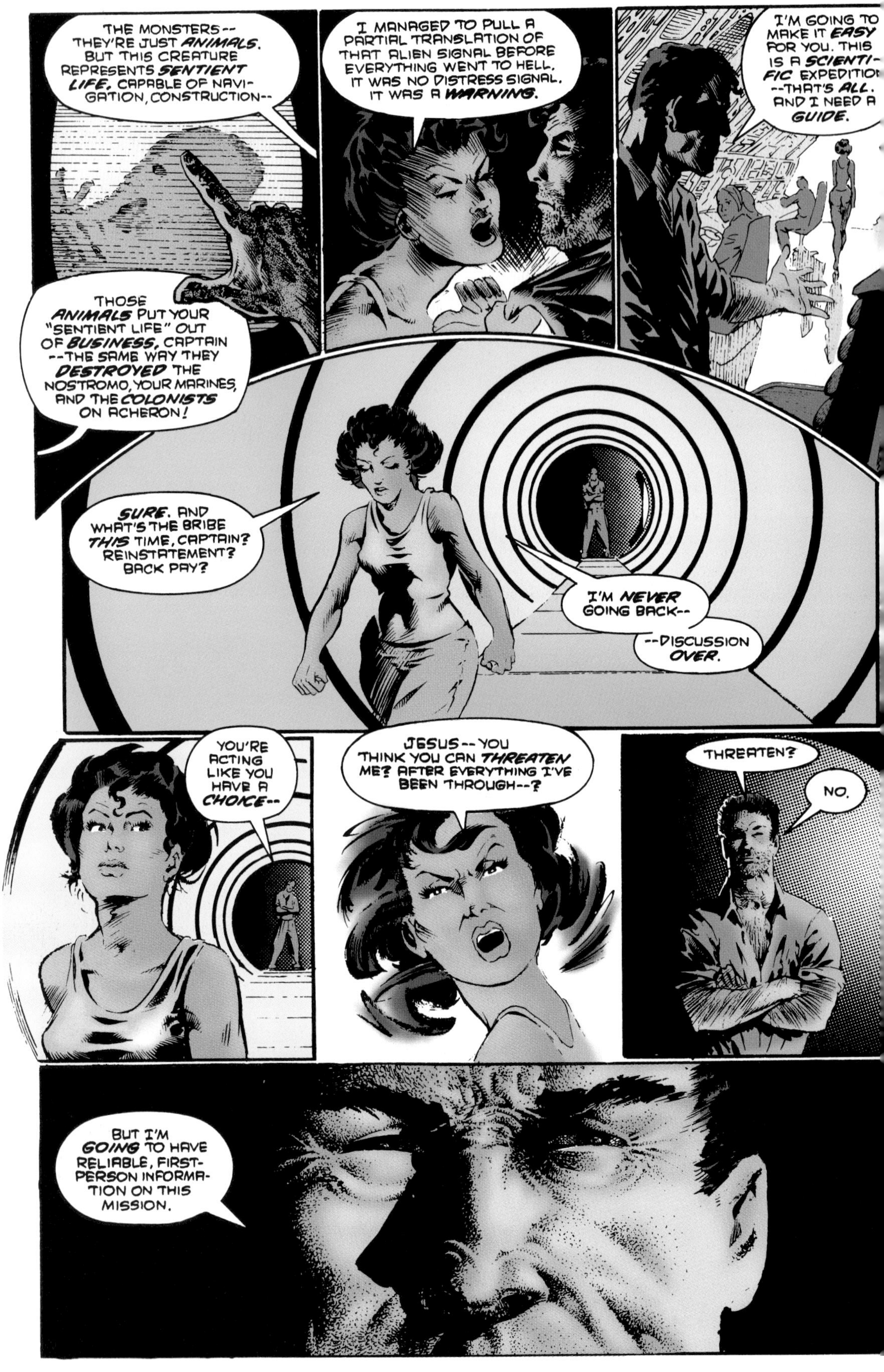
THE MONSTERS-- THEY'RE JUST ANIMALS. BUT THIS CREATURE REPRESENTS SENTIENT LIFE. CAPABLE OF NAVIGATION, CONSTRUCTION--
THOSE ANIMALS PUT YOUR "SENTIENT LIFE" OUT OF BUSINESS, CAPTAIN --THE SAME WAY THEY DESTROYED THE NOSTROMO, YOUR MARINES, AND THE COLONISTS ON ACHERON!
I MANAGED TO PULL A PARTIAL TRANSLATION OF THAT ALIEN SIGNAL BEFORE EVERYTHING WENT TO HELL. IT WAS NO DISTRESS SIGNAL. IT WAS A WARNING.
I'M GOING TO MAKE IT EASY FOR YOU. THIS IS A SCIENTIFIC EXPEDITION --THAT'S ALL. AND I NEED A GUIDE.
SURE. AND WHAT'S THE BRIBE THIS TIME, CAPTAIN? REINSTATEMENT? BACK PAY?
I'M NEVER GOING BACK--
--DISCUSSION OVER.
YOU'RE ACTING LIKE YOU HAVE A CHOICE--
JESUS--YOU THINK YOU CAN THREATEN ME? AFTER EVERYTHING I'VE BEEN THROUGH--?
THREATEN?
NO.
BUT I'M GOING TO HAVE RELIABLE, FIRST-PERSON INFORMATION ON THIS MISSION.

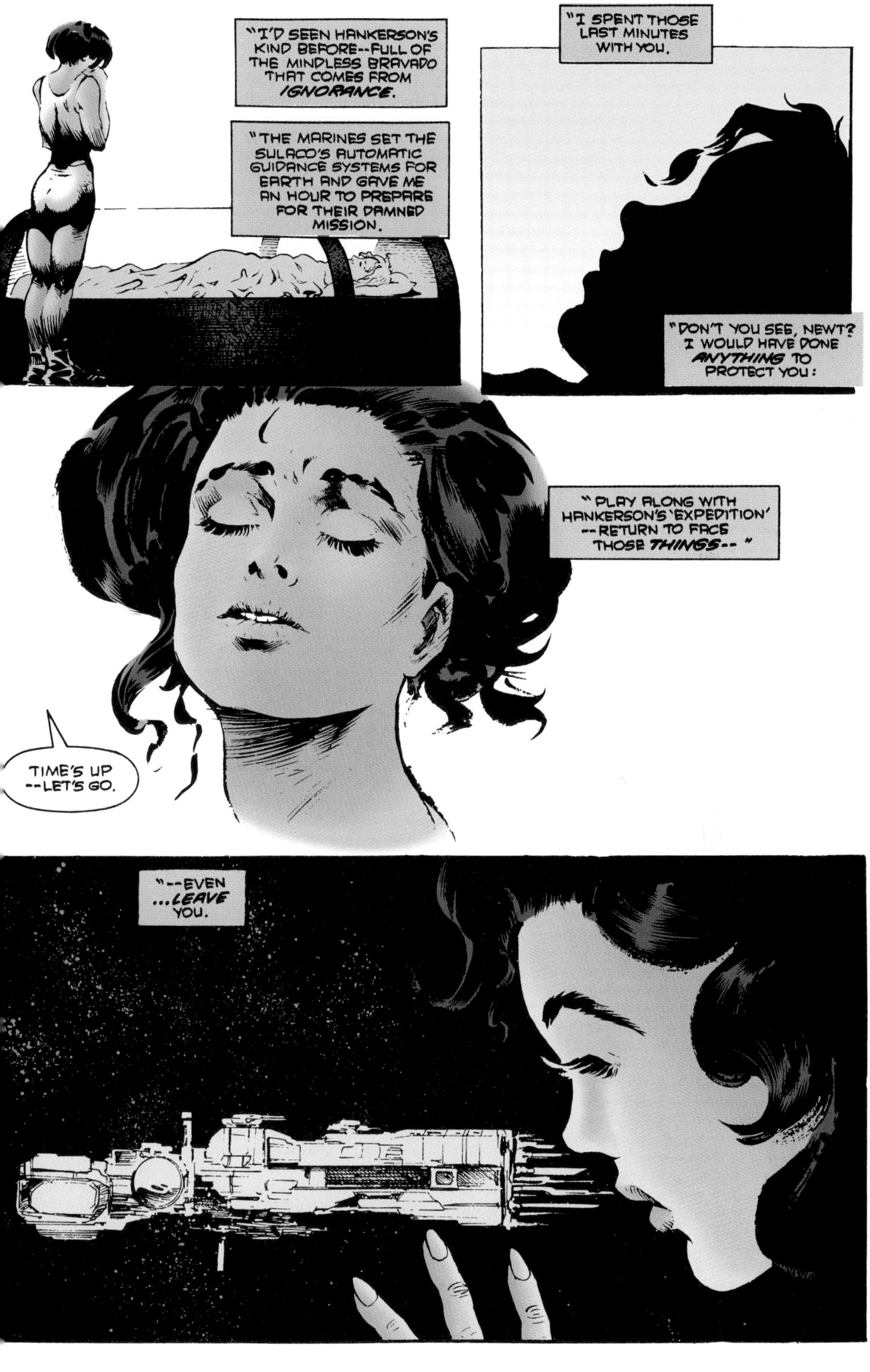
"I'D SEEN HANKERSON'S KIND BEFORE--FULL OF THE MINDLESS BRAVADO THAT COMES FROM *IGNORANCE*.
"THE MARINES SET THE SULACO'S AUTOMATIC GUIDANCE SYSTEMS FOR EARTH AND GAVE ME AN HOUR TO PREPARE FOR THEIR DAMNED MISSION.
"I SPENT THOSE LAST MINUTES WITH YOU.
"DON'T YOU SEE, NEWT? I WOULD HAVE DONE *ANYTHING* TO PROTECT YOU:
" PLAY ALONG WITH HANKERSON'S 'EXPEDITION' --RETURN TO FACE THOSE *THINGS*-- "
TIME'S UP --LET'S GO.
"--EVEN ...*LEAVE* YOU.

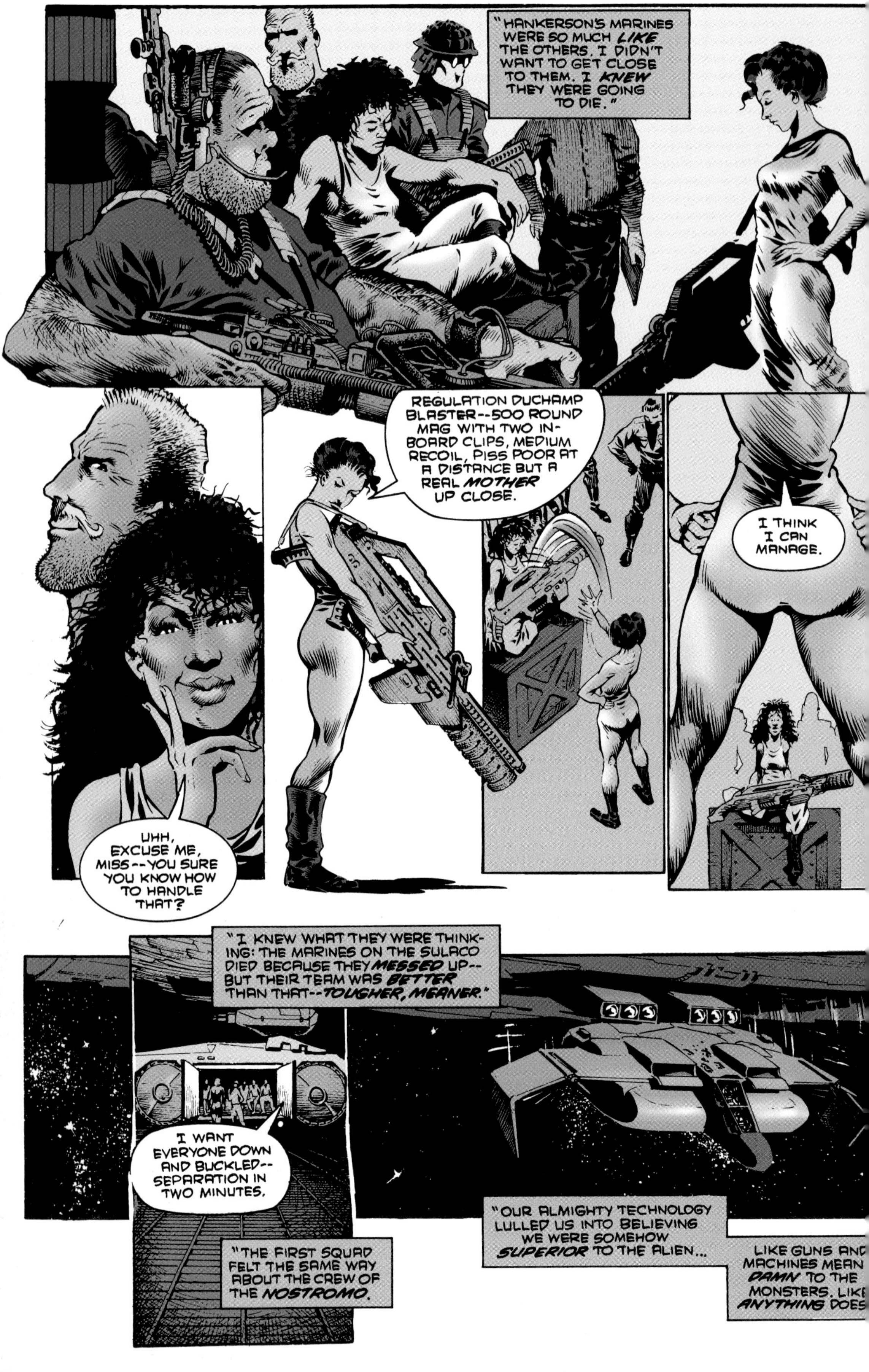
"HANKERSON'S MARINES WERE SO MUCH LIKE THE OTHERS. I DIDN'T WANT TO GET CLOSE TO THEM. I KNEW THEY WERE GOING TO DIE."
REGULATION DUCHAMP BLASTER--500 ROUND MAG WITH TWO IN-BOARD CLIPS, MEDIUM RECOIL, PISS POOR AT A DISTANCE BUT A REAL MOTHER UP CLOSE.
UHH, EXCUSE ME, MISS--YOU SURE YOU KNOW HOW TO HANDLE THAT?
I THINK I CAN MANAGE.
"I KNEW WHAT THEY WERE THINK-ING: THE MARINES ON THE SULACO DIED BECAUSE THEY MESSED UP--BUT THEIR TEAM WAS BETTER THAN THAT--TOUGHER, MEANER."
I WANT EVERYONE DOWN AND BUCKLED--SEPARATION IN TWO MINUTES.
"THE FIRST SQUAD FELT THE SAME WAY ABOUT THE CREW OF THE NOSTROMO.
"OUR ALMIGHTY TECHNOLOGY LULLED US INTO BELIEVING WE WERE SOMEHOW SUPERIOR TO THE ALIEN...
LIKE GUNS AND MACHINES MEAN DAMN TO THE MONSTERS. LIKE ANYTHING DOES

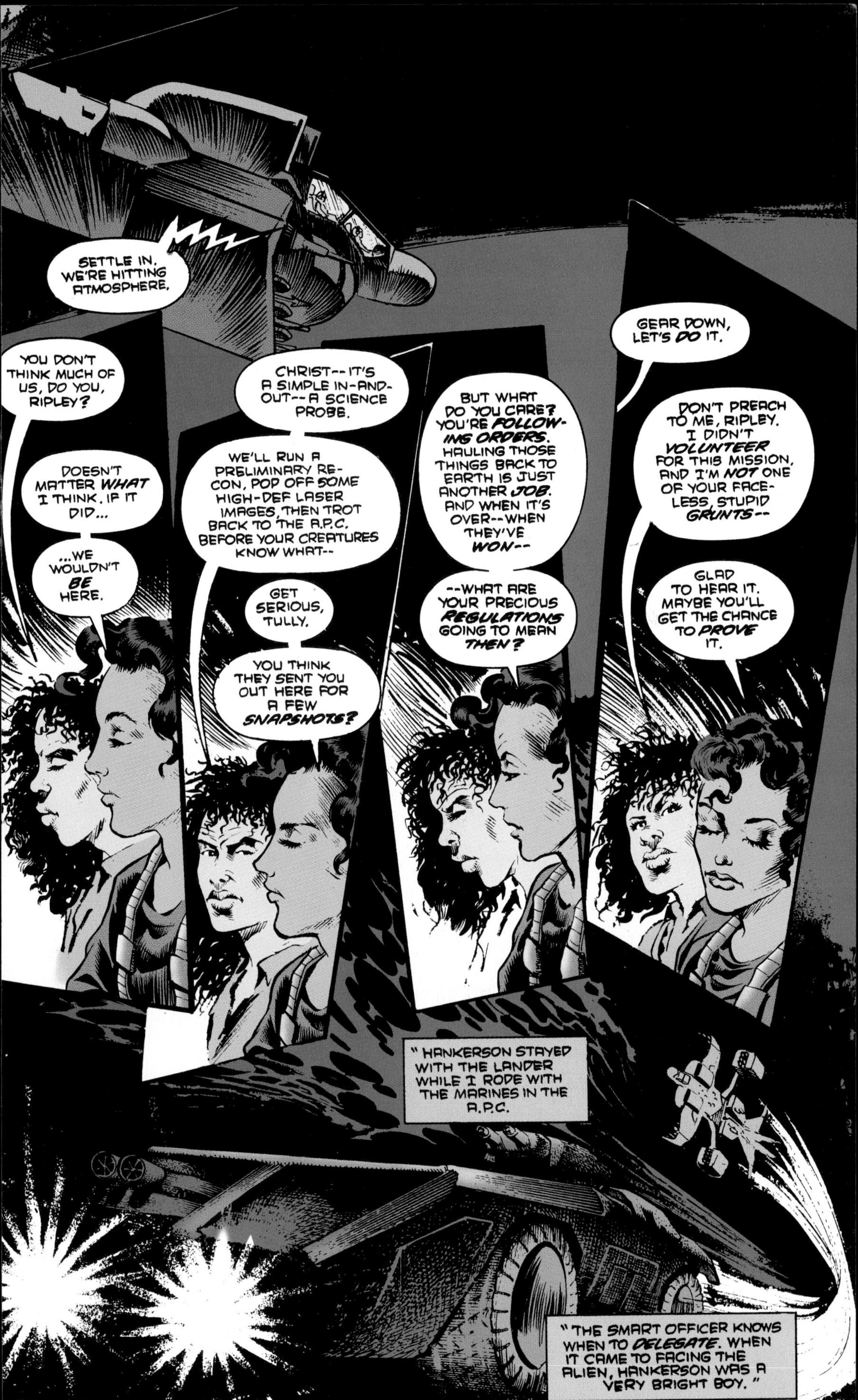
SETTLE IN. WE'RE HITTING ATMOSPHERE.
YOU DON'T THINK MUCH OF US, DO YOU, RIPLEY?
DOESN'T MATTER WHAT I THINK. IF IT DID...
...WE WOULDN'T BE HERE.
CHRIST-- IT'S A SIMPLE IN-AND-OUT-- A SCIENCE PROBE.
WE'LL RUN A PRELIMINARY RE-CON, POP OFF SOME HIGH-DEF LASER IMAGES, THEN TROT BACK TO THE A.P.C. BEFORE YOUR CREATURES KNOW WHAT--
GET SERIOUS, TULLY.
YOU THINK THEY SENT YOU OUT HERE FOR A FEW SNAPSHOTS?
BUT WHAT DO YOU CARE? YOU'RE FOLLOWING ORDERS. HAULING THOSE THINGS BACK TO EARTH IS JUST ANOTHER JOB. AND WHEN IT'S OVER-- WHEN THEY'VE WON--
--WHAT ARE YOUR PRECIOUS REGULATIONS GOING TO MEAN THEN?
GEAR DOWN, LET'S DO IT.
DON'T PREACH TO ME, RIPLEY. I DIDN'T VOLUNTEER FOR THIS MISSION, AND I'M NOT ONE OF YOUR FACELESS, STUPID GRUNTS--
GLAD TO HEAR IT. MAYBE YOU'LL GET THE CHANCE TO PROVE IT.
"HANKERSON STAYED WITH THE LANDER WHILE I RODE WITH THE MARINES IN THE A.P.C.
"THE SMART OFFICER KNOWS WHEN TO DELEGATE. WHEN IT CAME TO FACING THE ALIEN, HANKERSON WAS A VERY BRIGHT BOY."

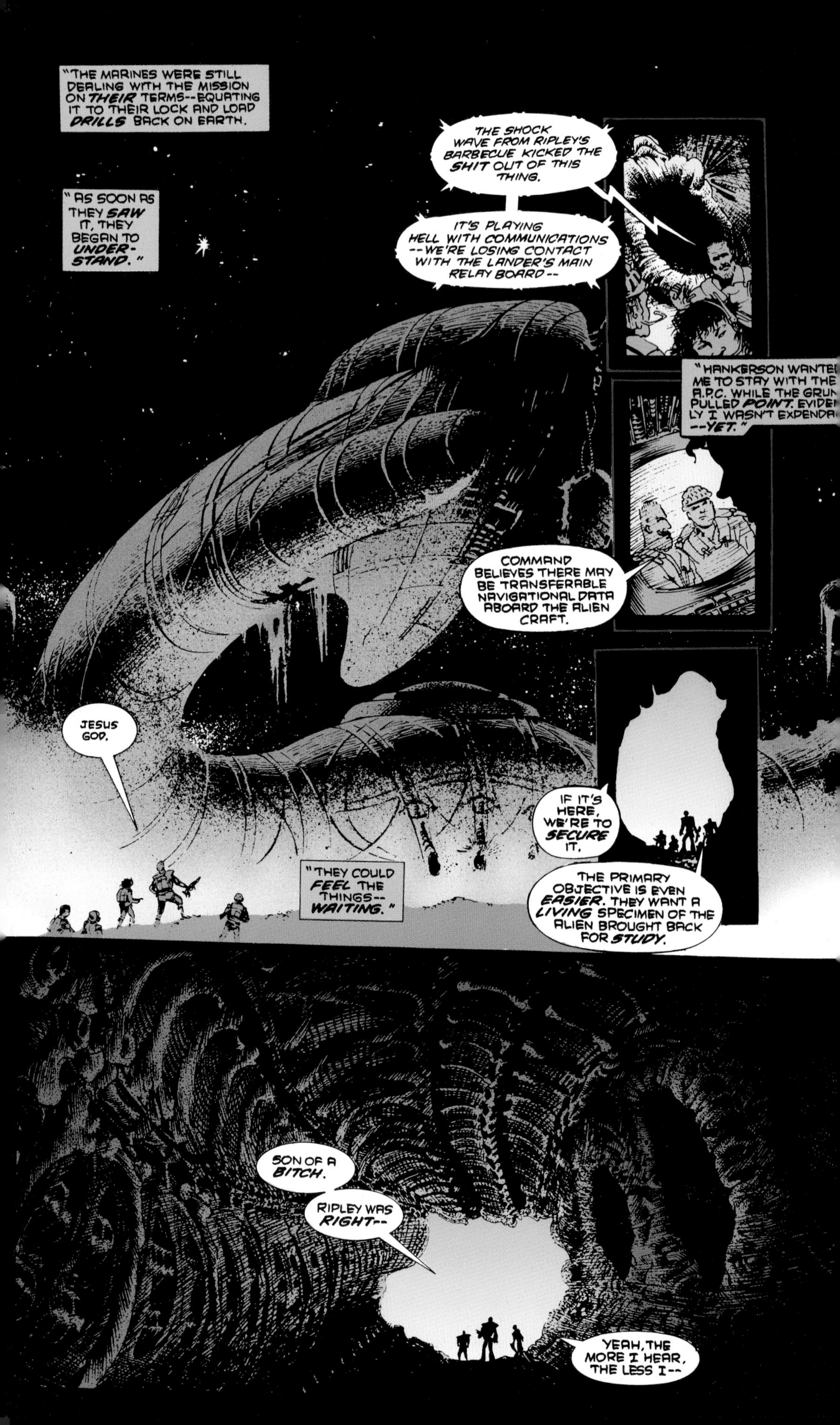
"THE MARINES WERE STILL DEALING WITH THE MISSION ON THEIR TERMS--EQUATING IT TO THEIR LOCK AND LOAD DRILLS BACK ON EARTH.
"AS SOON AS THEY SAW IT, THEY BEGAN TO UNDER-STAND."
THE SHOCK WAVE FROM RIPLEY'S BARBECUE KICKED THE SHIT OUT OF THIS THING.
IT'S PLAYING HELL WITH COMMUNICATIONS --WE'RE LOSING CONTACT WITH THE LANDER'S MAIN RELAY BOARD--
"HANKERSON WANTE ME TO STAY WITH THE A.P.C. WHILE THE GRUN PULLED POINT. EVIDEN LY I WASN'T EXPENDA --YET."
COMMAND BELIEVES THERE MAY BE TRANSFERABLE NAVIGATIONAL DATA ABOARD THE ALIEN CRAFT.
JESUS GOD.
IF IT'S HERE, WE'RE TO SECURE IT.
"THEY COULD FEEL THE THINGS-- WAITING."
THE PRIMARY OBJECTIVE IS EVEN EASIER. THEY WANT A LIVING SPECIMEN OF THE ALIEN BROUGHT BACK FOR STUDY.
SON OF A BITCH.
RIPLEY WAS RIGHT--
YEAH, THE MORE I HEAR, THE LESS I--

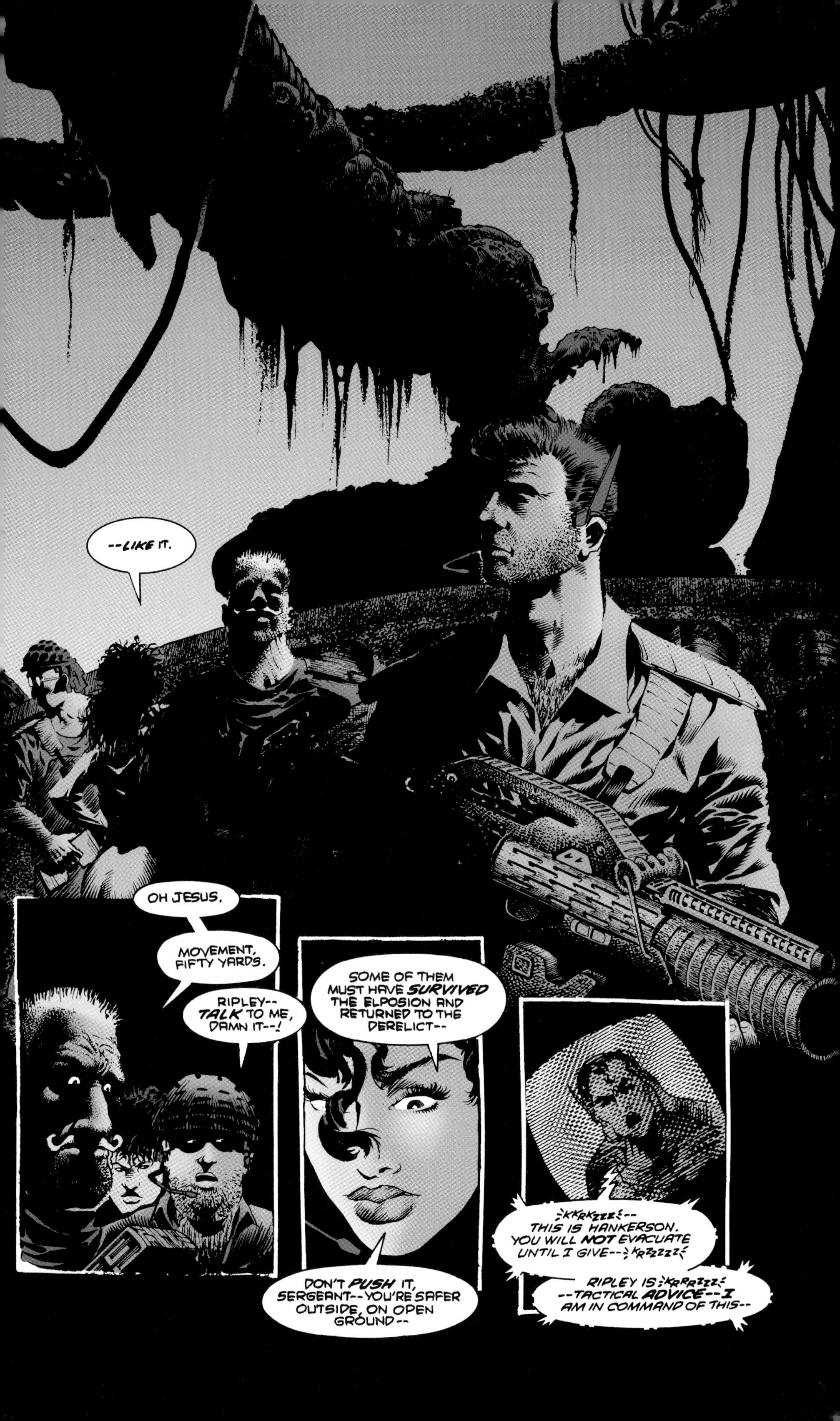
--LIKE IT.
OH JESUS.
MOVEMENT, FIFTY YARDS.
RIPLEY-- TALK TO ME, DAMN IT--!
SOME OF THEM MUST HAVE SURVIVED THE ELPOSION AND RETURNED TO THE DERELICT--
DON'T PUSH IT, SERGEANT--YOU'RE SAFER OUTSIDE, ON OPEN GROUND--
KKRKZZZ-- THIS IS HANKERSON. YOU WILL NOT EVACUATE UNTIL I GIVE-- KRZZZZZ
RIPLEY IS KRRRZZZ --TACTICAL ADVICE--I AM IN COMMAND OF THIS--

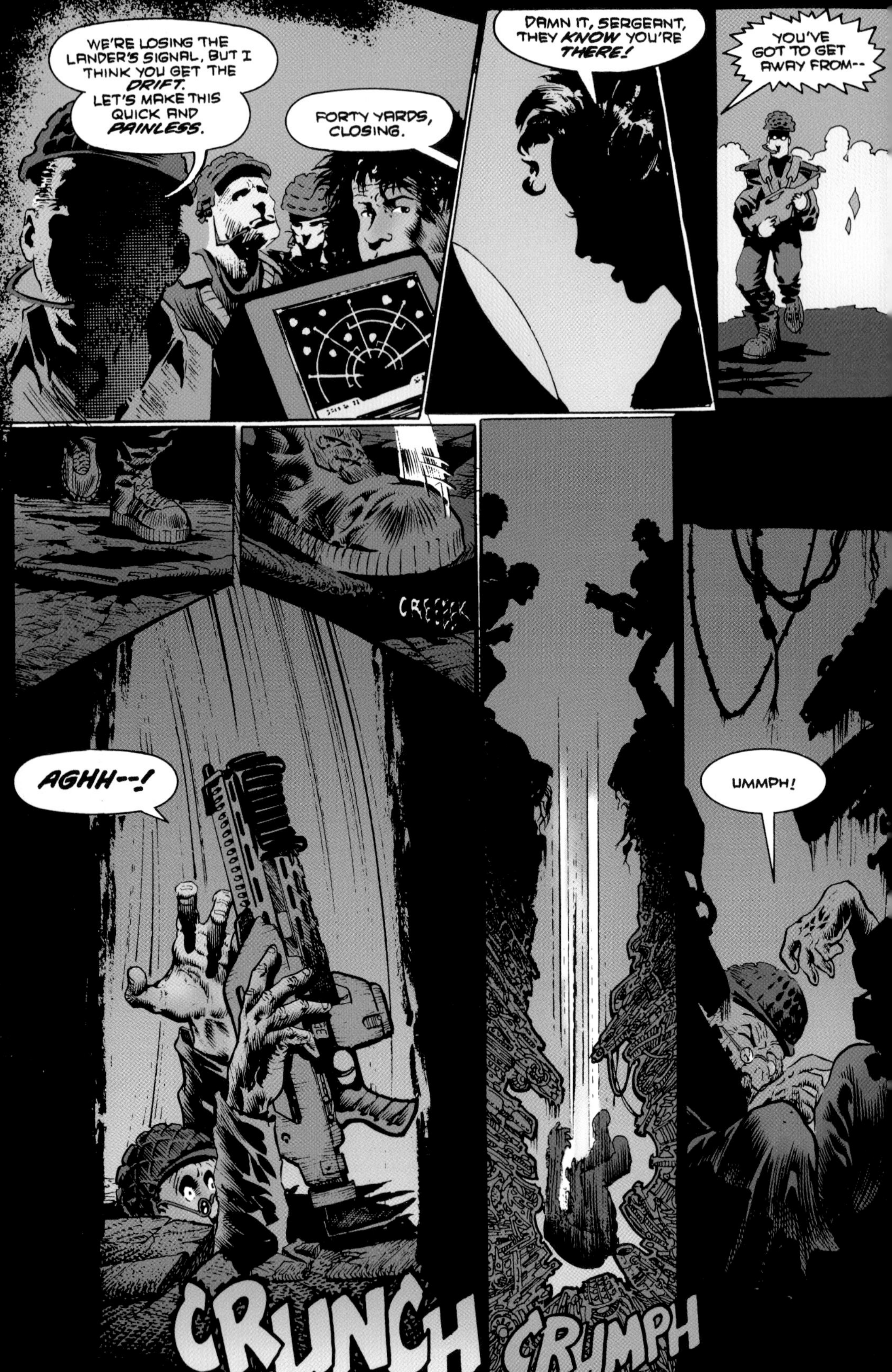
WE'RE LOSING THE LANDER'S SIGNAL, BUT I THINK YOU GET THE DRIFT. LET'S MAKE THIS QUICK AND PAINLESS.
FORTY YARDS, CLOSING.
DAMN IT, SERGEANT, THEY KNOW YOU'RE THERE!
YOU'VE GOT TO GET AWAY FROM--
CREEEEK
AGHH--!
UMMPH!
CRUNCH
CRUMPH

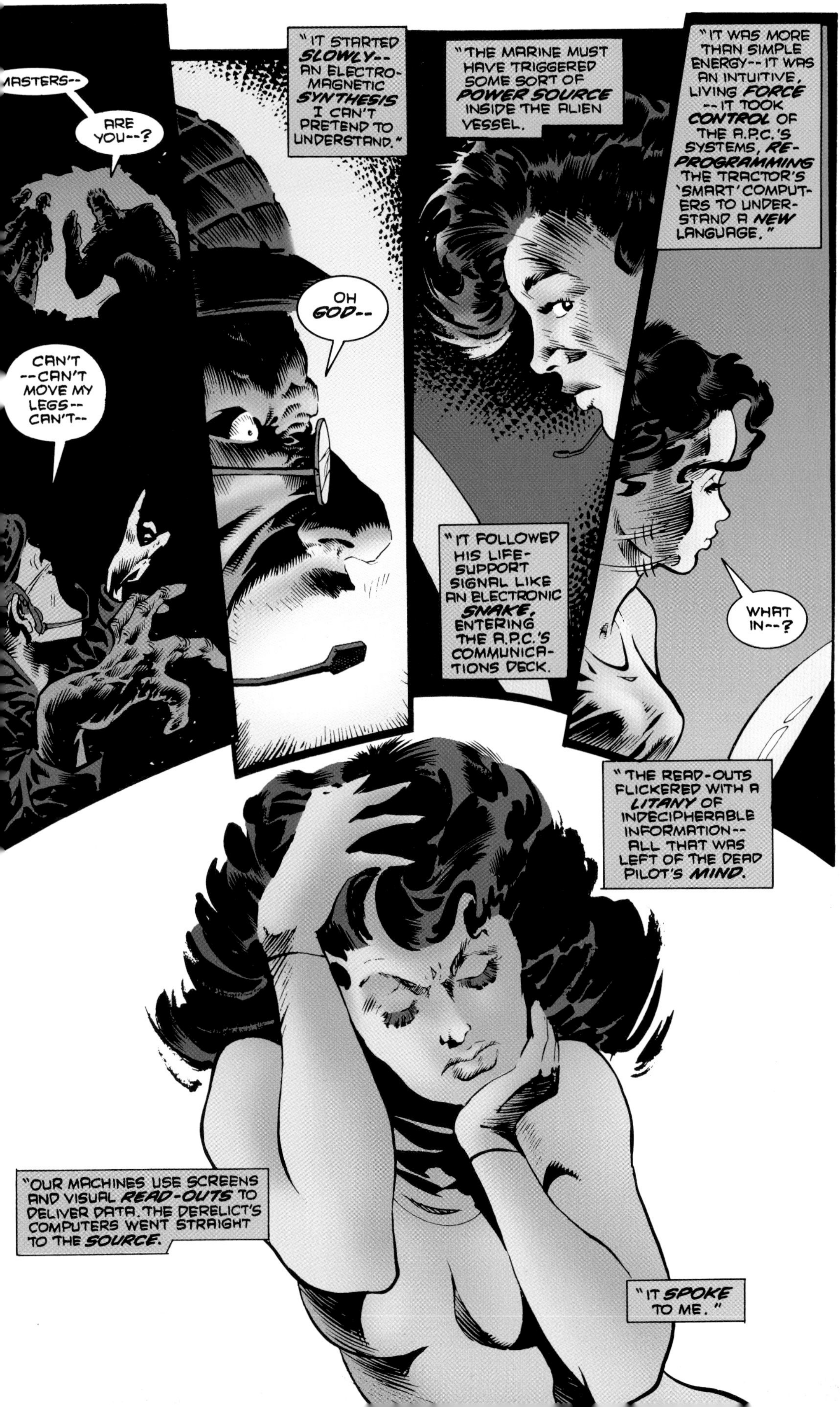

MASTERS--
ARE YOU--?
CAN'T --CAN'T MOVE MY LEGS-- CAN'T--
"IT STARTED SLOWLY-- AN ELECTRO-MAGNETIC SYNTHESIS I CAN'T PRETEND TO UNDERSTAND."
OH GOD--
"THE MARINE MUST HAVE TRIGGERED SOME SORT OF POWER SOURCE INSIDE THE ALIEN VESSEL.
"IT FOLLOWED HIS LIFE-SUPPORT SIGNAL LIKE AN ELECTRONIC SNAKE, ENTERING THE A.P.C.'S COMMUNICA-TIONS DECK.
"IT WAS MORE THAN SIMPLE ENERGY-- IT WAS AN INTUITIVE, LIVING FORCE --IT TOOK CONTROL OF THE A.P.C.'S SYSTEMS, RE-PROGRAMMING THE TRACTOR'S 'SMART' COMPUT-ERS TO UNDER-STAND A NEW LANGUAGE."
WHAT IN--?
"THE READ-OUTS FLICKERED WITH A LITANY OF INDECIPHERABLE INFORMATION-- ALL THAT WAS LEFT OF THE DEAD PILOT'S MIND.
"OUR MACHINES USE SCREENS AND VISUAL READ-OUTS TO DELIVER DATA. THE DERELICT'S COMPUTERS WENT STRAIGHT TO THE SOURCE.
"IT SPOKE TO ME."

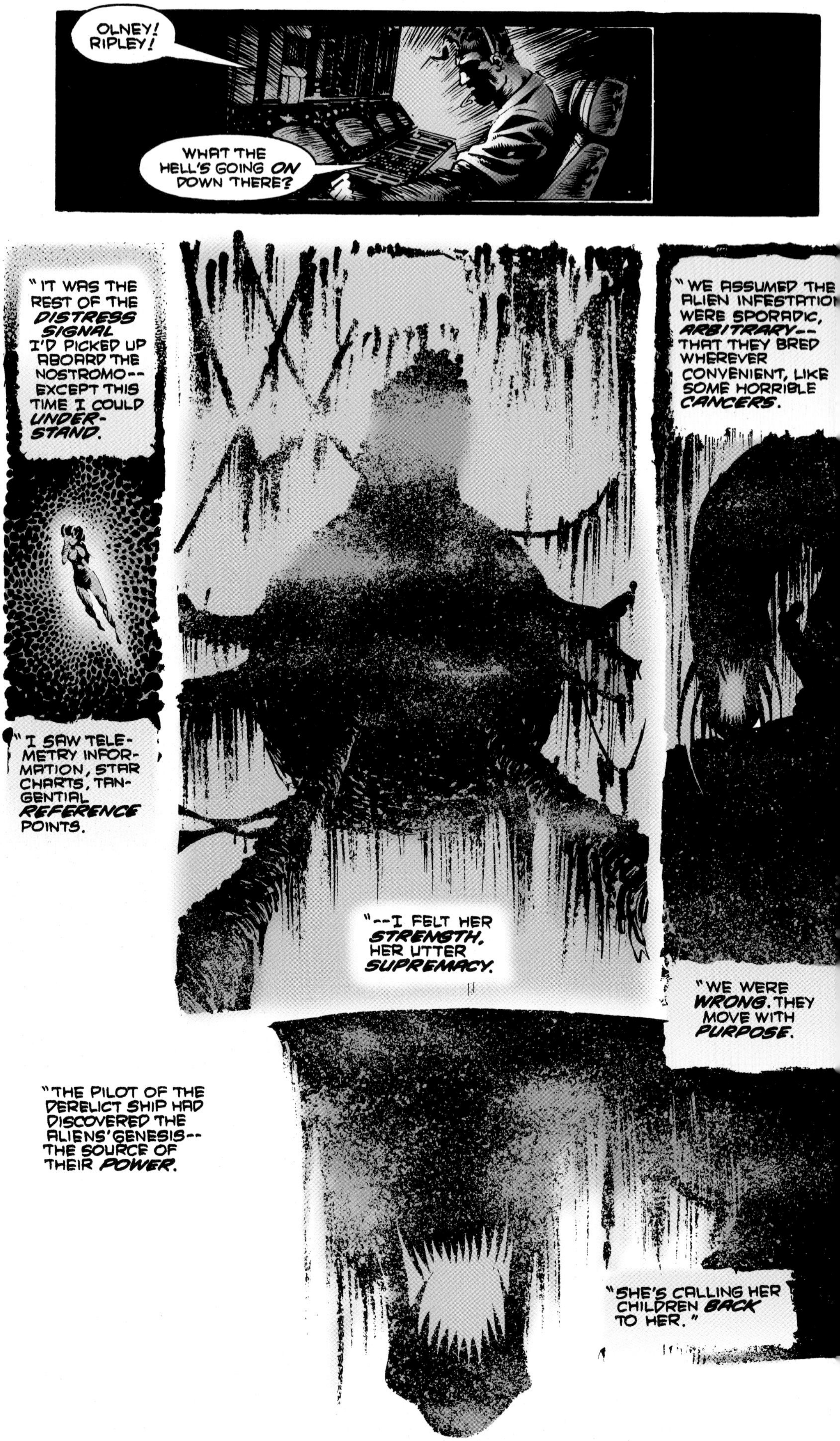
OLNEY! RIPLEY!
WHAT THE HELL'S GOING ON DOWN THERE?
"IT WAS THE REST OF THE DISTRESS SIGNAL I'D PICKED UP ABOARD THE NOSTROMO--EXCEPT THIS TIME I COULD UNDERSTAND.
"I SAW TELEMETRY INFORMATION, STAR CHARTS, TANGENTIAL REFERENCE POINTS.
"--I FELT HER STRENGTH, HER UTTER SUPREMACY.
"WE ASSUMED THE ALIEN INFESTATIO WERE SPORADIC, ARBITRARY--THAT THEY BRED WHEREVER CONVENIENT, LIKE SOME HORRIBLE CANCERS.
"WE WERE WRONG. THEY MOVE WITH PURPOSE.
"THE PILOT OF THE DERELICT SHIP HAD DISCOVERED THE ALIENS' GENESIS--THE SOURCE OF THEIR POWER.
"SHE'S CALLING HER CHILDREN BACK TO HER."

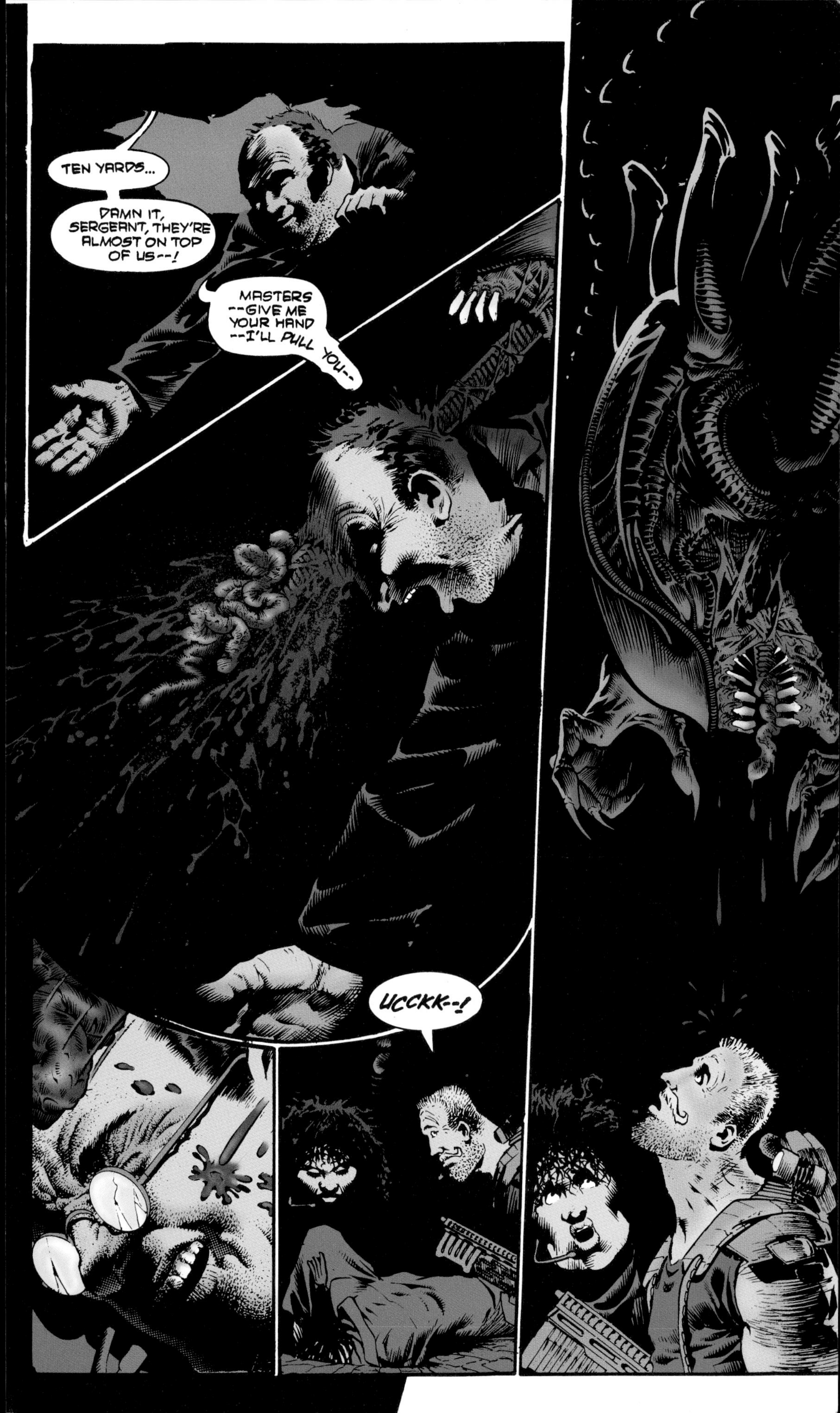
TEN YARDS...
DAMN IT, SERGEANT, THEY'RE ALMOST ON TOP OF US--!
MASTERS --GIVE ME YOUR HAND --I'LL PULL YOU--
UCCKK--!

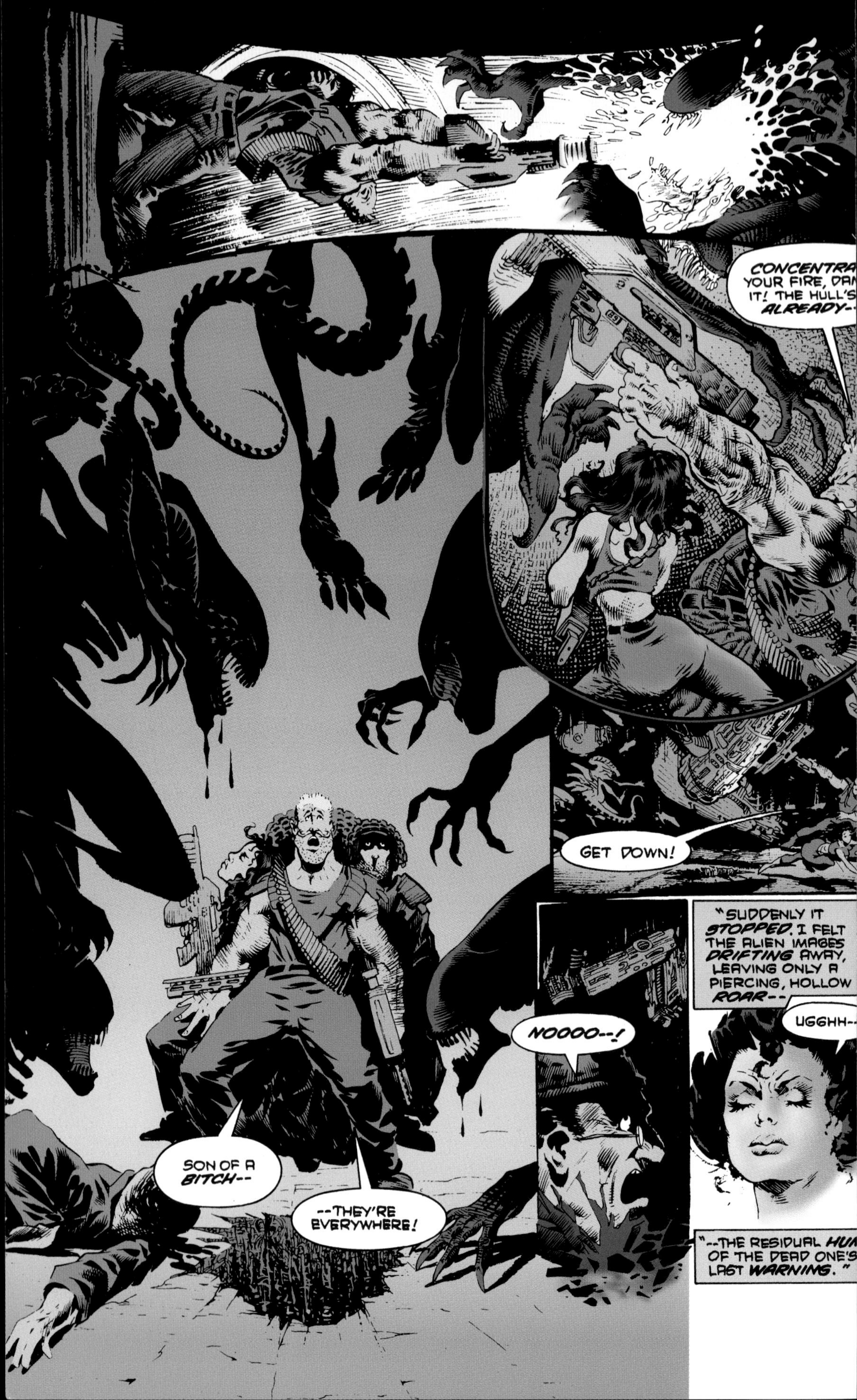

CONCENTRA
YOUR FIRE, DAM
IT! THE HULL'S
ALREADY--
GET DOWN!
"SUDDENLY IT STOPPED. I FELT THE ALIEN IMAGES DRIFTING AWAY, LEAVING ONLY A PIERCING, HOLLOW ROAR--
UGGHH--
NOOOO--!
SON OF A BITCH--
--THEY'RE EVERYWHERE!
"--THE RESIDUAL HUM OF THE DEAD ONE'S LAST WARNING."

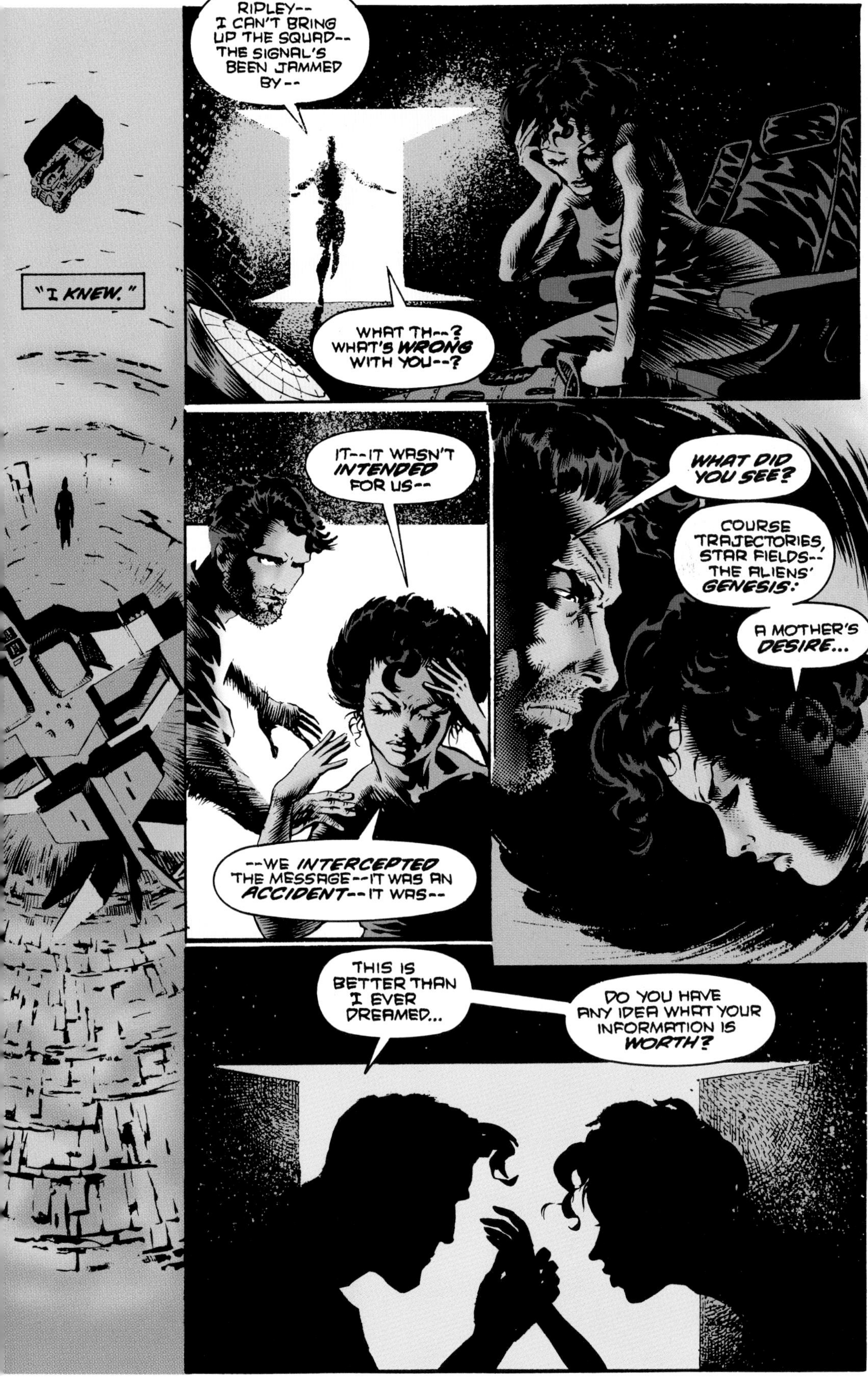
RIPLEY-- I CAN'T BRING UP THE SQUAD-- THE SIGNAL'S BEEN JAMMED BY--
"I KNEW."
WHAT TH--? WHAT'S WRONG WITH YOU--?
IT--IT WASN'T INTENDED FOR US--
--WE INTERCEPTED THE MESSAGE--IT WAS AN ACCIDENT--IT WAS--
WHAT DID YOU SEE?
COURSE TRAJECTORIES, STAR FIELDS-- THE ALIENS' GENESIS:
A MOTHER'S DESIRE...
THIS IS BETTER THAN I EVER DREAMED...
DO YOU HAVE ANY IDEA WHAT YOUR INFORMATION IS WORTH?

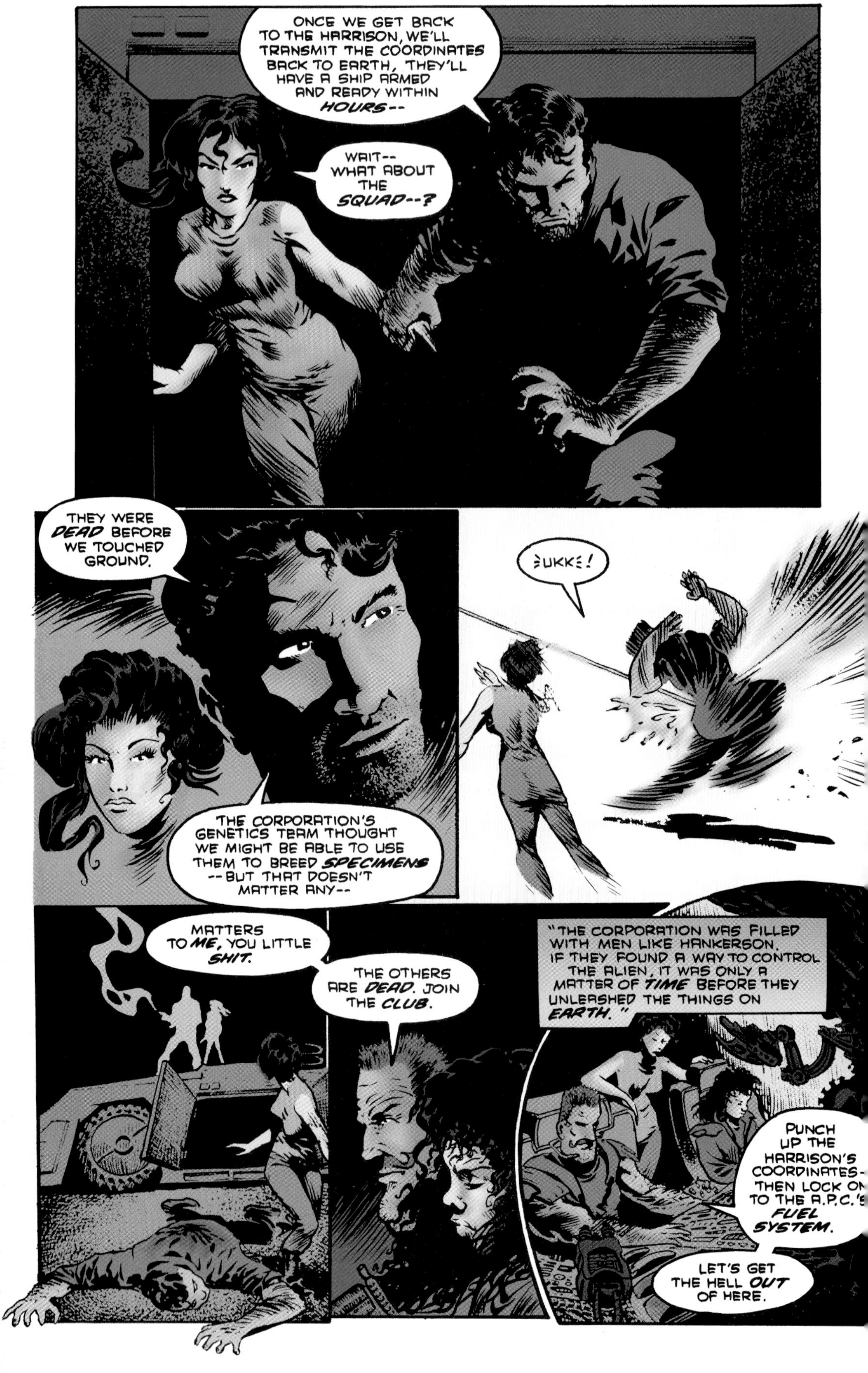
ONCE WE GET BACK TO THE HARRISON, WE'LL TRANSMIT THE COORDINATES BACK TO EARTH, THEY'LL HAVE A SHIP ARMED AND READY WITHIN HOURS--
WAIT-- WHAT ABOUT THE SQUAD--?
THEY WERE DEAD BEFORE WE TOUCHED GROUND.
THE CORPORATION'S GENETICS TEAM THOUGHT WE MIGHT BE ABLE TO USE THEM TO BREED SPECIMENS --BUT THAT DOESN'T MATTER ANY--
UKK!
MATTERS TO ME, YOU LITTLE SHIT.
THE OTHERS ARE DEAD. JOIN THE CLUB.
"THE CORPORATION WAS FILLED WITH MEN LIKE HANKERSON. IF THEY FOUND A WAY TO CONTROL THE ALIEN, IT WAS ONLY A MATTER OF TIME BEFORE THEY UNLEASHED THE THINGS ON EARTH."
PUNCH UP THE HARRISON'S COORDINATES-- THEN LOCK ON TO THE A.P.C.'S FUEL SYSTEM.
LET'S GET THE HELL OUT OF HERE.

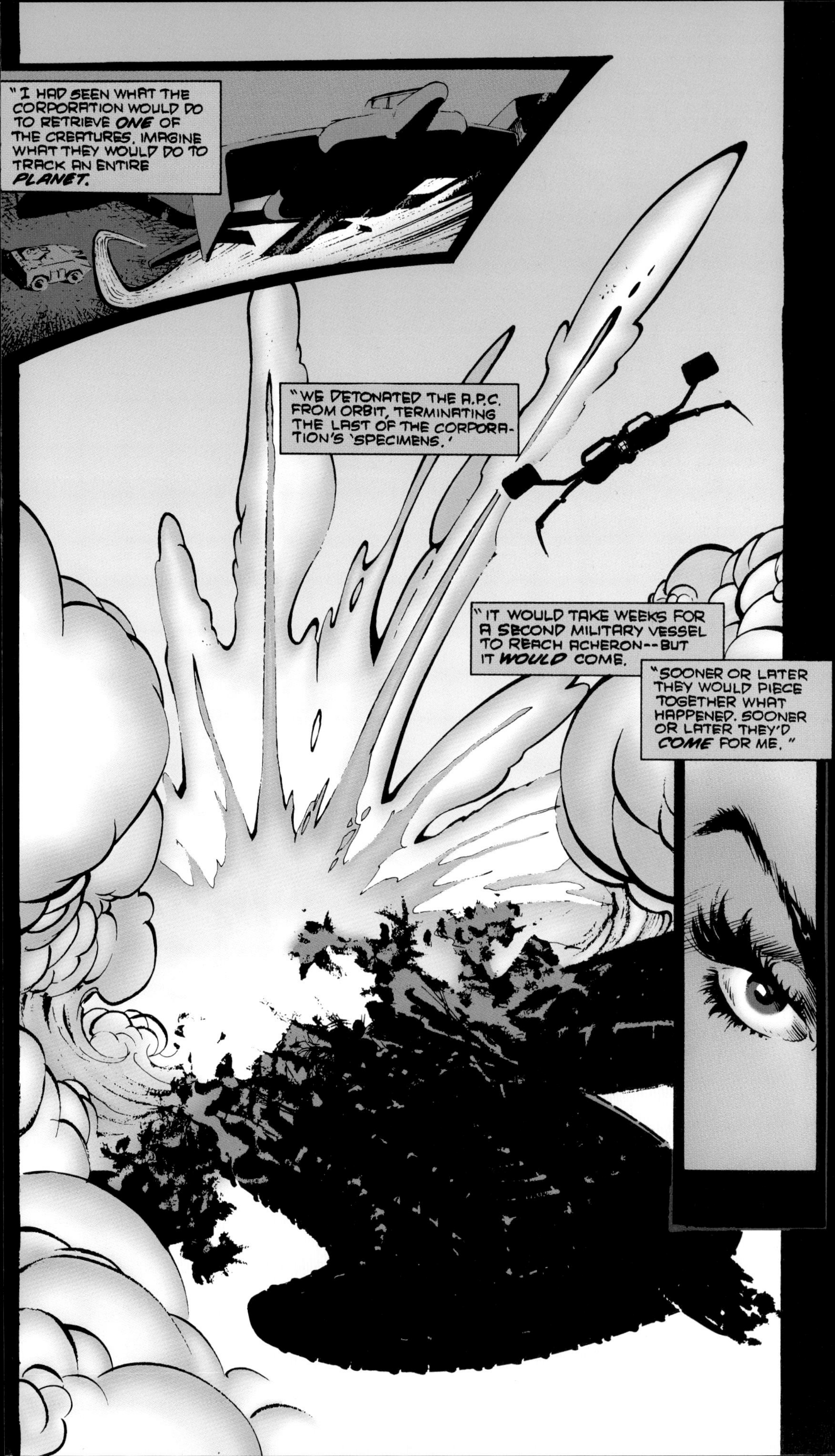
"I HAD SEEN WHAT THE CORPORATION WOULD DO TO RETRIEVE ONE OF THE CREATURES. IMAGINE WHAT THEY WOULD DO TO TRACK AN ENTIRE PLANET.
"WE DETONATED THE A.P.C. FROM ORBIT, TERMINATING THE LAST OF THE CORPORATION'S 'SPECIMENS.'
"IT WOULD TAKE WEEKS FOR A SECOND MILITARY VESSEL TO REACH ACHERON--BUT IT WOULD COME.
"SOONER OR LATER THEY WOULD PIECE TOGETHER WHAT HAPPENED. SOONER OR LATER THEY'D COME FOR ME."

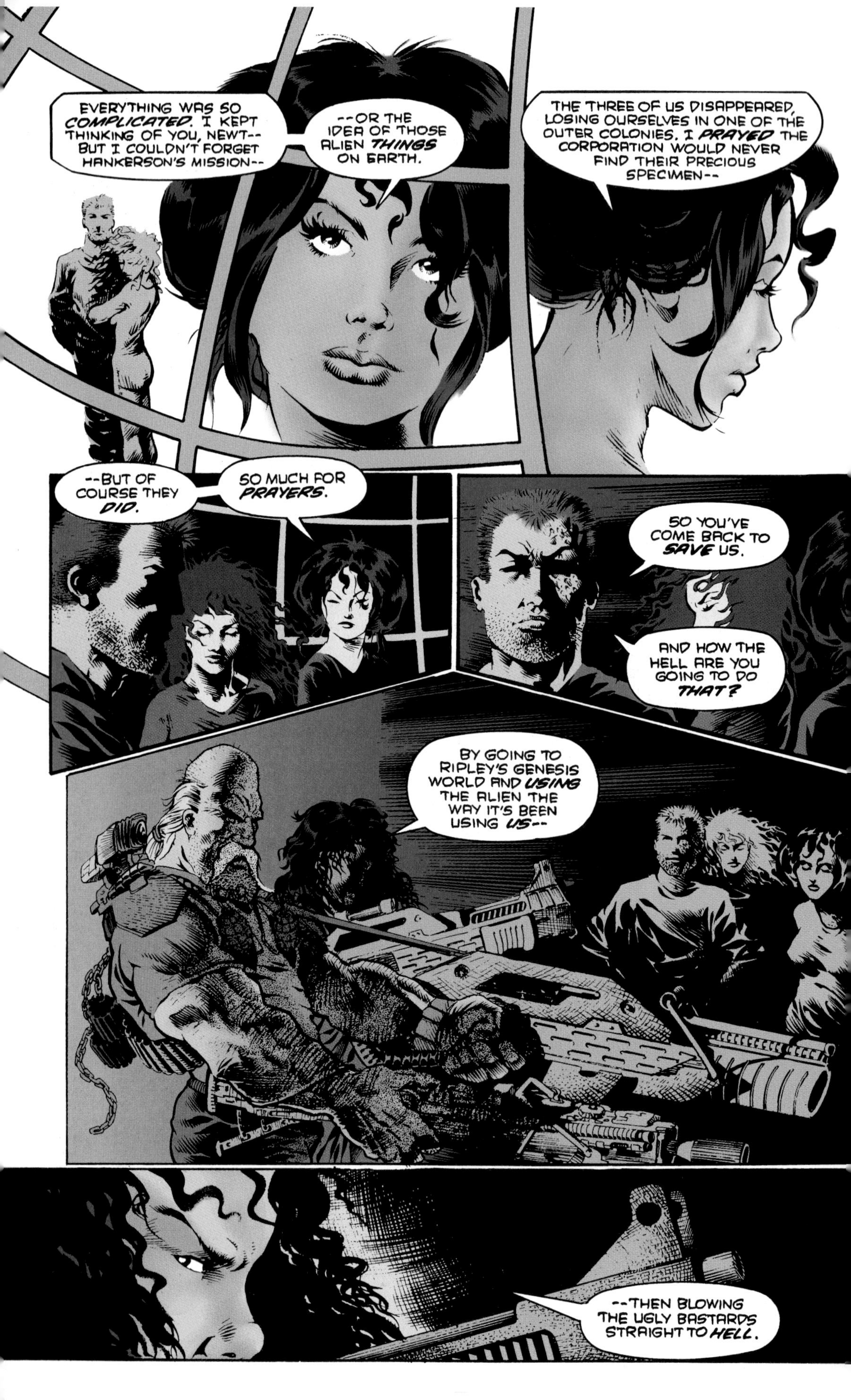
EVERYTHING WAS SO *COMPLICATED*. I KEPT THINKING OF YOU, NEWT-- BUT I COULDN'T FORGET HANKERSON'S MISSION--
--OR THE IDEA OF THOSE ALIEN *THINGS* ON EARTH.
THE THREE OF US DISAPPEARED, LOSING OURSELVES IN ONE OF THE OUTER COLONIES. I *PRAYED* THE CORPORATION WOULD NEVER FIND THEIR PRECIOUS SPECIMEN--
--BUT OF COURSE THEY *DID*.
SO MUCH FOR *PRAYERS*.
SO YOU'VE COME BACK TO *SAVE* US.
AND HOW THE HELL ARE YOU GOING TO DO *THAT?*
BY GOING TO RIPLEY'S GENESIS WORLD AND *USING* THE ALIEN THE WAY IT'S BEEN USING *US*--
--THEN BLOWING THE UGLY BASTARDS STRAIGHT TO *HELL*.

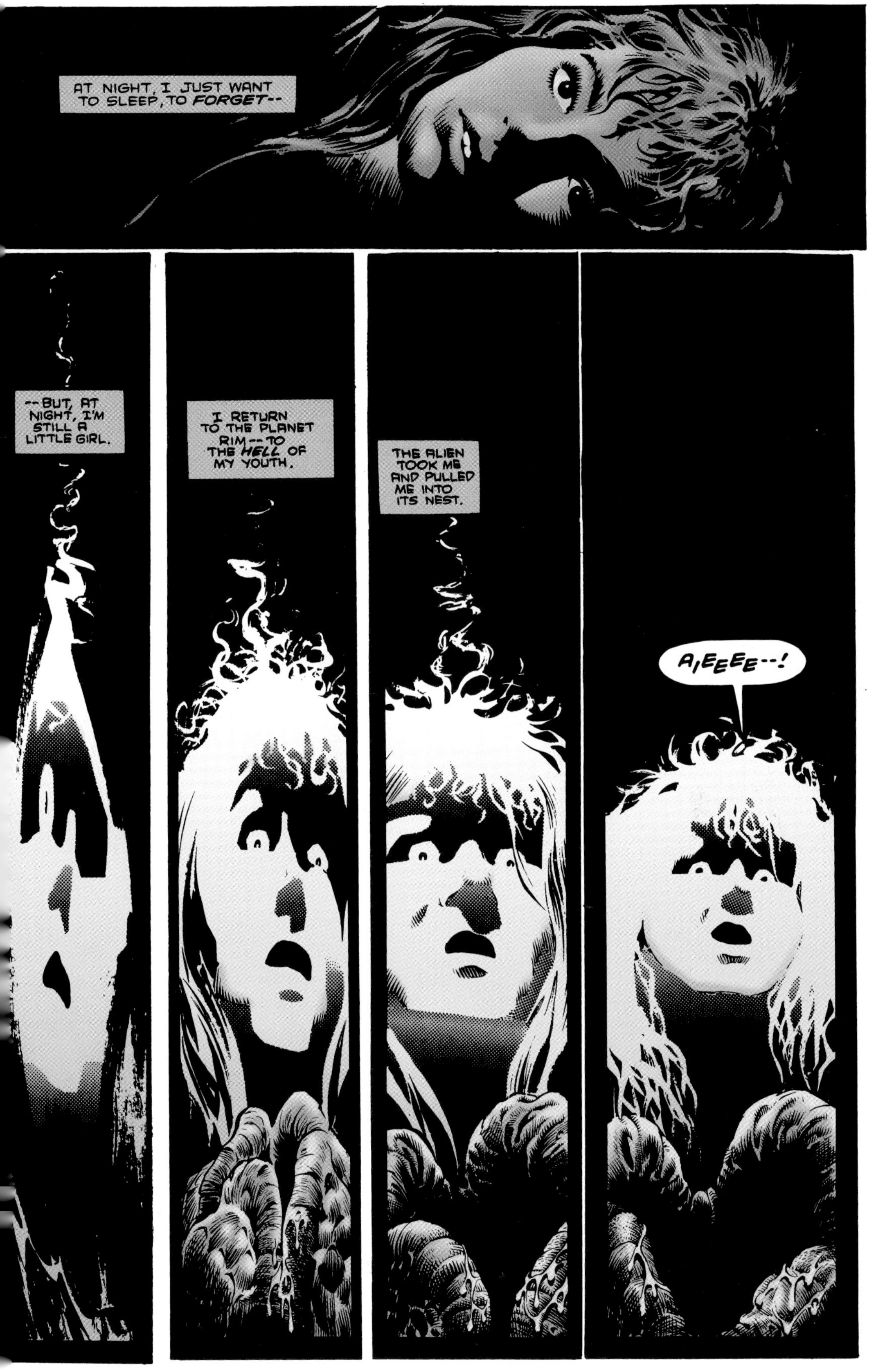
AT NIGHT, I JUST WANT TO SLEEP, TO *FORGET*--
--BUT, AT NIGHT, I'M STILL A LITTLE GIRL.
I RETURN TO THE PLANET RIM--TO THE *HELL* OF MY YOUTH.
THE ALIEN TOOK ME AND PULLED ME INTO ITS NEST.
AIEEEE--!

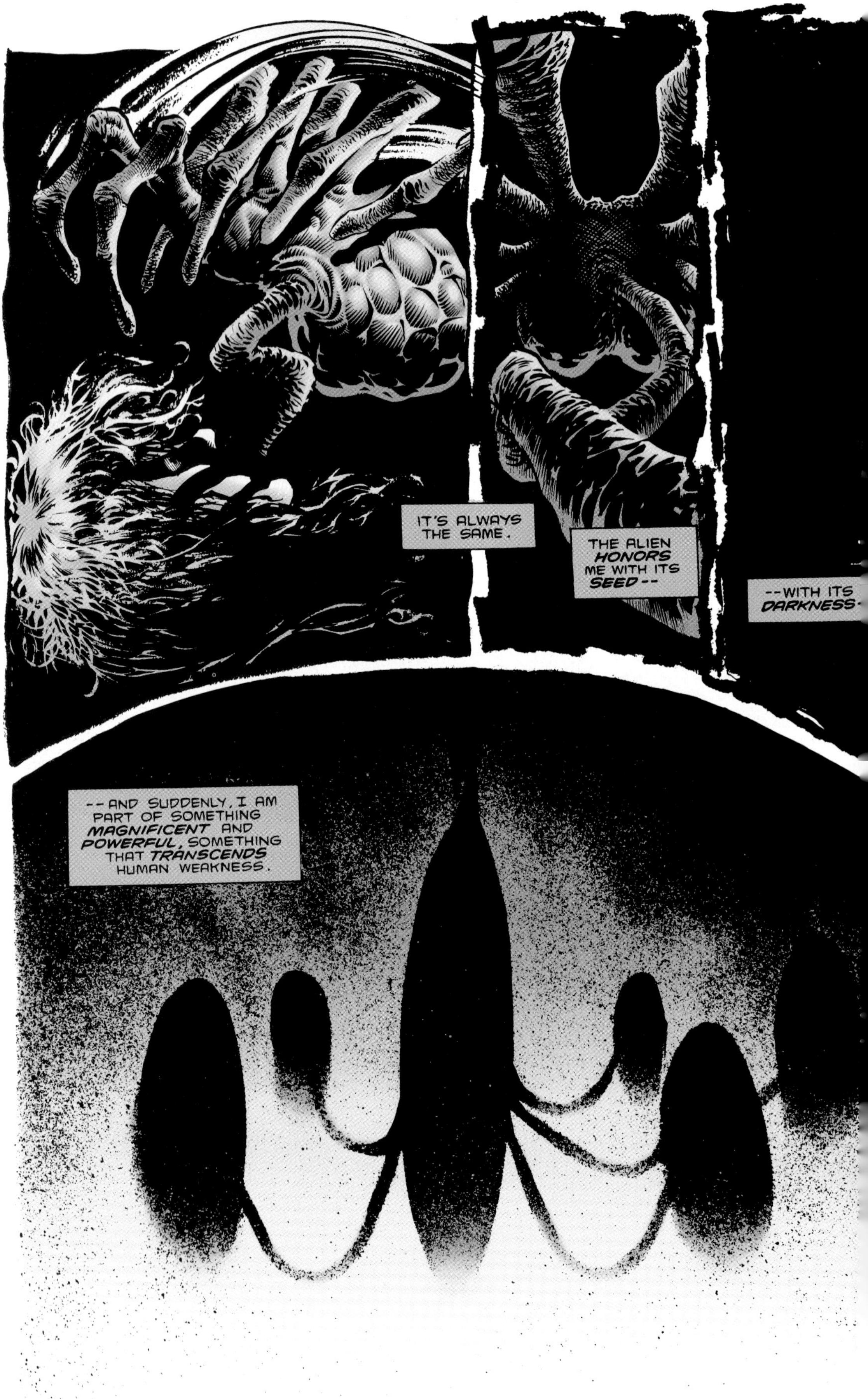
IT'S ALWAYS THE SAME.
THE ALIEN HONORS ME WITH ITS SEED--
--WITH ITS DARKNESS-
--AND SUDDENLY, I AM PART OF SOMETHING MAGNIFICENT AND POWERFUL, SOMETHING THAT TRANSCENDS HUMAN WEAKNESS.

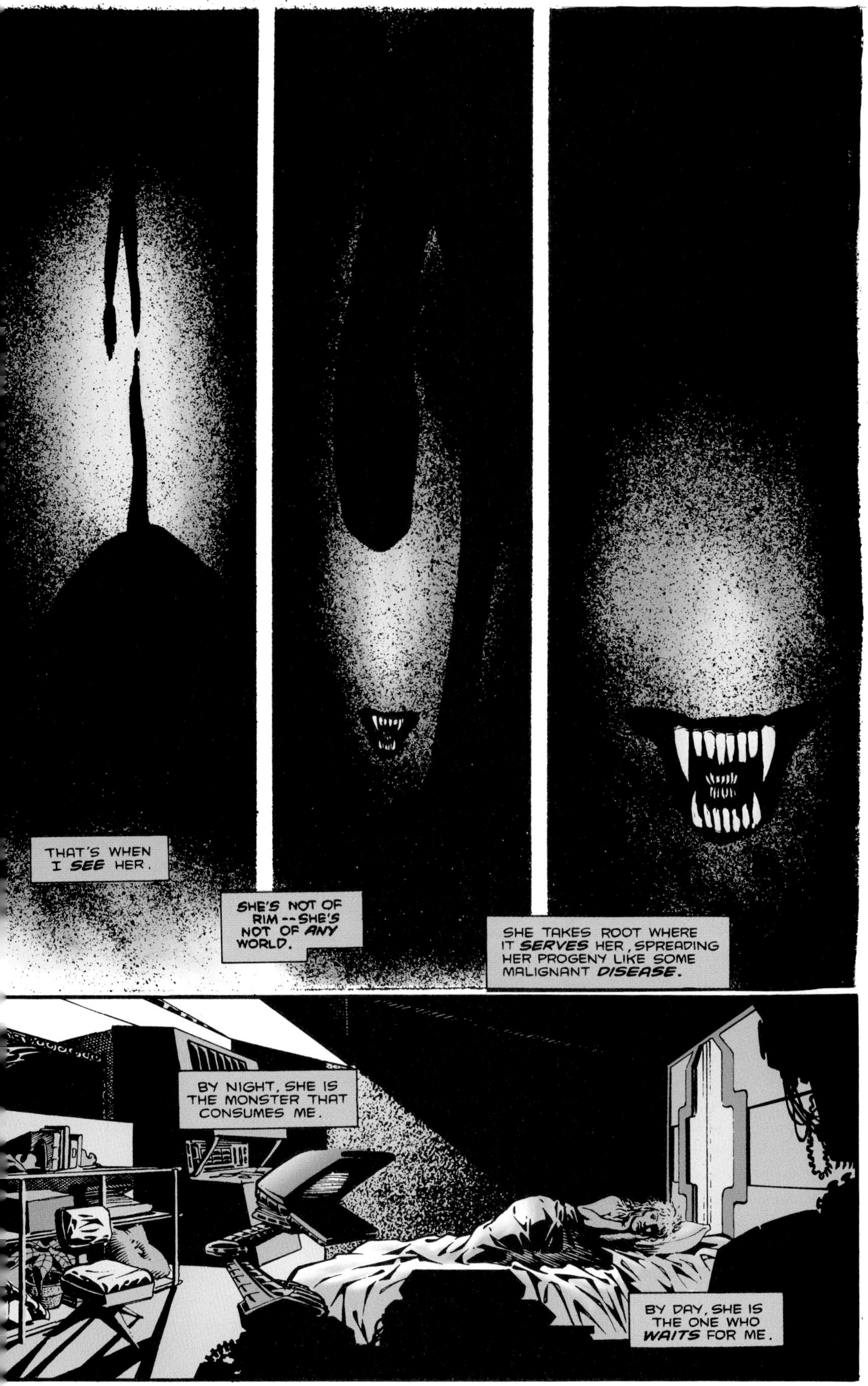
THAT'S WHEN I SEE HER.
SHE'S NOT OF RIM--SHE'S NOT OF ANY WORLD.
SHE TAKES ROOT WHERE IT SERVES HER, SPREADING HER PROGENY LIKE SOME MALIGNANT DISEASE.
BY NIGHT, SHE IS THE MONSTER THAT CONSUMES ME.
BY DAY, SHE IS THE ONE WHO WAITS FOR ME.

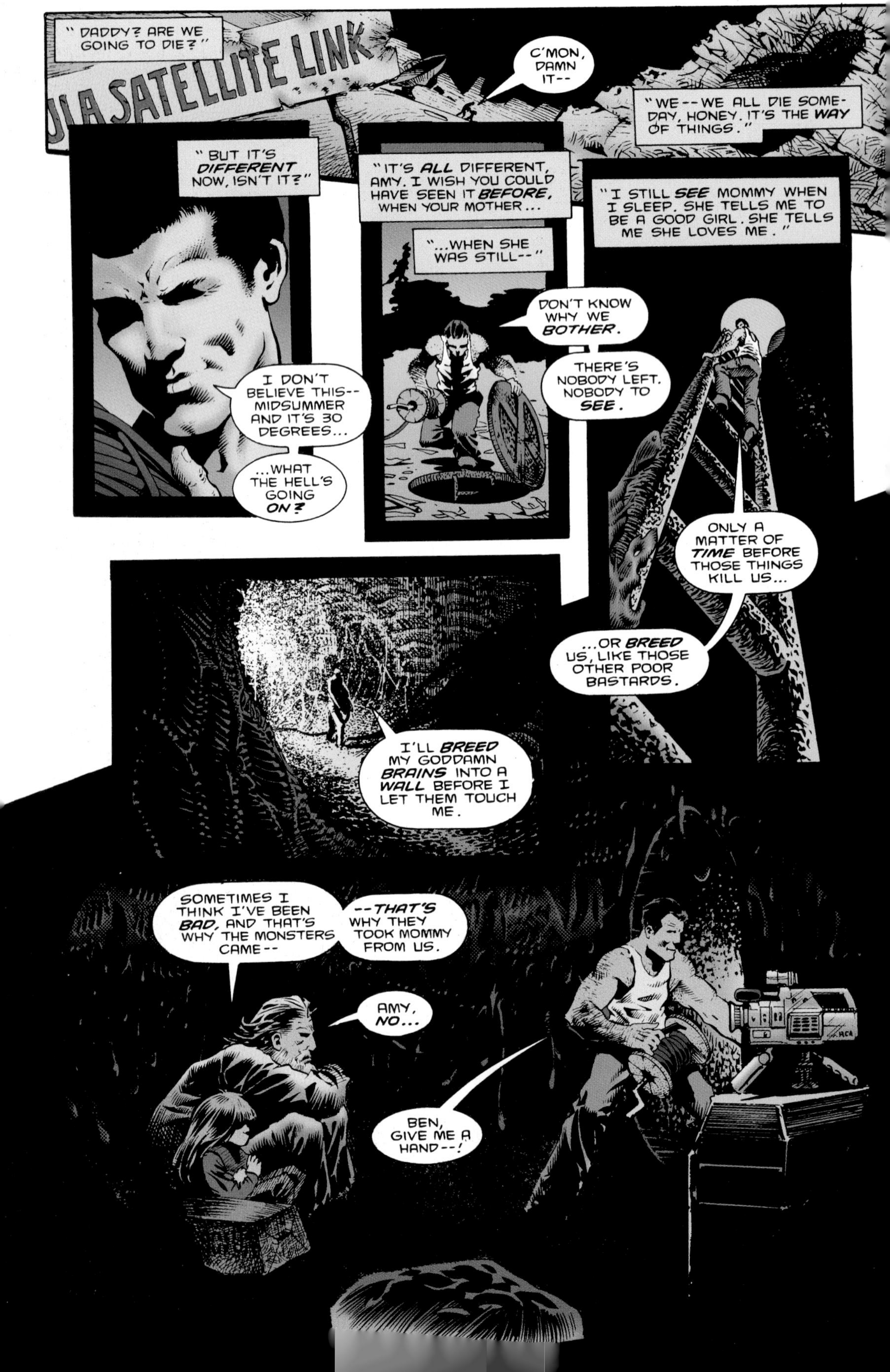

"DADDY? ARE WE GOING TO DIE?"
JLA SATELLITE LINK
C'MON, DAMN IT--
"WE--WE ALL DIE SOME-DAY, HONEY. IT'S THE WAY OF THINGS."
"BUT IT'S DIFFERENT NOW, ISN'T IT?"
I DON'T BELIEVE THIS-- MIDSUMMER AND IT'S 30 DEGREES...
...WHAT THE HELL'S GOING ON?
"IT'S ALL DIFFERENT, AMY. I WISH YOU COULD HAVE SEEN IT BEFORE, WHEN YOUR MOTHER...
"...WHEN SHE WAS STILL--"
DON'T KNOW WHY WE BOTHER.
THERE'S NOBODY LEFT. NOBODY TO SEE.
"I STILL SEE MOMMY WHEN I SLEEP. SHE TELLS ME TO BE A GOOD GIRL. SHE TELLS ME SHE LOVES ME."
ONLY A MATTER OF TIME BEFORE THOSE THINGS KILL US...
...OR BREED US, LIKE THOSE OTHER POOR BASTARDS.
I'LL BREED MY GODDAMN BRAINS INTO A WALL BEFORE I LET THEM TOUCH ME.
SOMETIMES I THINK I'VE BEEN BAD, AND THAT'S WHY THE MONSTERS CAME--
--THAT'S WHY THEY TOOK MOMMY FROM US.
AMY, NO...
BEN, GIVE ME A HAND--!

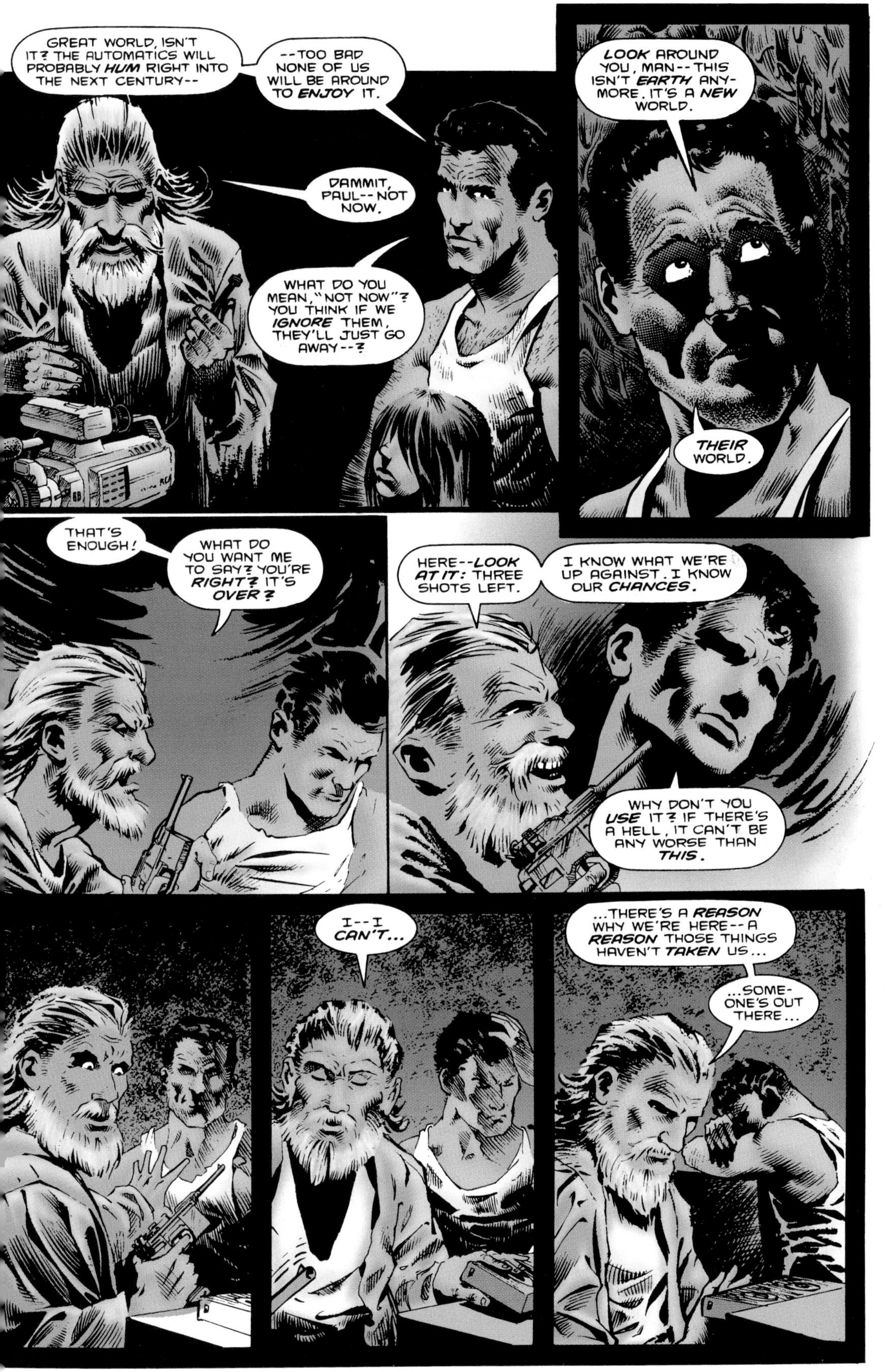
GREAT WORLD, ISN'T IT? THE AUTOMATICS WILL PROBABLY HUM RIGHT INTO THE NEXT CENTURY--
--TOO BAD NONE OF US WILL BE AROUND TO ENJOY IT.
DAMMIT, PAUL--NOT NOW.
WHAT DO YOU MEAN, "NOT NOW"? YOU THINK IF WE IGNORE THEM, THEY'LL JUST GO AWAY--?
LOOK AROUND YOU, MAN--THIS ISN'T EARTH ANYMORE. IT'S A NEW WORLD.
THEIR WORLD.
THAT'S ENOUGH!
WHAT DO YOU WANT ME TO SAY? YOU'RE RIGHT? IT'S OVER?
HERE--LOOK AT IT: THREE SHOTS LEFT.
I KNOW WHAT WE'RE UP AGAINST. I KNOW OUR CHANCES.
WHY DON'T YOU USE IT? IF THERE'S A HELL, IT CAN'T BE ANY WORSE THAN THIS.
I--I CAN'T...
...THERE'S A REASON WHY WE'RE HERE--A REASON THOSE THINGS HAVEN'T TAKEN US...
...SOMEONE'S OUT THERE...

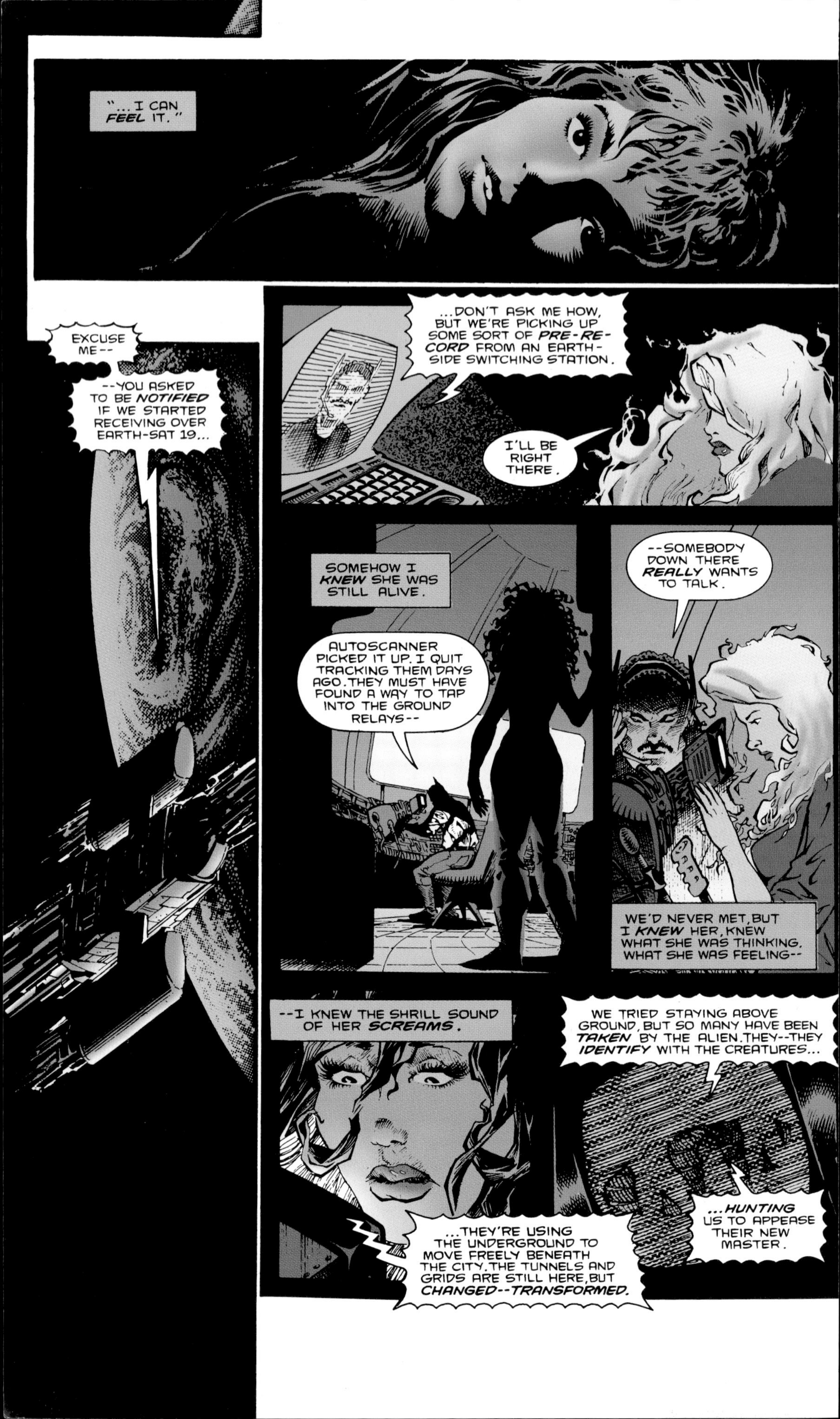
"...I CAN FEEL IT."
EXCUSE ME--
--YOU ASKED TO BE NOTIFIED IF WE STARTED RECEIVING OVER EARTH-SAT 19...
...DON'T ASK ME HOW, BUT WE'RE PICKING UP SOME SORT OF PRE-RECORD FROM AN EARTH-SIDE SWITCHING STATION.
I'LL BE RIGHT THERE.
SOMEHOW I KNEW SHE WAS STILL ALIVE.
AUTOSCANNER PICKED IT UP. I QUIT TRACKING THEM DAYS AGO. THEY MUST HAVE FOUND A WAY TO TAP INTO THE GROUND RELAYS--
--SOMEBODY DOWN THERE REALLY WANTS TO TALK.
WE'D NEVER MET, BUT I KNEW HER, KNEW WHAT SHE WAS THINKING, WHAT SHE WAS FEELING--
--I KNEW THE SHRILL SOUND OF HER SCREAMS.
WE TRIED STAYING ABOVE GROUND, BUT SO MANY HAVE BEEN TAKEN BY THE ALIEN. THEY--THEY IDENTIFY WITH THE CREATURES...
...HUNTING US TO APPEASE THEIR NEW MASTER.
...THEY'RE USING THE UNDERGROUND TO MOVE FREELY BENEATH THE CITY. THE TUNNELS AND GRIDS ARE STILL HERE, BUT CHANGED--TRANSFORMED.

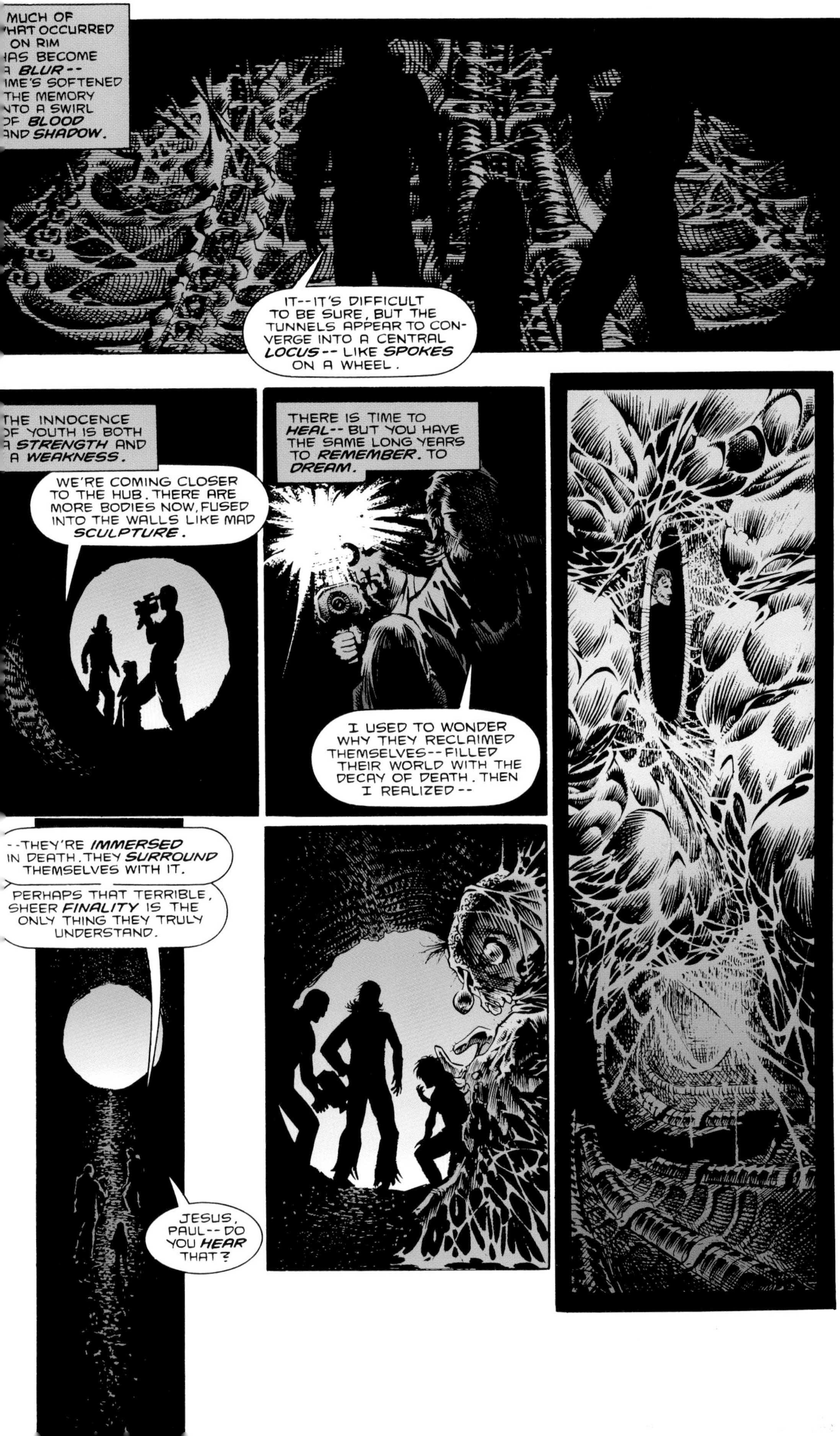
MUCH OF WHAT OCCURRED ON RIM HAS BECOME A BLUR-- TIME'S SOFTENED THE MEMORY INTO A SWIRL OF BLOOD AND SHADOW.
IT--IT'S DIFFICULT TO BE SURE, BUT THE TUNNELS APPEAR TO CONVERGE INTO A CENTRAL LOCUS-- LIKE SPOKES ON A WHEEL.
THE INNOCENCE OF YOUTH IS BOTH A STRENGTH AND A WEAKNESS.
WE'RE COMING CLOSER TO THE HUB. THERE ARE MORE BODIES NOW, FUSED INTO THE WALLS LIKE MAD SCULPTURE.
THERE IS TIME TO HEAL-- BUT YOU HAVE THE SAME LONG YEARS TO REMEMBER. TO DREAM.
I USED TO WONDER WHY THEY RECLAIMED THEMSELVES--FILLED THEIR WORLD WITH THE DECAY OF DEATH. THEN I REALIZED--
--THEY'RE IMMERSED IN DEATH. THEY SURROUND THEMSELVES WITH IT.
PERHAPS THAT TERRIBLE, SHEER FINALITY IS THE ONLY THING THEY TRULY UNDERSTAND.
JESUS, PAUL--DO YOU HEAR THAT?

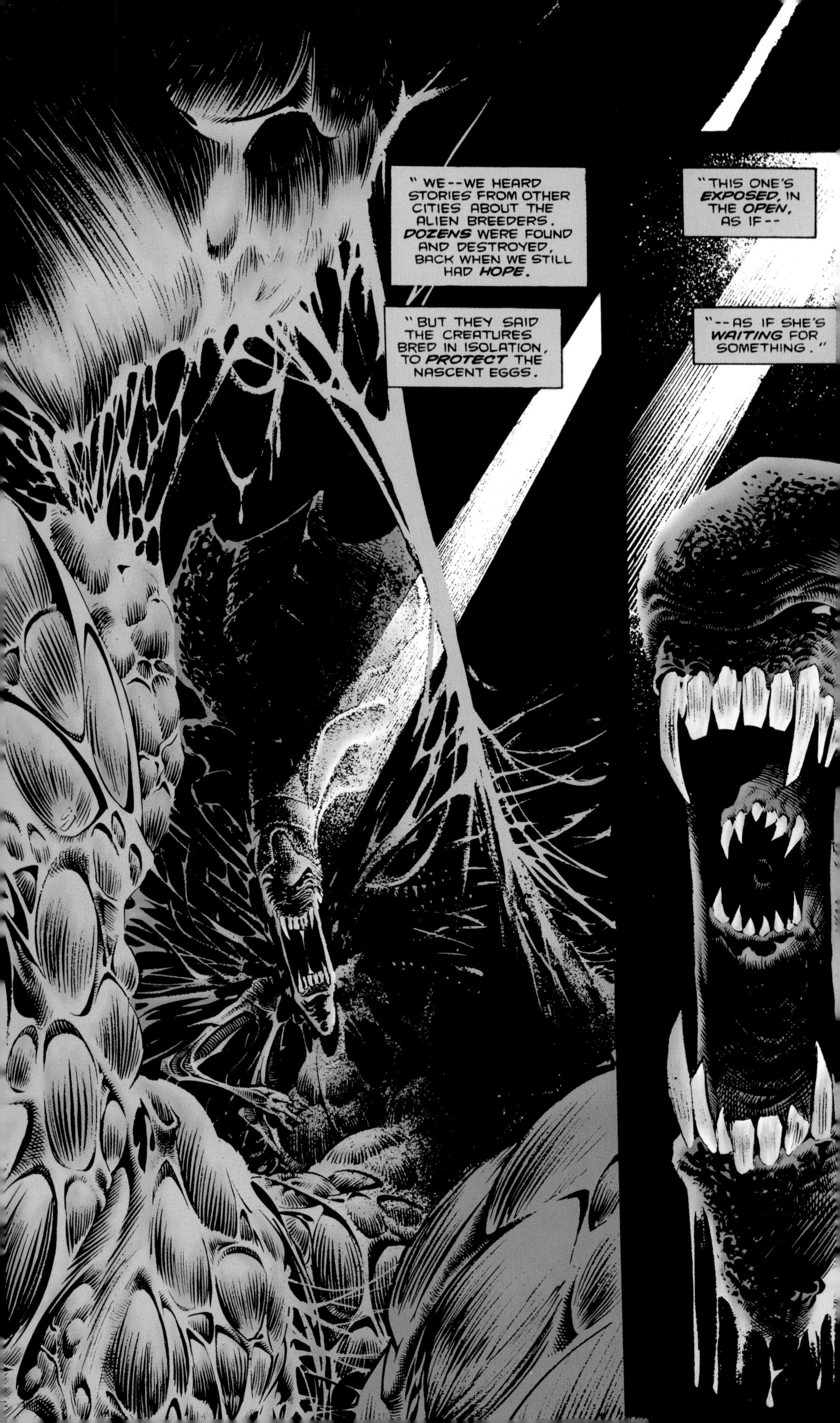
" WE--WE HEARD STORIES FROM OTHER CITIES ABOUT THE ALIEN BREEDERS. DOZENS WERE FOUND AND DESTROYED, BACK WHEN WE STILL HAD HOPE.
" BUT THEY SAID THE CREATURES BRED IN ISOLATION, TO PROTECT THE NASCENT EGGS.
"THIS ONE'S EXPOSED, IN THE OPEN, AS IF--
"--AS IF SHE'S WAITING FOR SOMETHING."

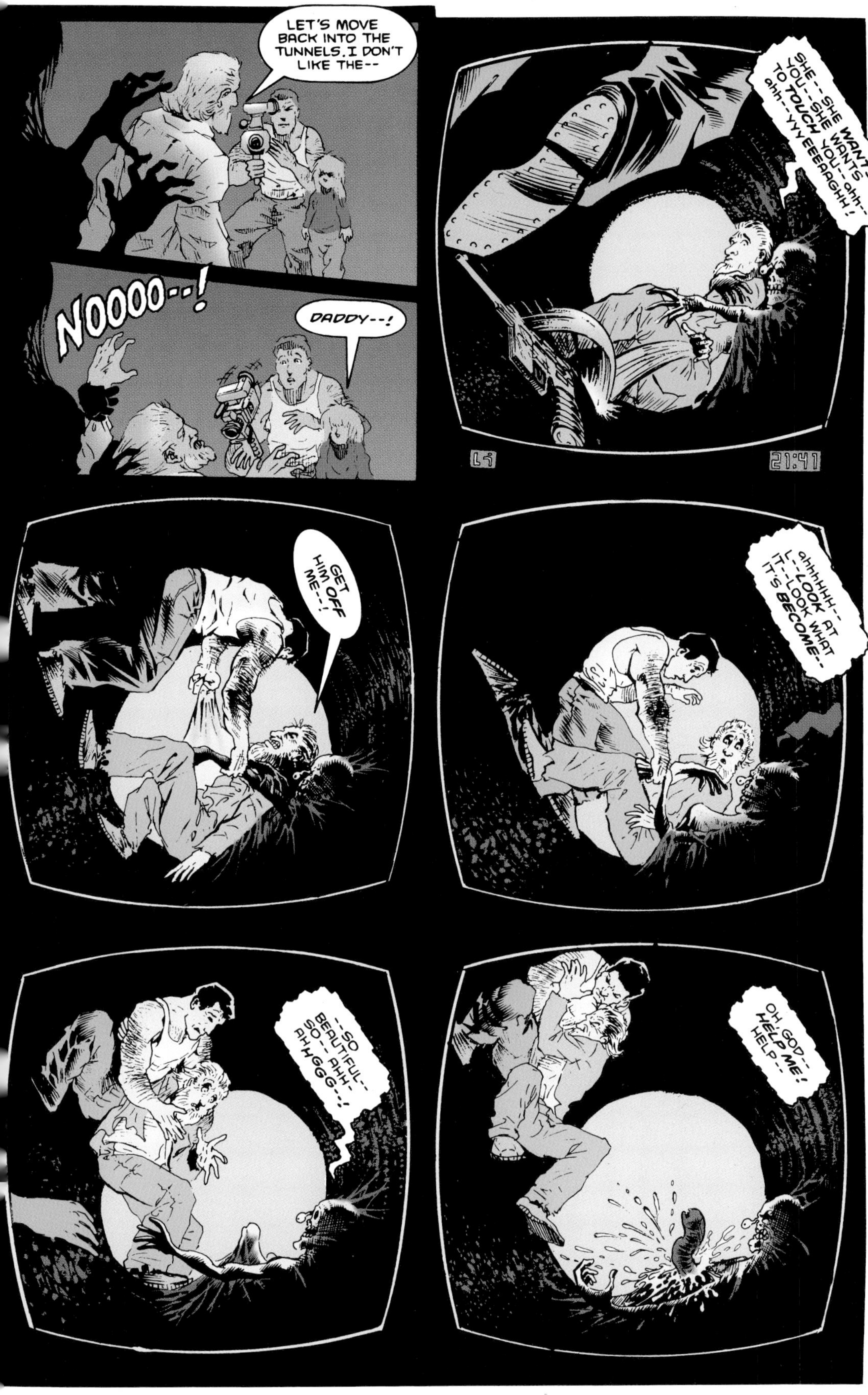
LET'S MOVE BACK INTO THE TUNNELS, I DON'T LIKE THE--
SHE--SHE WANTS YOU--SHE WANTS TO TOUCH YOU--ahh--ahh--YYYEEEAAGHH!
NOOOO--!
DADDY--!
21:41
GET HIM OFF ME--!
ahhhhHH--L--LOOK AT IT--LOOK WHAT IT'S BECOME--
--SO BEAUTIFUL--SO--AHH-AHHGGG--!
OH, GOD--HELP ME! HELP--

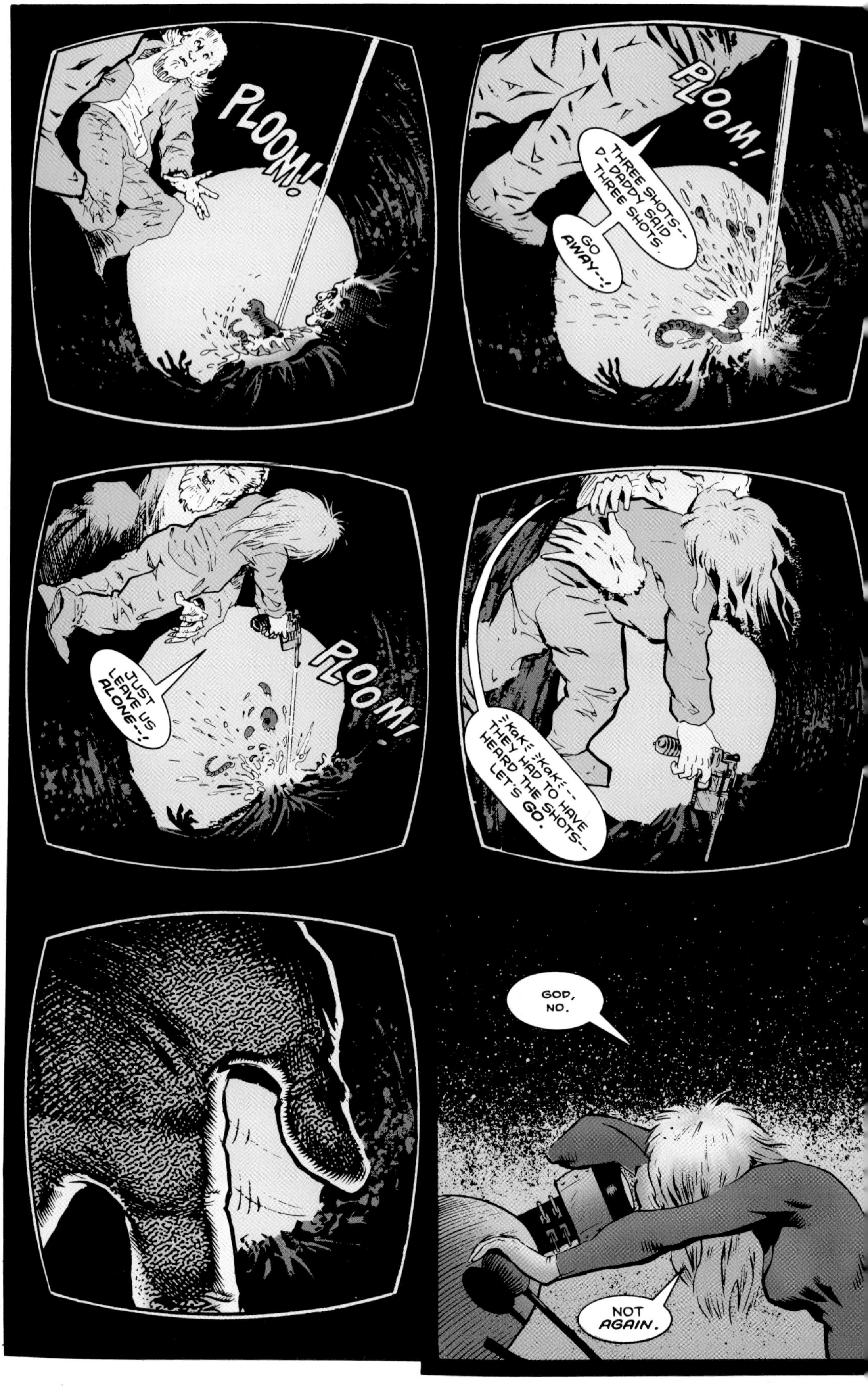
PLOOM!
PLOOM!
THREE SHOTS-- D-DADDY SAID THREE SHOTS.
GO AWAY--!
PLOOM!
JUST LEAVE US ALONE--!
KAK KAK-- THEY HAD TO HAVE HEARD THE SHOTS-- LET'S GO.
GOD, NO.
NOT AGAIN.

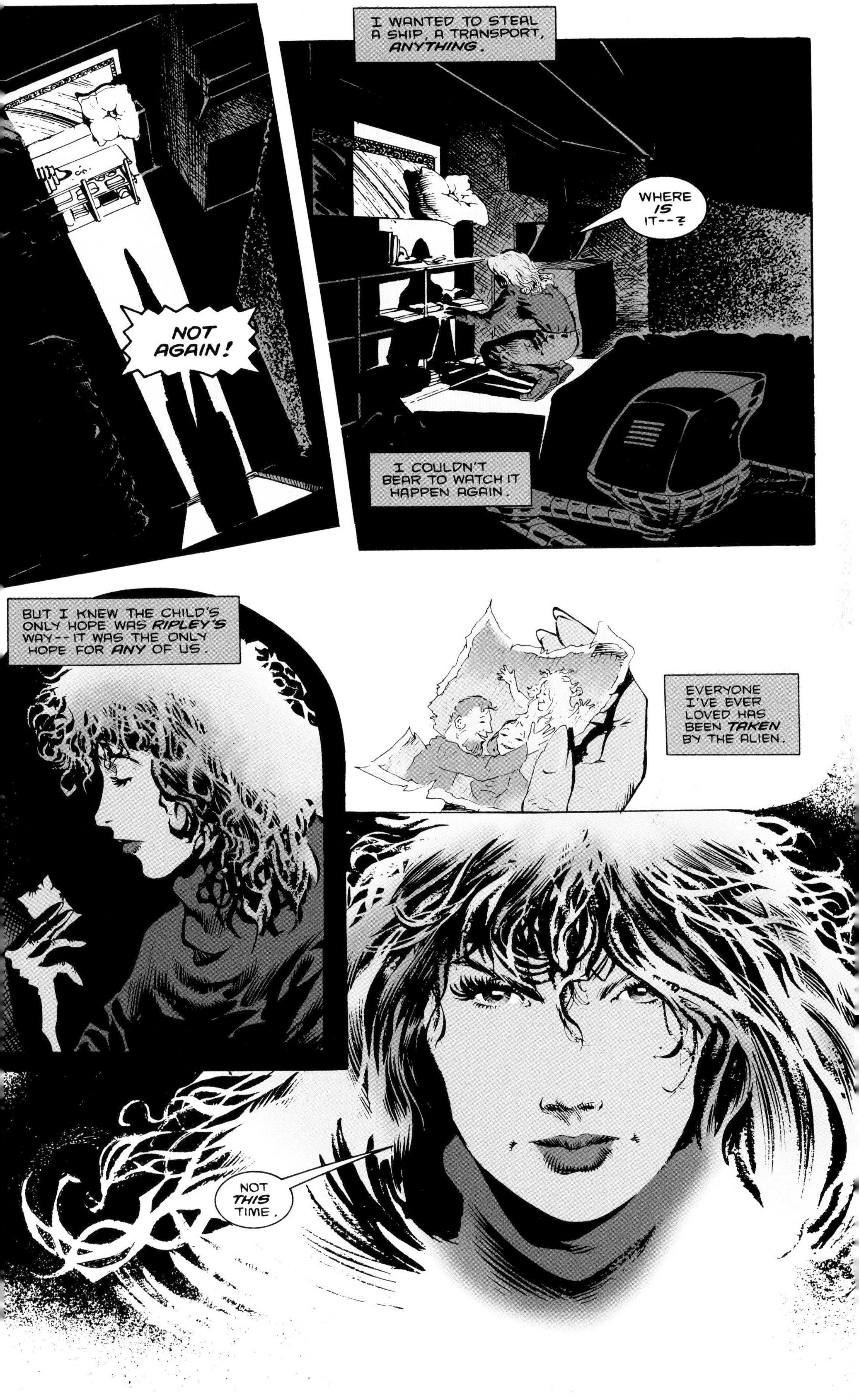

NOT AGAIN!
I WANTED TO STEAL A SHIP, A TRANSPORT, ANYTHING.
WHERE IS IT--?
I COULDN'T BEAR TO WATCH IT HAPPEN AGAIN.
BUT I KNEW THE CHILD'S ONLY HOPE WAS RIPLEY'S WAY--IT WAS THE ONLY HOPE FOR ANY OF US.
EVERYONE I'VE EVER LOVED HAS BEEN TAKEN BY THE ALIEN.
NOT THIS TIME.

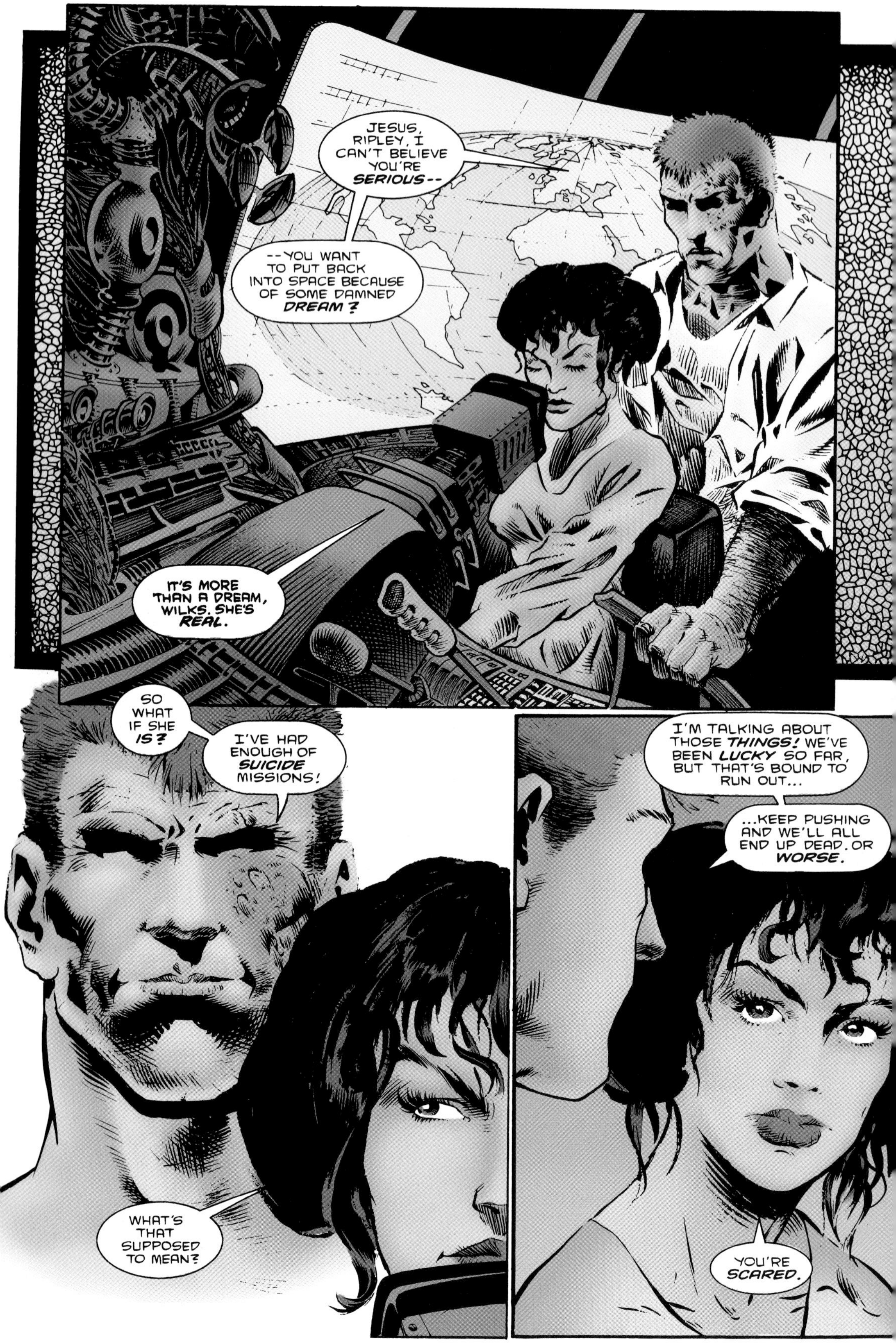
JESUS, RIPLEY, I CAN'T BELIEVE YOU'RE SERIOUS--
--YOU WANT TO PUT BACK INTO SPACE BECAUSE OF SOME DAMNED DREAM?
IT'S MORE THAN A DREAM, WILKS. SHE'S REAL.
SO WHAT IF SHE IS?
I'VE HAD ENOUGH OF SUICIDE MISSIONS!
WHAT'S THAT SUPPOSED TO MEAN?
I'M TALKING ABOUT THOSE THINGS! WE'VE BEEN LUCKY SO FAR, BUT THAT'S BOUND TO RUN OUT...
...KEEP PUSHING AND WE'LL ALL END UP DEAD. OR WORSE.
YOU'RE SCARED.

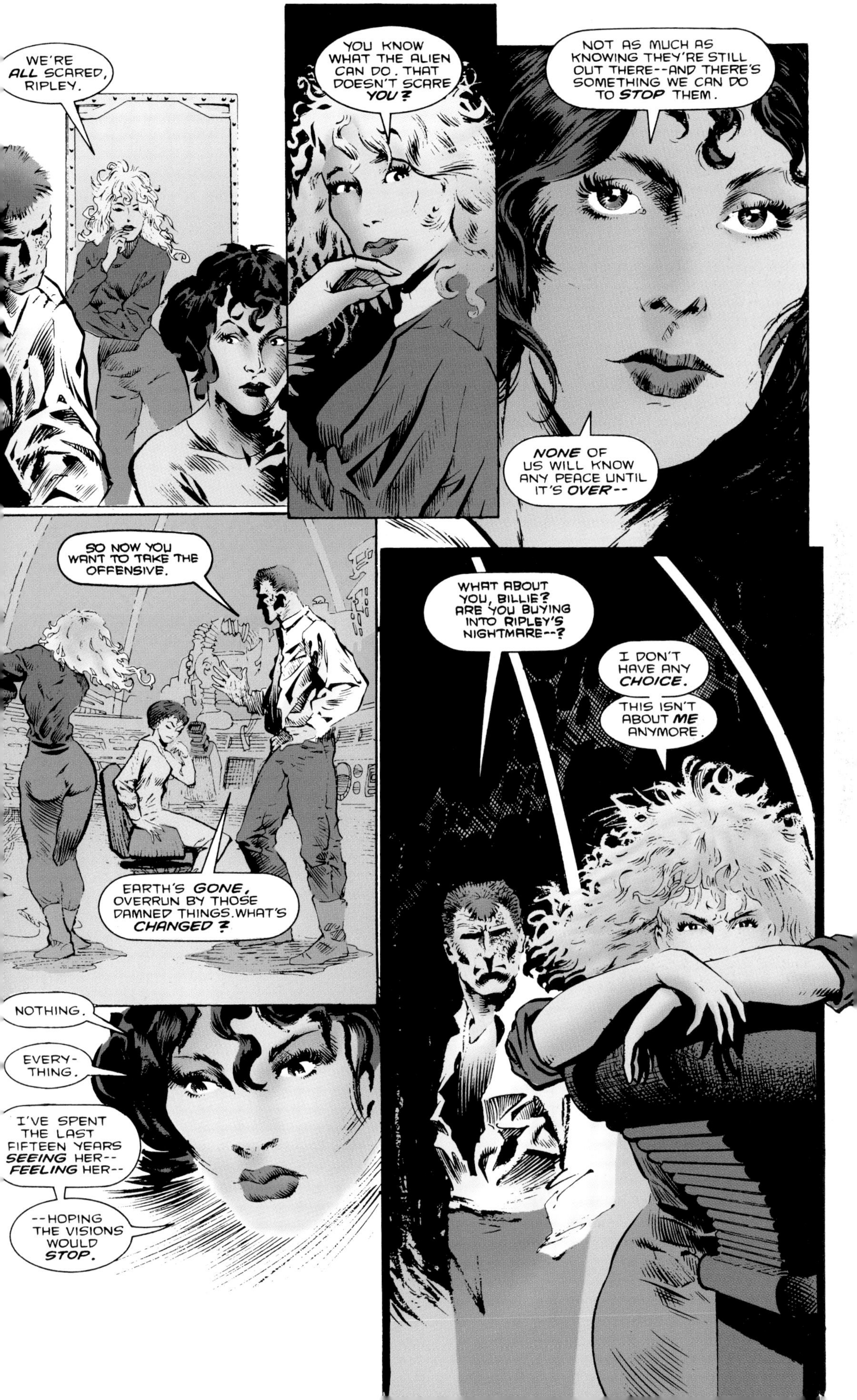
WE'RE ALL SCARED, RIPLEY.
YOU KNOW WHAT THE ALIEN CAN DO. THAT DOESN'T SCARE YOU?
NOT AS MUCH AS KNOWING THEY'RE STILL OUT THERE--AND THERE'S SOMETHING WE CAN DO TO STOP THEM.
NONE OF US WILL KNOW ANY PEACE UNTIL IT'S OVER--
SO NOW YOU WANT TO TAKE THE OFFENSIVE.
EARTH'S GONE, OVERRUN BY THOSE DAMNED THINGS. WHAT'S CHANGED?
NOTHING.
EVERY-THING.
I'VE SPENT THE LAST FIFTEEN YEARS SEEING HER--FEELING HER--
--HOPING THE VISIONS WOULD STOP.
WHAT ABOUT YOU, BILLIE? ARE YOU BUYING INTO RIPLEY'S NIGHTMARE--?
I DON'T HAVE ANY CHOICE.
THIS ISN'T ABOUT ME ANYMORE.

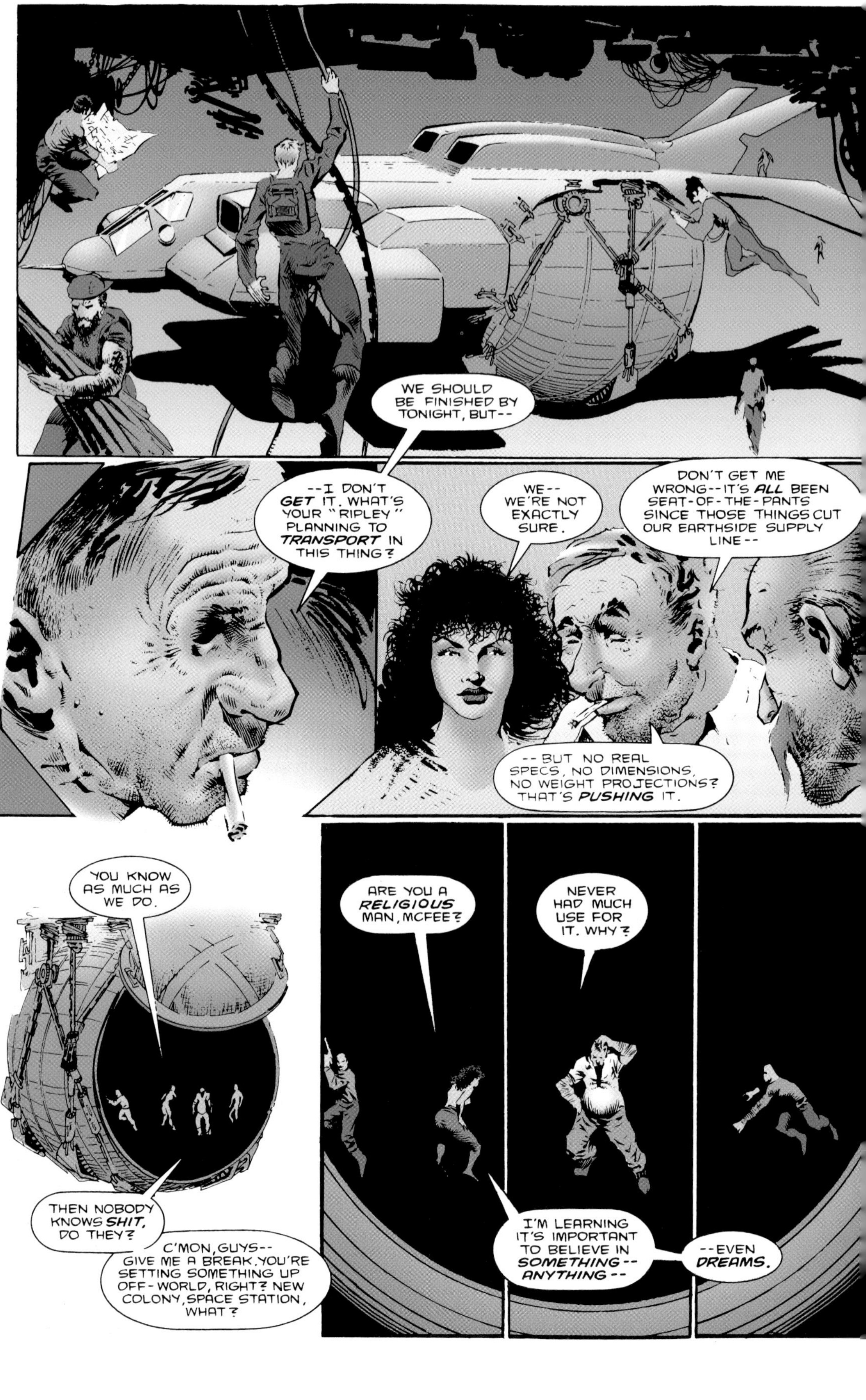
WE SHOULD BE FINISHED BY TONIGHT, BUT--
--I DON'T GET IT. WHAT'S YOUR "RIPLEY" PLANNING TO TRANSPORT IN THIS THING?
WE-- WE'RE NOT EXACTLY SURE.
DON'T GET ME WRONG--IT'S ALL BEEN SEAT-OF-THE-PANTS SINCE THOSE THINGS CUT OUR EARTHSIDE SUPPLY LINE--
--BUT NO REAL SPECS, NO DIMENSIONS, NO WEIGHT PROJECTIONS? THAT'S PUSHING IT.
YOU KNOW AS MUCH AS WE DO.
THEN NOBODY KNOWS SHIT, DO THEY?
C'MON, GUYS-- GIVE ME A BREAK. YOU'RE SETTING SOMETHING UP OFF-WORLD, RIGHT? NEW COLONY, SPACE STATION, WHAT?
ARE YOU A RELIGIOUS MAN, MCFEE?
NEVER HAD MUCH USE FOR IT. WHY?
I'M LEARNING IT'S IMPORTANT TO BELIEVE IN SOMETHING-- ANYTHING--
--EVEN DREAMS.

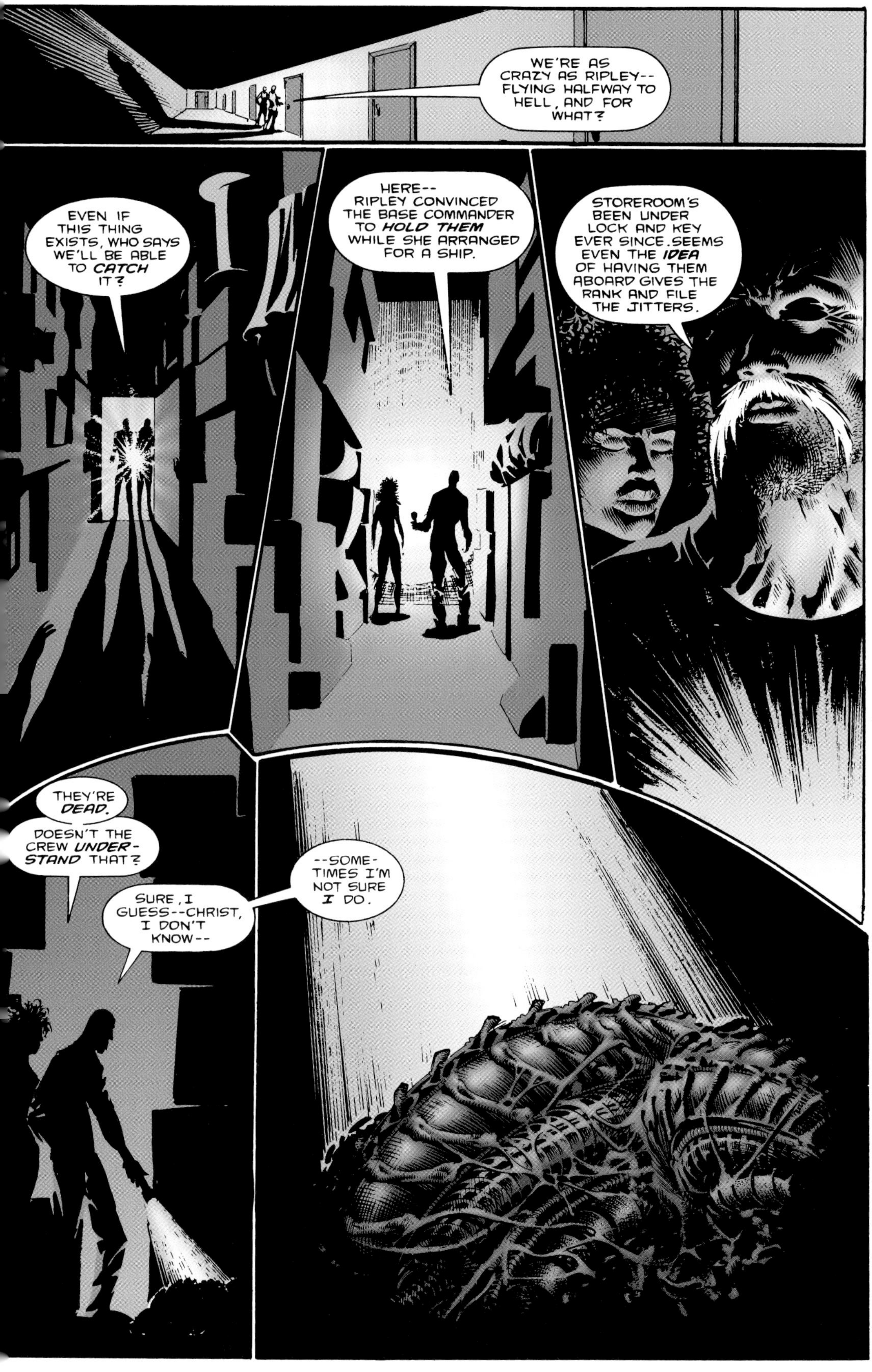
WE'RE AS CRAZY AS RIPLEY-- FLYING HALFWAY TO HELL, AND FOR WHAT?
EVEN IF THIS THING EXISTS, WHO SAYS WE'LL BE ABLE TO *CATCH* IT?
HERE-- RIPLEY CONVINCED THE BASE COMMANDER TO *HOLD THEM* WHILE SHE ARRANGED FOR A SHIP.
STOREROOM'S BEEN UNDER LOCK AND KEY EVER SINCE. SEEMS EVEN THE *IDEA* OF HAVING THEM ABOARD GIVES THE RANK AND FILE THE JITTERS.
THEY'RE *DEAD.*
DOESN'T THE CREW *UNDERSTAND* THAT?
SURE, I GUESS--CHRIST, I DON'T KNOW--
--SOMETIMES I'M NOT SURE *I* DO.

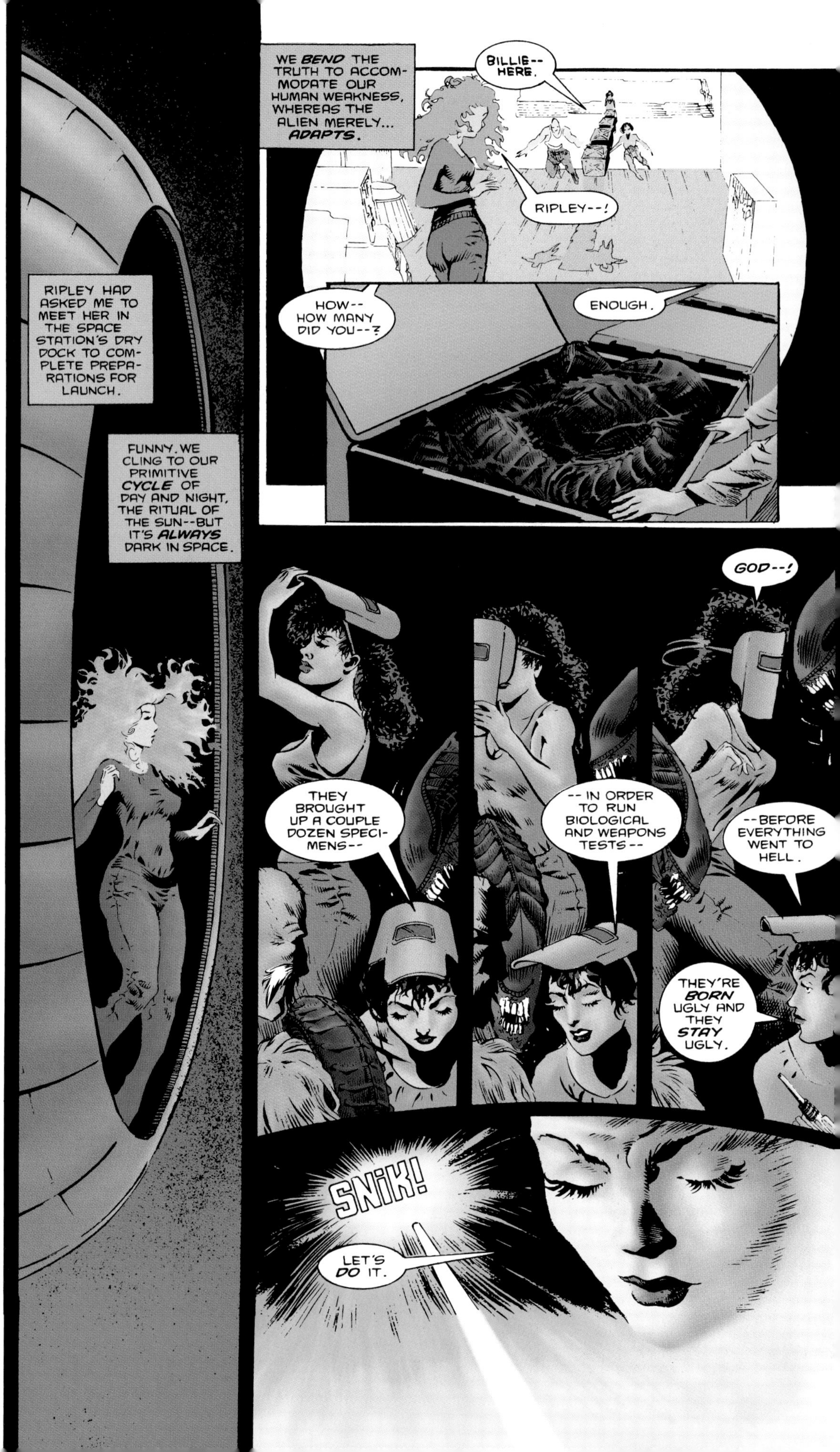
WE BEND THE TRUTH TO ACCOMMODATE OUR HUMAN WEAKNESS, WHEREAS THE ALIEN MERELY... ADAPTS.
BILLIE-- HERE.
RIPLEY--!
RIPLEY HAD ASKED ME TO MEET HER IN THE SPACE STATION'S DRY DOCK TO COMPLETE PREPARATIONS FOR LAUNCH.
FUNNY. WE CLING TO OUR PRIMITIVE CYCLE OF DAY AND NIGHT, THE RITUAL OF THE SUN--BUT IT'S ALWAYS DARK IN SPACE.
HOW-- HOW MANY DID YOU--?
ENOUGH.
GOD--!
THEY BROUGHT UP A COUPLE DOZEN SPECIMENS--
-- IN ORDER TO RUN BIOLOGICAL AND WEAPONS TESTS --
--BEFORE EVERYTHING WENT TO HELL.
THEY'RE BORN UGLY AND THEY STAY UGLY.
SNIK!
LET'S DO IT.

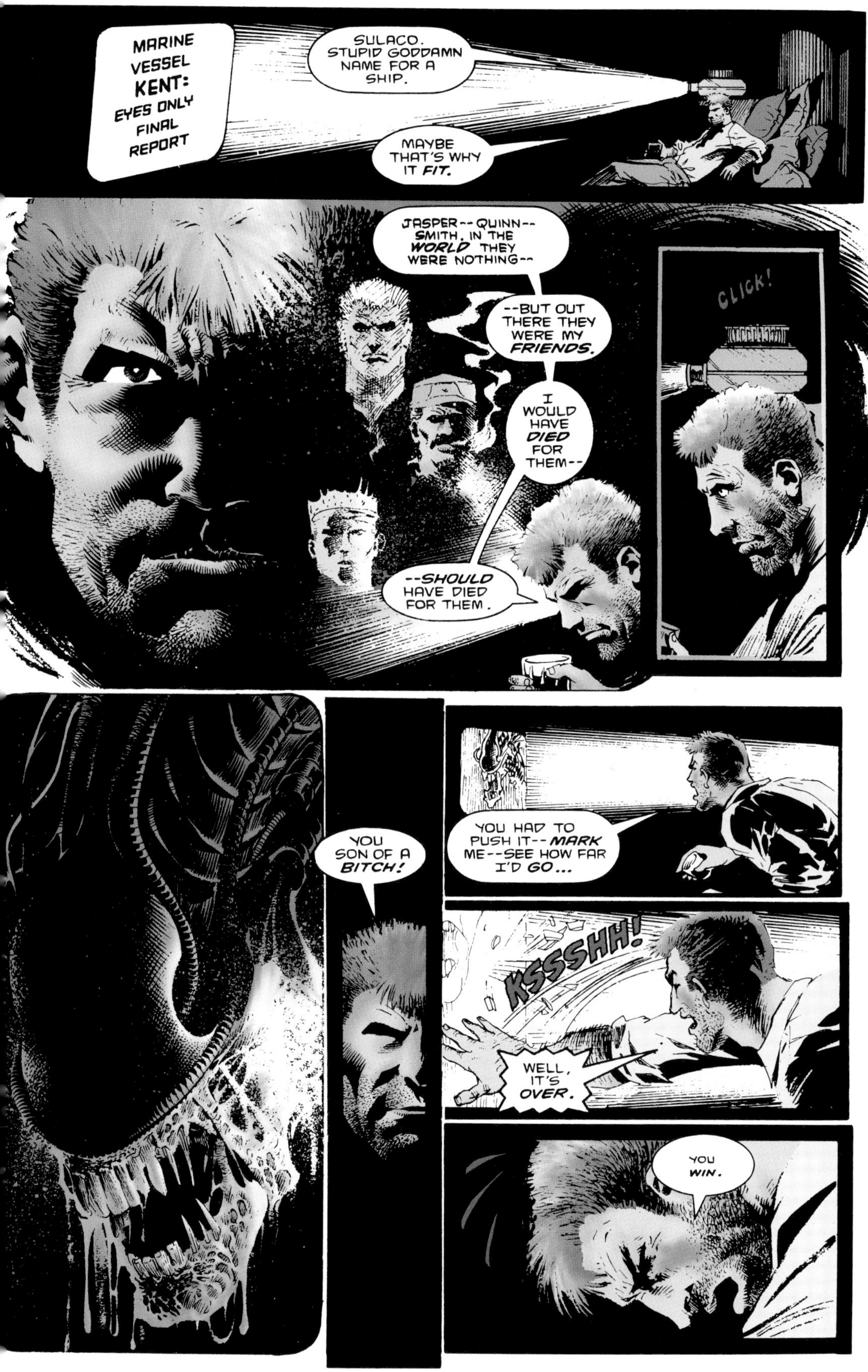
MARINE VESSEL KENT: EYES ONLY FINAL REPORT
SULACO. STUPID GODDAMN NAME FOR A SHIP.
MAYBE THAT'S WHY IT FIT.
JASPER--QUINN--SMITH, IN THE WORLD THEY WERE NOTHING--
--BUT OUT THERE THEY WERE MY FRIENDS.
I WOULD HAVE DIED FOR THEM--
--SHOULD HAVE DIED FOR THEM.
CLICK!
YOU SON OF A BITCH!
YOU HAD TO PUSH IT--MARK ME--SEE HOW FAR I'D GO...
KSSSHH!
WELL, IT'S OVER.
YOU WIN.

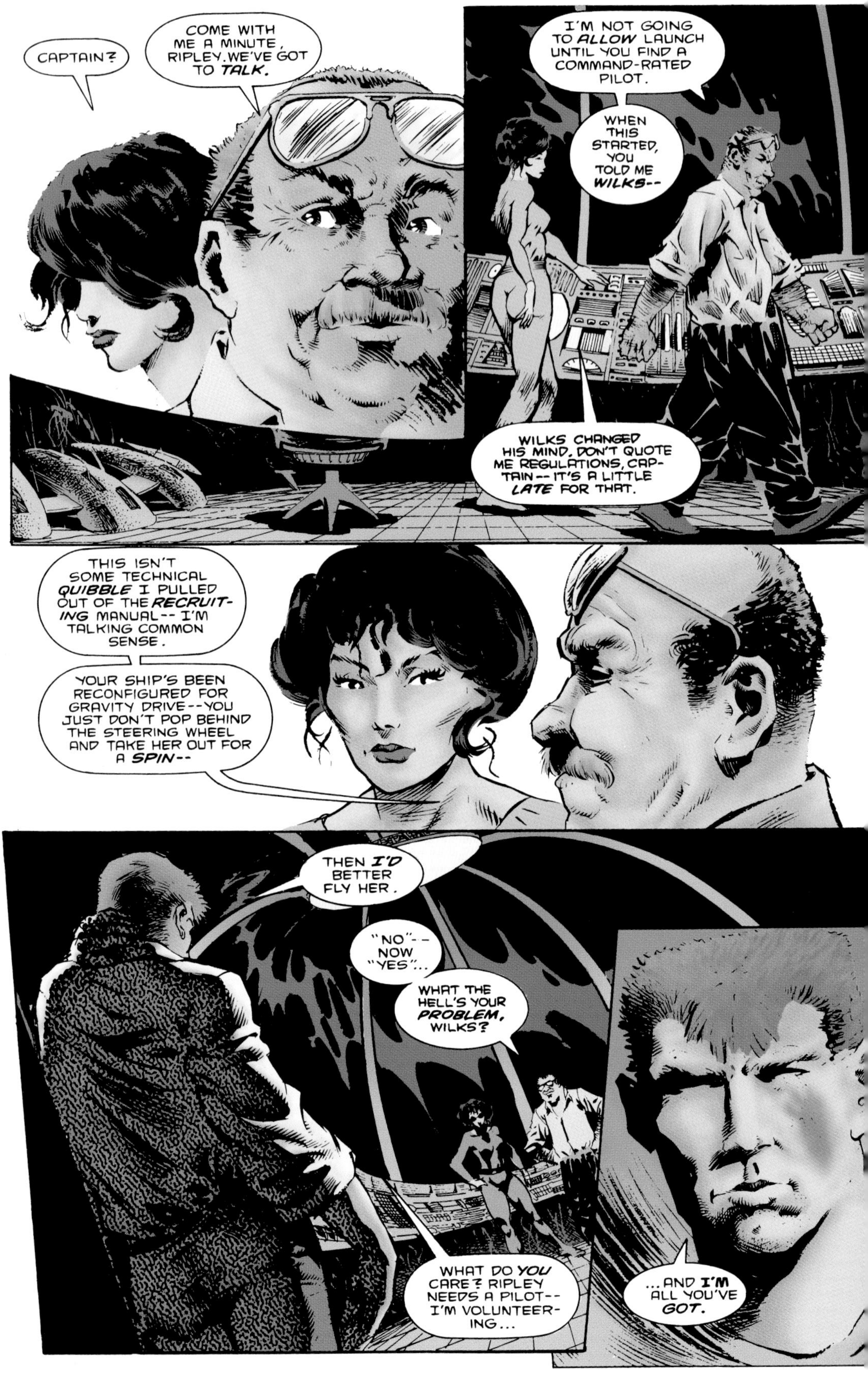

CAPTAIN?
COME WITH ME A MINUTE, RIPLEY. WE'VE GOT TO TALK.
I'M NOT GOING TO ALLOW LAUNCH UNTIL YOU FIND A COMMAND-RATED PILOT.
WHEN THIS STARTED, YOU TOLD ME WILKS--
WILKS CHANGED HIS MIND. DON'T QUOTE ME REGULATIONS, CAPTAIN-- IT'S A LITTLE LATE FOR THAT.
THIS ISN'T SOME TECHNICAL QUIBBLE I PULLED OUT OF THE RECRUITING MANUAL-- I'M TALKING COMMON SENSE.
YOUR SHIP'S BEEN RECONFIGURED FOR GRAVITY DRIVE--YOU JUST DON'T POP BEHIND THE STEERING WHEEL AND TAKE HER OUT FOR A SPIN--
THEN I'D BETTER FLY HER.
"NO"-- NOW "YES"...
WHAT THE HELL'S YOUR PROBLEM, WILKS?
WHAT DO YOU CARE? RIPLEY NEEDS A PILOT-- I'M VOLUNTEERING...
...AND I'M ALL YOU'VE GOT.

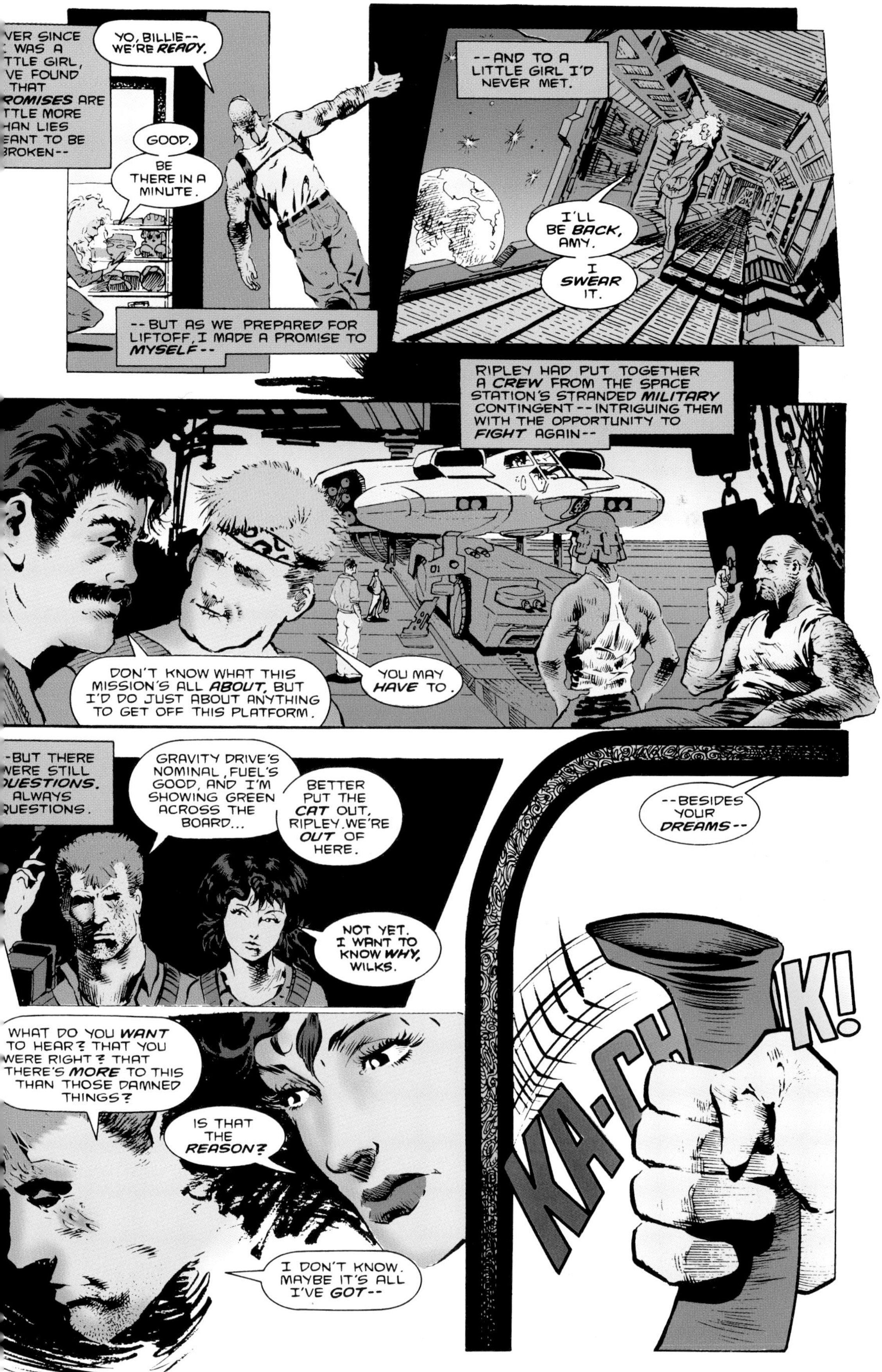
VER SINCE
WAS A
TTLE GIRL,
VE FOUND
THAT
ROMISES ARE
TTLE MORE
HAN LIES
EANT TO BE
BROKEN--
YO, BILLIE-- WE'RE READY.
GOOD.
BE THERE IN A MINUTE.
--BUT AS WE PREPARED FOR LIFTOFF, I MADE A PROMISE TO MYSELF--
--AND TO A LITTLE GIRL I'D NEVER MET.
I'LL BE BACK, AMY.
I SWEAR IT.
RIPLEY HAD PUT TOGETHER A CREW FROM THE SPACE STATION'S STRANDED MILITARY CONTINGENT--INTRIGUING THEM WITH THE OPPORTUNITY TO FIGHT AGAIN--
DON'T KNOW WHAT THIS MISSION'S ALL ABOUT, BUT I'D DO JUST ABOUT ANYTHING TO GET OFF THIS PLATFORM.
YOU MAY HAVE TO.
-BUT THERE
VERE STILL
UESTIONS.
ALWAYS
UESTIONS.
GRAVITY DRIVE'S NOMINAL, FUEL'S GOOD, AND I'M SHOWING GREEN ACROSS THE BOARD...
BETTER PUT THE CAT OUT, RIPLEY. WE'RE OUT OF HERE.
NOT YET. I WANT TO KNOW WHY, WILKS.
WHAT DO YOU WANT TO HEAR? THAT YOU WERE RIGHT? THAT THERE'S MORE TO THIS THAN THOSE DAMNED THINGS?
IS THAT THE REASON?
I DON'T KNOW. MAYBE IT'S ALL I'VE GOT--
--BESIDES YOUR DREAMS--
KA-CH K!

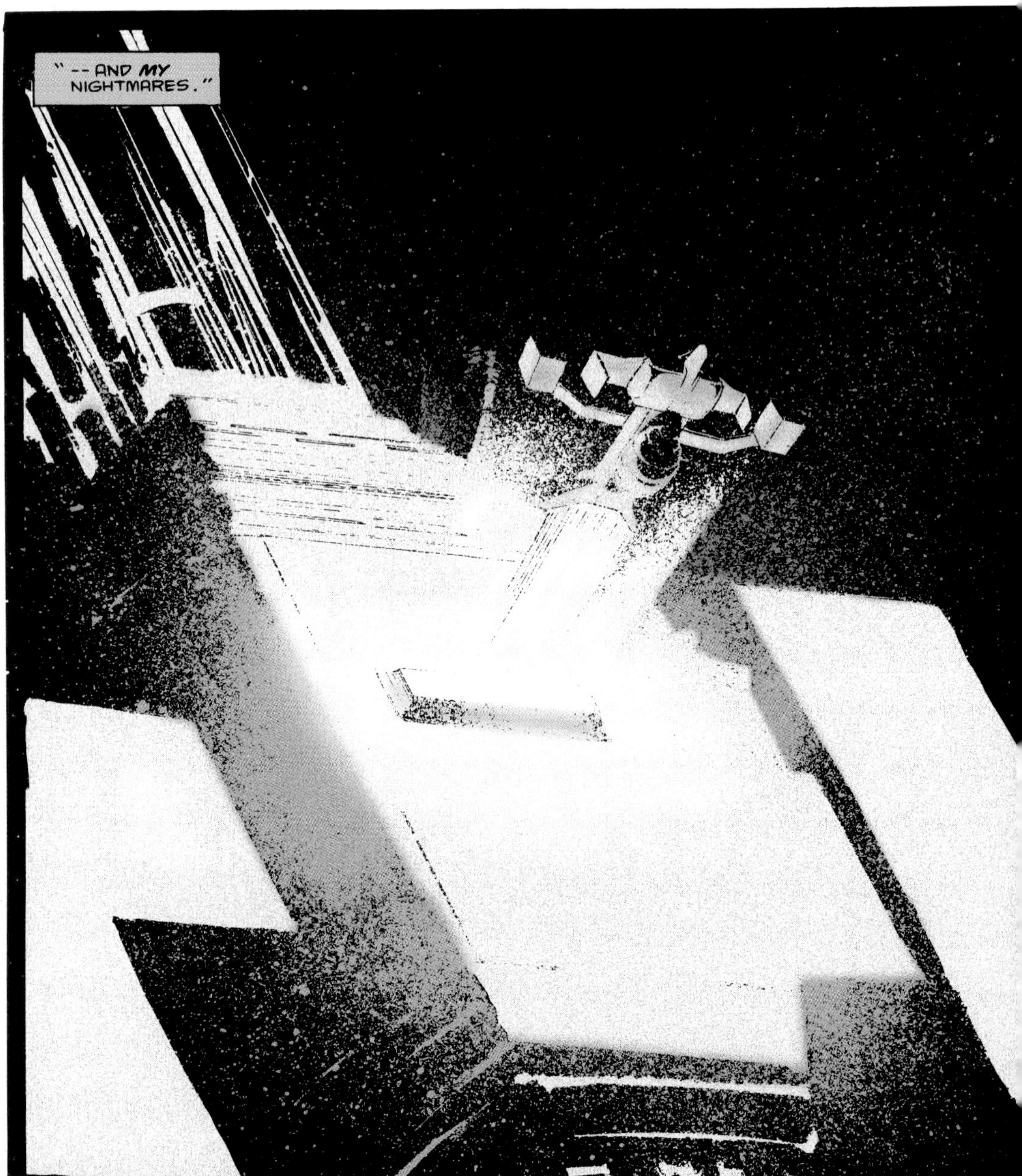
"--AND *MY* NIGHTMARES."

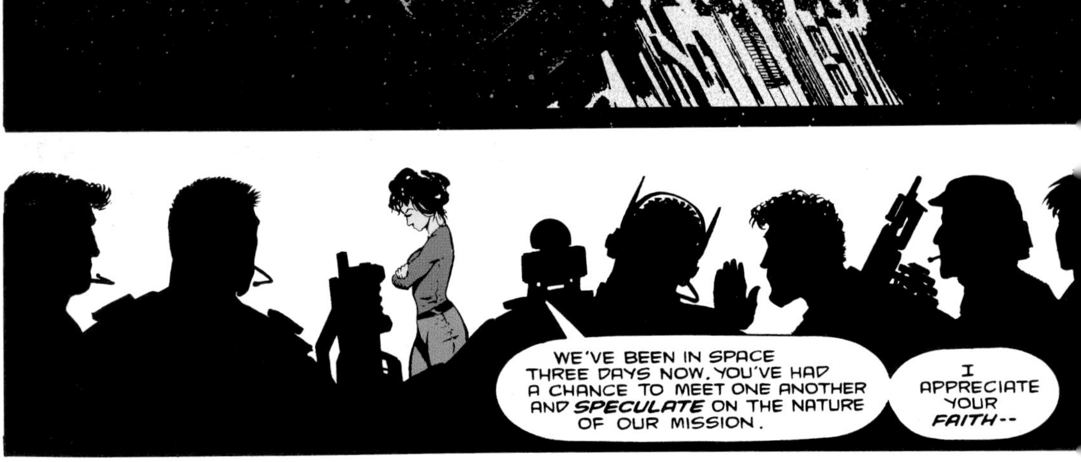
WE'VE BEEN IN SPACE THREE DAYS NOW. YOU'VE HAD A CHANCE TO MEET ONE ANOTHER AND *SPECULATE* ON THE NATURE OF OUR MISSION.
I APPRECIATE YOUR *FAITH*--

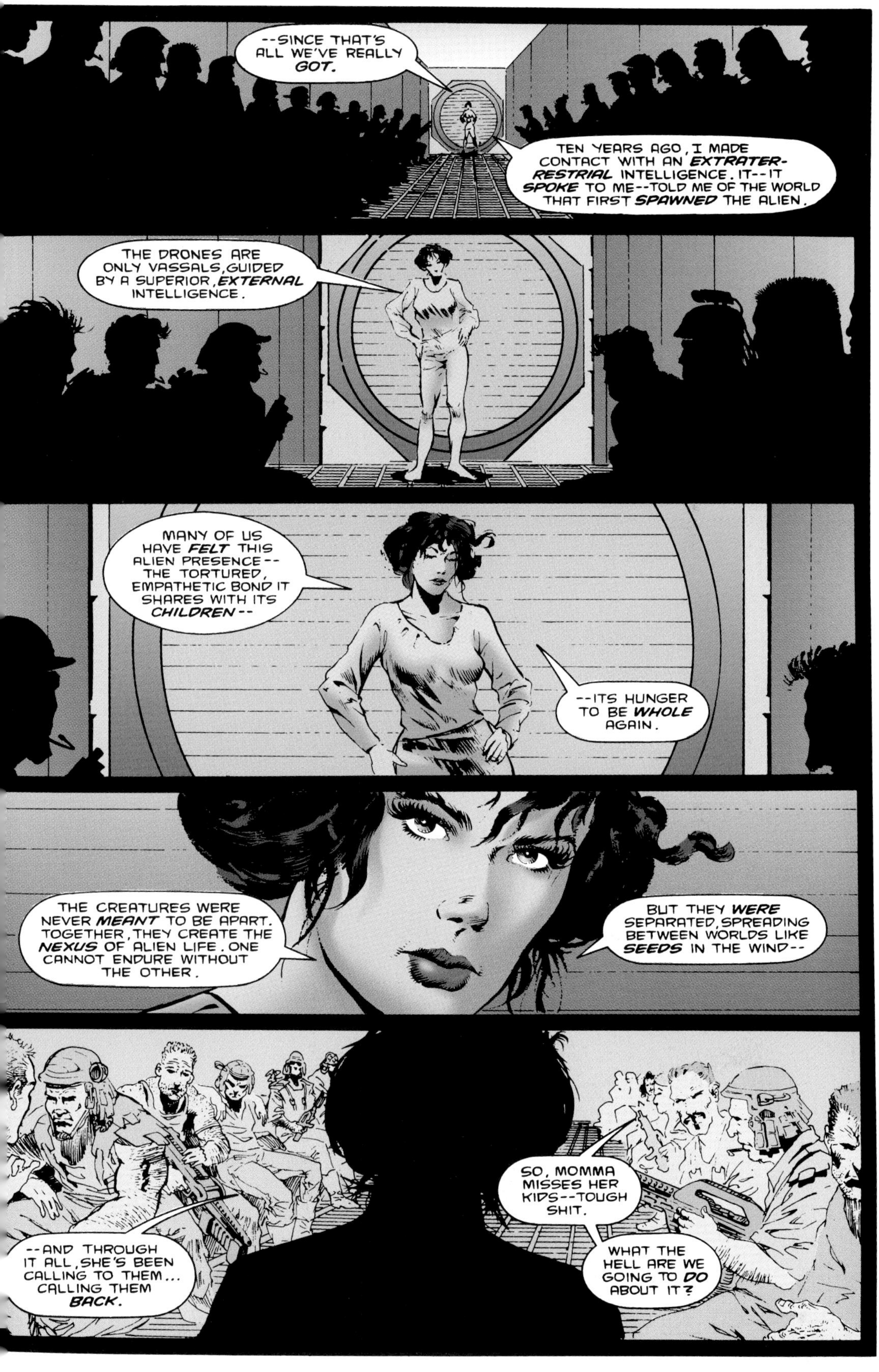
--SINCE THAT'S ALL WE'VE REALLY GOT.
TEN YEARS AGO, I MADE CONTACT WITH AN EXTRATER-RESTRIAL INTELLIGENCE. IT--IT SPOKE TO ME--TOLD ME OF THE WORLD THAT FIRST SPAWNED THE ALIEN.
THE DRONES ARE ONLY VASSALS, GUIDED BY A SUPERIOR, EXTERNAL INTELLIGENCE.
MANY OF US HAVE FELT THIS ALIEN PRESENCE-- THE TORTURED, EMPATHETIC BOND IT SHARES WITH ITS CHILDREN--
--ITS HUNGER TO BE WHOLE AGAIN.
THE CREATURES WERE NEVER MEANT TO BE APART. TOGETHER, THEY CREATE THE NEXUS OF ALIEN LIFE. ONE CANNOT ENDURE WITHOUT THE OTHER.
BUT THEY WERE SEPARATED, SPREADING BETWEEN WORLDS LIKE SEEDS IN THE WIND--
--AND THROUGH IT ALL, SHE'S BEEN CALLING TO THEM... CALLING THEM BACK.
SO, MOMMA MISSES HER KIDS--TOUGH SHIT.
WHAT THE HELL ARE WE GOING TO DO ABOUT IT?

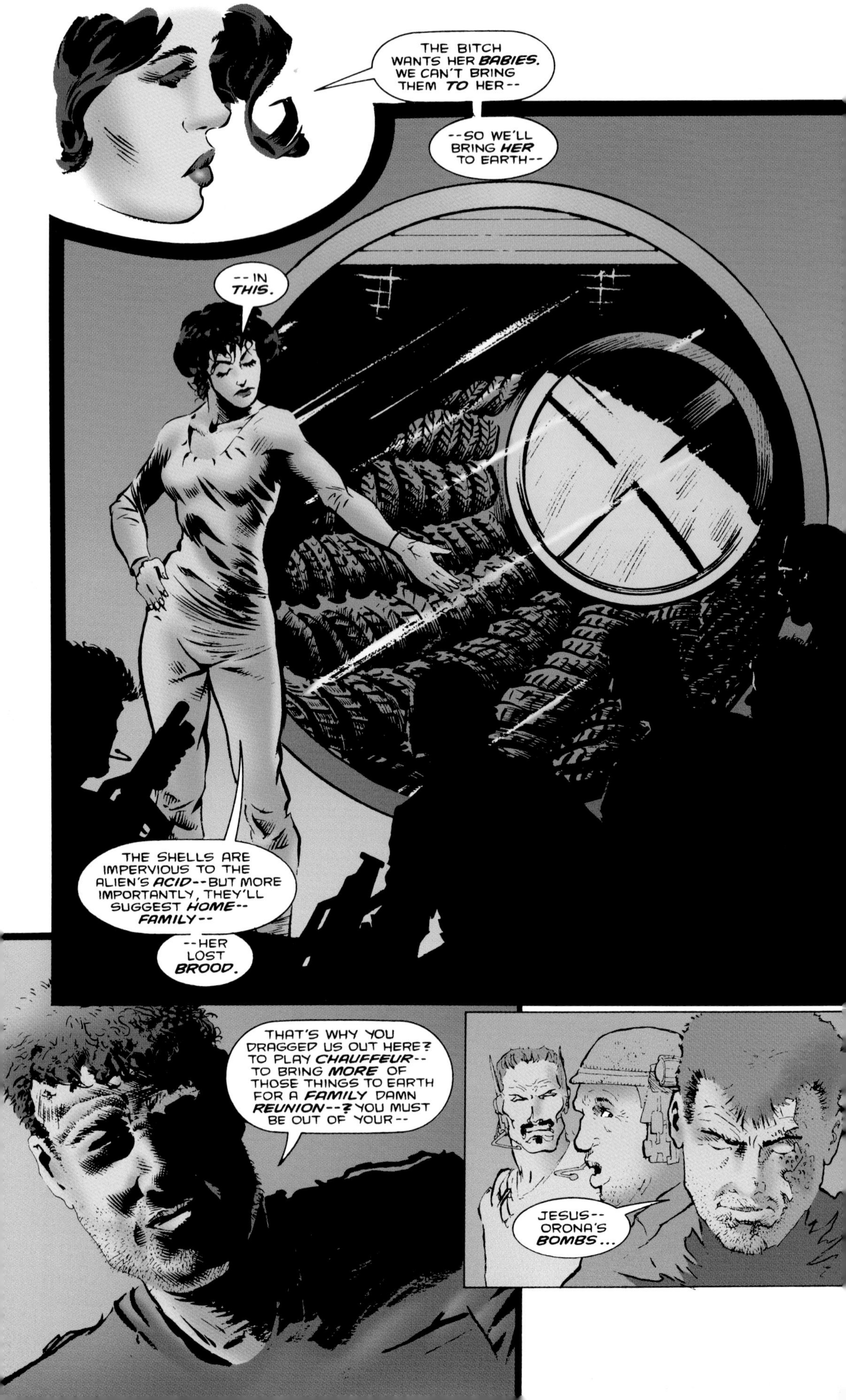
THE BITCH WANTS HER BABIES. WE CAN'T BRING THEM TO HER--
--SO WE'LL BRING HER TO EARTH--
--IN THIS.
THE SHELLS ARE IMPERVIOUS TO THE ALIEN'S ACID--BUT MORE IMPORTANTLY, THEY'LL SUGGEST HOME--FAMILY--
--HER LOST BROOD.
THAT'S WHY YOU DRAGGED US OUT HERE? TO PLAY CHAUFFEUR--TO BRING MORE OF THOSE THINGS TO EARTH FOR A FAMILY DAMN REUNION--? YOU MUST BE OUT OF YOUR--
JESUS--ORONA'S BOMBS...

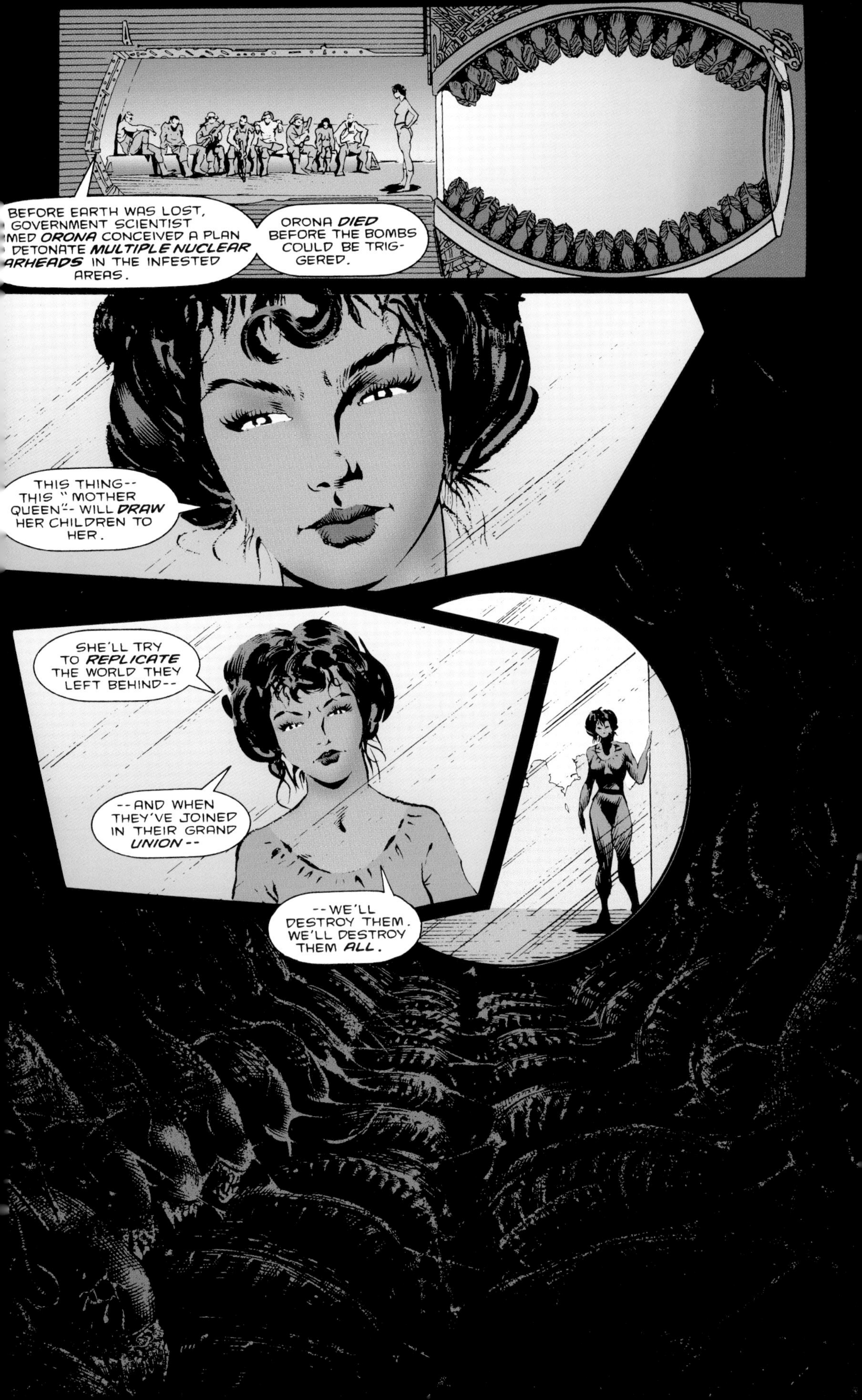
BEFORE EARTH WAS LOST, GOVERNMENT SCIENTIST MED ORONA CONCEIVED A PLAN DETONATE MULTIPLE NUCLEAR ARHEADS IN THE INFESTED AREAS.
ORONA DIED BEFORE THE BOMBS COULD BE TRIG-GERED.
THIS THING-- THIS "MOTHER QUEEN"-- WILL DRAW HER CHILDREN TO HER.
SHE'LL TRY TO REPLICATE THE WORLD THEY LEFT BEHIND--
--AND WHEN THEY'VE JOINED IN THEIR GRAND UNION--
--WE'LL DESTROY THEM. WE'LL DESTROY THEM ALL.

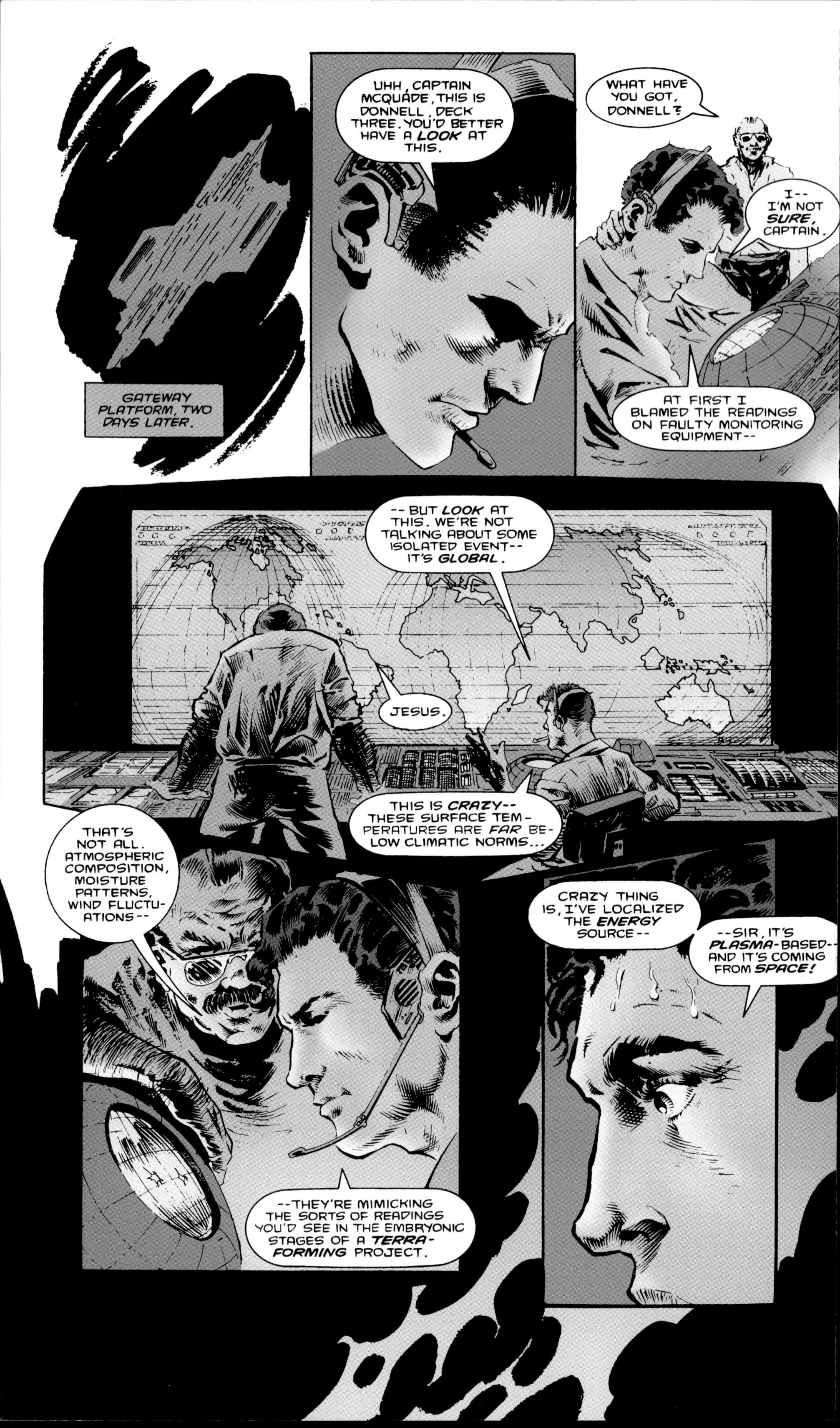
GATEWAY PLATFORM, TWO DAYS LATER.
UHH, CAPTAIN MCQUADE, THIS IS DONNELL, DECK THREE. YOU'D BETTER HAVE A LOOK AT THIS.
WHAT HAVE YOU GOT, DONNELL?
I-- I'M NOT SURE, CAPTAIN.
AT FIRST I BLAMED THE READINGS ON FAULTY MONITORING EQUIPMENT--
-- BUT LOOK AT THIS. WE'RE NOT TALKING ABOUT SOME ISOLATED EVENT-- IT'S GLOBAL.
JESUS.
THIS IS CRAZY-- THESE SURFACE TEM-PERATURES ARE FAR BE-LOW CLIMATIC NORMS...
THAT'S NOT ALL. ATMOSPHERIC COMPOSITION, MOISTURE PATTERNS, WIND FLUCTU-ATIONS--
--THEY'RE MIMICKING THE SORTS OF READINGS YOU'D SEE IN THE EMBRYONIC STAGES OF A TERRA-FORMING PROJECT.
CRAZY THING IS, I'VE LOCALIZED THE ENERGY SOURCE--
--SIR, IT'S PLASMA-BASED-- AND IT'S COMING FROM SPACE!

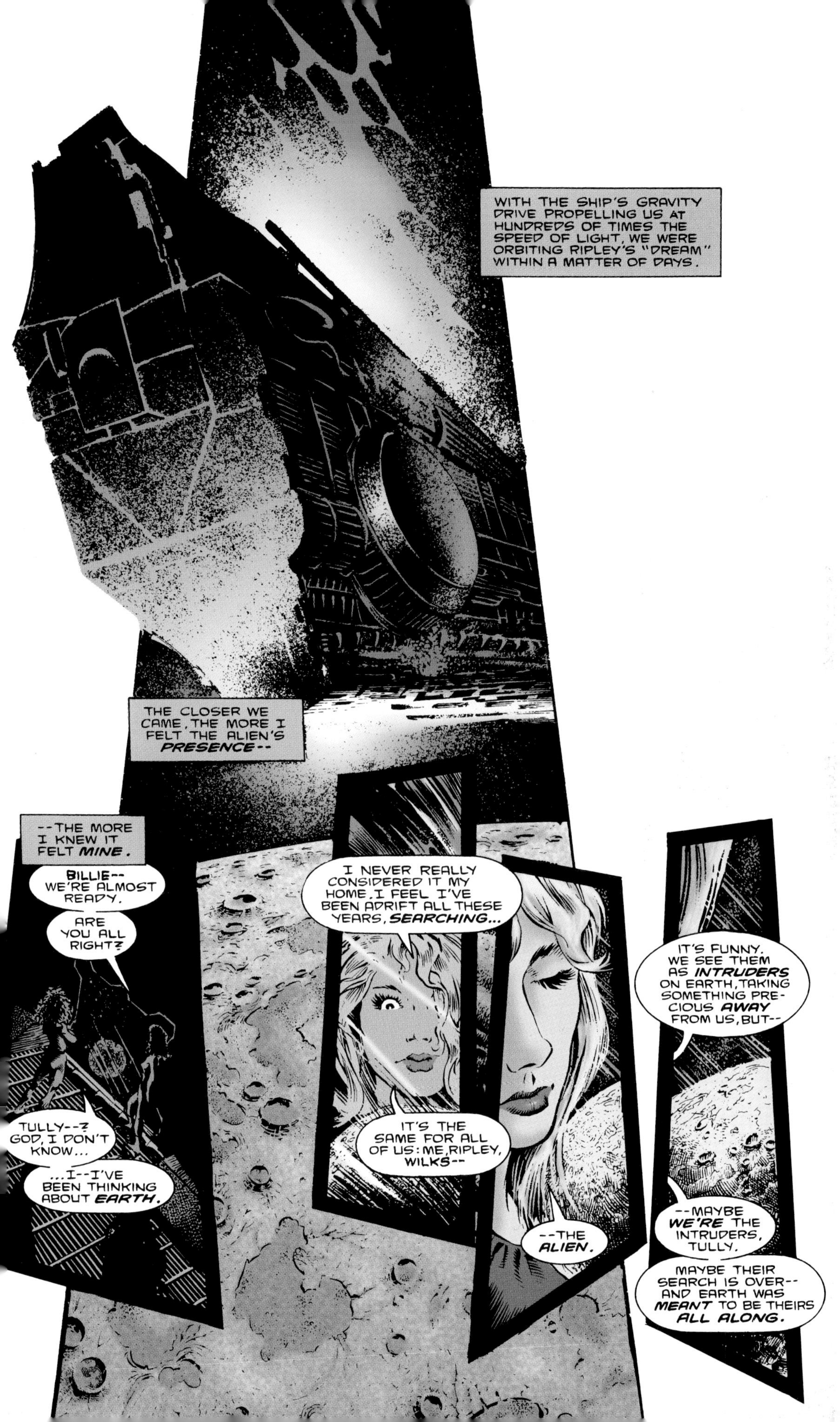
WITH THE SHIP'S GRAVITY DRIVE PROPELLING US AT HUNDREDS OF TIMES THE SPEED OF LIGHT, WE WERE ORBITING RIPLEY'S "DREAM" WITHIN A MATTER OF DAYS.
THE CLOSER WE CAME, THE MORE I FELT THE ALIEN'S *PRESENCE*--
--THE MORE I KNEW IT FELT *MINE*.
BILLIE-- WE'RE ALMOST READY.
ARE YOU ALL RIGHT?
TULLY--? GOD, I DON'T KNOW...
...I--I'VE BEEN THINKING ABOUT *EARTH*.
I NEVER REALLY CONSIDERED IT MY HOME. I FEEL I'VE BEEN ADRIFT ALL THESE YEARS, *SEARCHING*...
IT'S THE SAME FOR ALL OF US: ME, RIPLEY, WILKS--
--THE *ALIEN*.
IT'S FUNNY. WE SEE THEM AS *INTRUDERS* ON EARTH, TAKING SOMETHING PRECIOUS *AWAY* FROM US, BUT--
--MAYBE *WE'RE* THE INTRUDERS, TULLY.
MAYBE THEIR SEARCH IS OVER-- AND EARTH WAS *MEANT* TO BE THEIRS *ALL ALONG*.

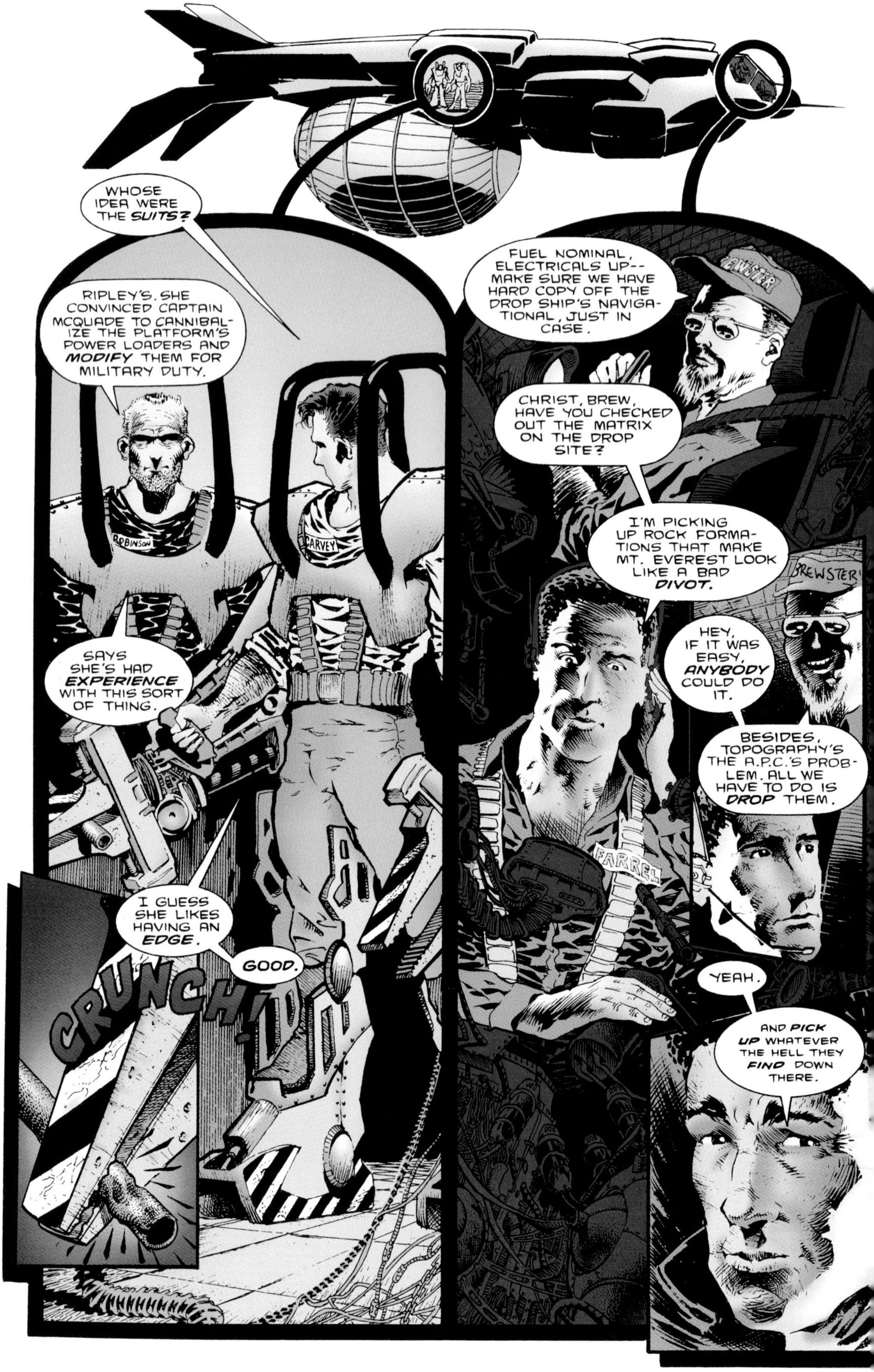
WHOSE IDEA WERE THE SUITS?
RIPLEY'S. SHE CONVINCED CAPTAIN MCQUADE TO CANNIBAL-IZE THE PLATFORM'S POWER LOADERS AND MODIFY THEM FOR MILITARY DUTY.
ROBINSON
GARVEY
SAYS SHE'S HAD EXPERIENCE WITH THIS SORT OF THING.
I GUESS SHE LIKES HAVING AN EDGE.
GOOD.
CRUNCH!
FUEL NOMINAL, ELECTRICALS UP-- MAKE SURE WE HAVE HARD COPY OFF THE DROP SHIP'S NAVIGA-TIONAL, JUST IN CASE.
CHRIST, BREW, HAVE YOU CHECKED OUT THE MATRIX ON THE DROP SITE?
I'M PICKING UP ROCK FORMA-TIONS THAT MAKE MT. EVEREST LOOK LIKE A BAD DIVOT.
BREWSTER
HEY, IF IT WAS EASY, ANYBODY COULD DO IT.
BESIDES, TOPOGRAPHY'S THE A.P.C.'S PROB-LEM. ALL WE HAVE TO DO IS DROP THEM.
FARREL
YEAH.
AND PICK UP WHATEVER THE HELL THEY FIND DOWN THERE.

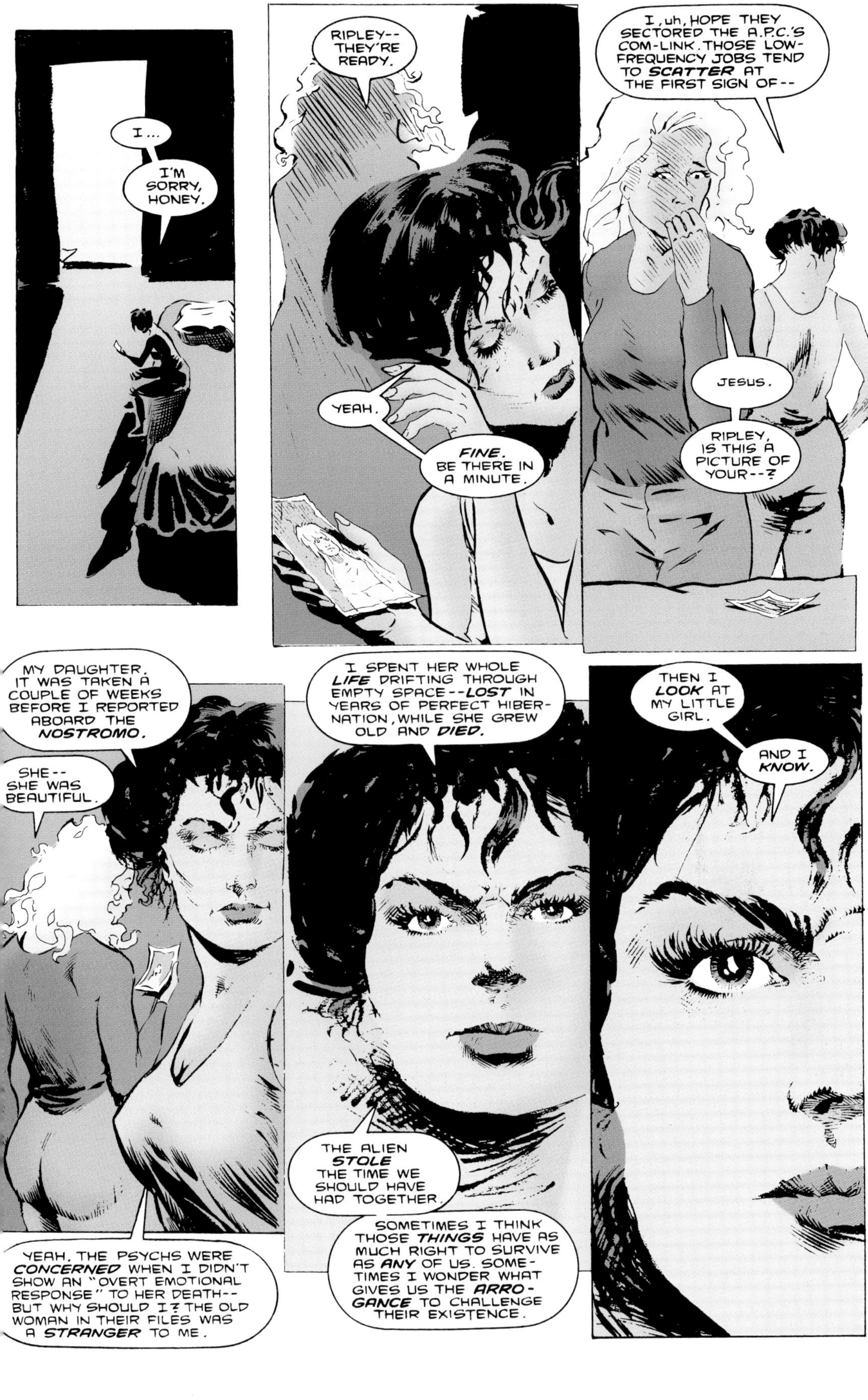
I...
I'M SORRY, HONEY.
RIPLEY-- THEY'RE READY.
YEAH.
FINE. BE THERE IN A MINUTE.
I, uh, HOPE THEY SECTORED THE A.P.C.'S COM-LINK. THOSE LOW-FREQUENCY JOBS TEND TO SCATTER AT THE FIRST SIGN OF--
JESUS.
RIPLEY, IS THIS A PICTURE OF YOUR--?
MY DAUGHTER. IT WAS TAKEN A COUPLE OF WEEKS BEFORE I REPORTED ABOARD THE NOSTROMO.
SHE-- SHE WAS BEAUTIFUL.
YEAH. THE PSYCHS WERE CONCERNED WHEN I DIDN'T SHOW AN "OVERT EMOTIONAL RESPONSE" TO HER DEATH-- BUT WHY SHOULD I? THE OLD WOMAN IN THEIR FILES WAS A STRANGER TO ME.
I SPENT HER WHOLE LIFE DRIFTING THROUGH EMPTY SPACE--LOST IN YEARS OF PERFECT HIBER-NATION, WHILE SHE GREW OLD AND DIED.
THE ALIEN STOLE THE TIME WE SHOULD HAVE HAD TOGETHER.
SOMETIMES I THINK THOSE THINGS HAVE AS MUCH RIGHT TO SURVIVE AS ANY OF US. SOME-TIMES I WONDER WHAT GIVES US THE ARRO-GANCE TO CHALLENGE THEIR EXISTENCE.
THEN I LOOK AT MY LITTLE GIRL.
AND I KNOW.

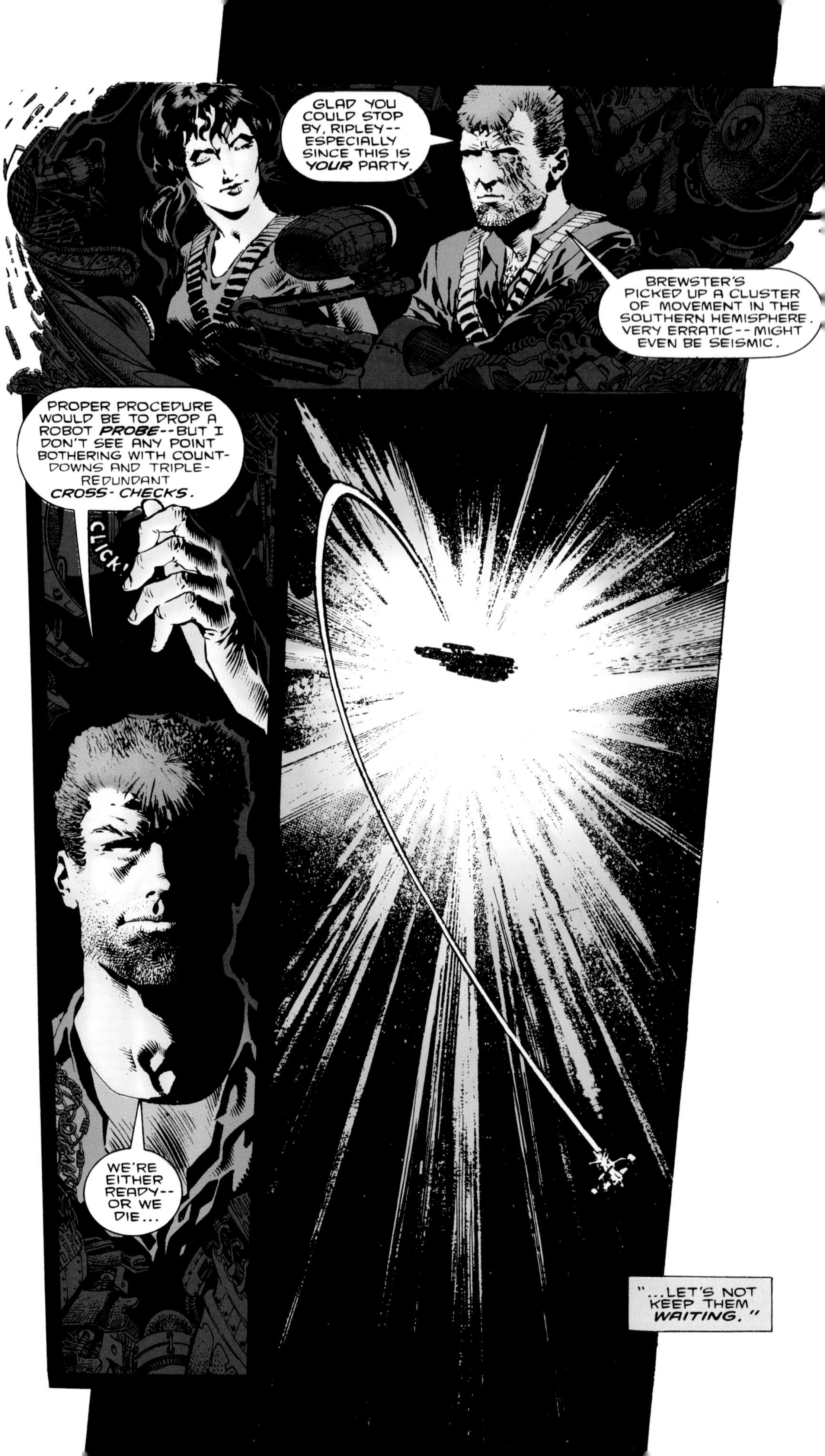
GLAD YOU COULD STOP BY, RIPLEY-- ESPECIALLY SINCE THIS IS *YOUR* PARTY.
BREWSTER'S PICKED UP A CLUSTER OF MOVEMENT IN THE SOUTHERN HEMISPHERE. VERY ERRATIC--MIGHT EVEN BE SEISMIC.
PROPER PROCEDURE WOULD BE TO DROP A ROBOT *PROBE*--BUT I DON'T SEE ANY POINT BOTHERING WITH COUNT-DOWNS AND TRIPLE-REDUNDANT *CROSS-CHECKS*.
CLICK!
WE'RE EITHER READY-- OR WE DIE...
"...LET'S NOT KEEP THEM *WAITING*."

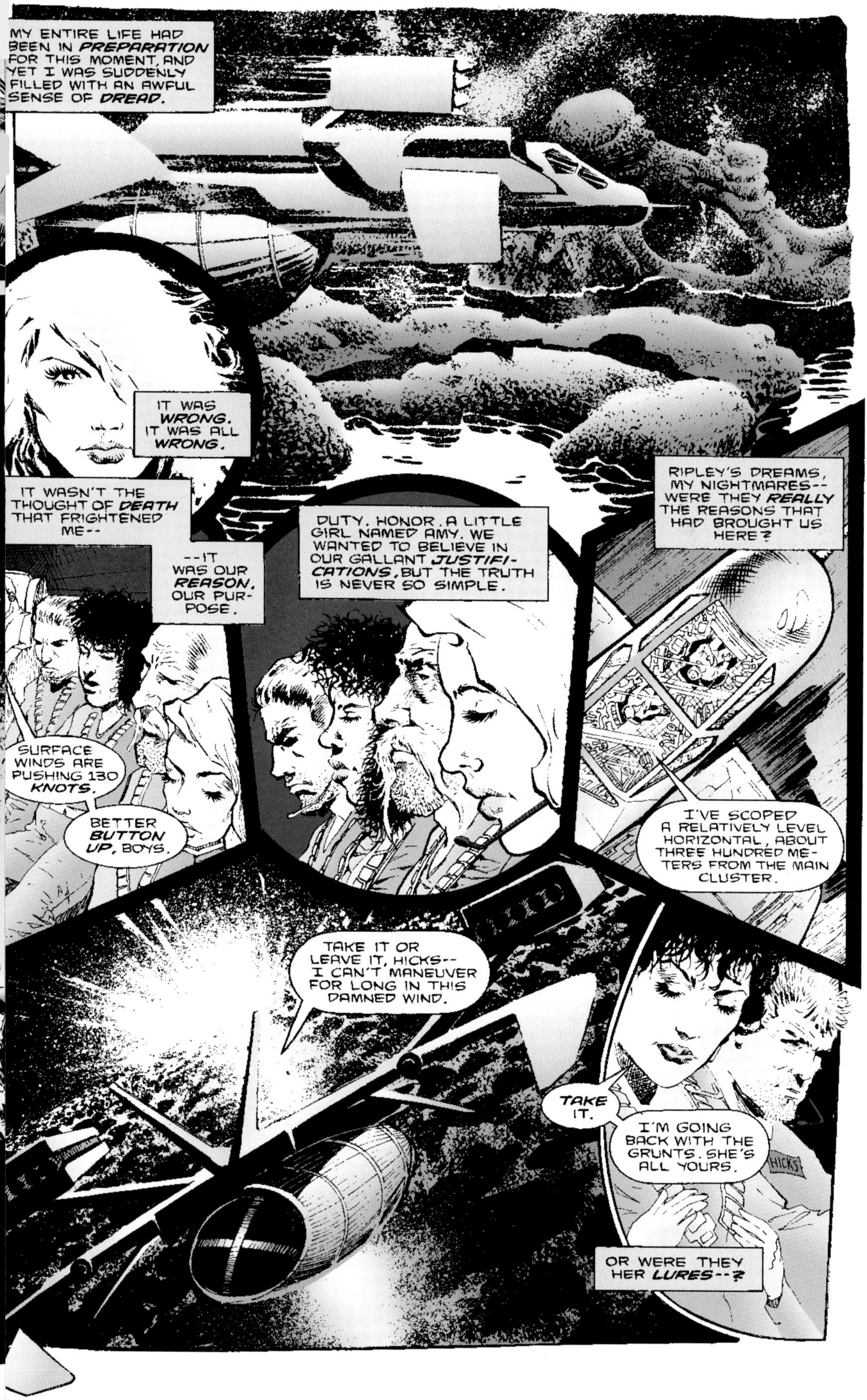
MY ENTIRE LIFE HAD BEEN IN *PREPARATION* FOR THIS MOMENT, AND YET I WAS SUDDENLY FILLED WITH AN AWFUL SENSE OF *DREAD*.
IT WAS *WRONG*. IT WAS ALL *WRONG*.
IT WASN'T THE THOUGHT OF *DEATH* THAT FRIGHTENED ME--
--IT WAS OUR *REASON*, OUR PURPOSE.
SURFACE WINDS ARE PUSHING 130 *KNOTS*.
BETTER *BUTTON UP*, BOYS.
DUTY. HONOR. A LITTLE GIRL NAMED AMY. WE WANTED TO BELIEVE IN OUR GALLANT *JUSTIFICATIONS*, BUT THE TRUTH IS NEVER SO SIMPLE.
RIPLEY'S DREAMS, MY NIGHTMARES-- WERE THEY *REALLY* THE REASONS THAT HAD BROUGHT US HERE?
I'VE SCOPED A RELATIVELY LEVEL HORIZONTAL, ABOUT THREE HUNDRED METERS FROM THE MAIN CLUSTER.
TAKE IT OR LEAVE IT, HICKS-- I CAN'T MANEUVER FOR LONG IN THIS DAMNED WIND.
TAKE IT.
I'M GOING BACK WITH THE GRUNTS. SHE'S ALL YOURS.
HICKS
OR WERE THEY HER *LURES*--?

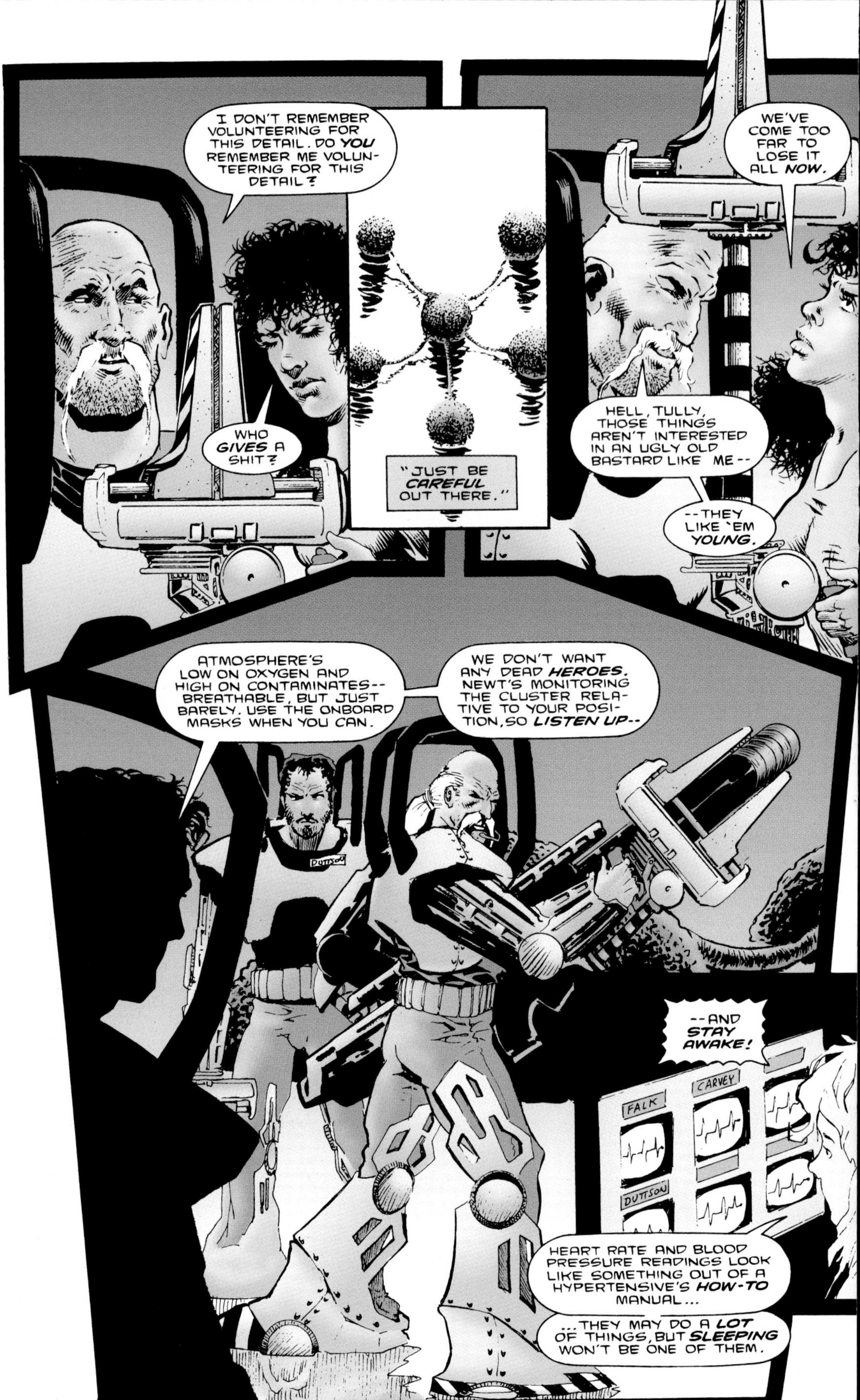

I DON'T REMEMBER VOLUNTEERING FOR THIS DETAIL. DO YOU REMEMBER ME VOLUNTEERING FOR THIS DETAIL?
WHO GIVES A SHIT?
"JUST BE CAREFUL OUT THERE."
WE'VE COME TOO FAR TO LOSE IT ALL NOW.
HELL, TULLY, THOSE THINGS AREN'T INTERESTED IN AN UGLY OLD BASTARD LIKE ME--
--THEY LIKE 'EM YOUNG.
ATMOSPHERE'S LOW ON OXYGEN AND HIGH ON CONTAMINATES--BREATHABLE, BUT JUST BARELY. USE THE ONBOARD MASKS WHEN YOU CAN.
WE DON'T WANT ANY DEAD HEROES. NEWT'S MONITORING THE CLUSTER RELATIVE TO YOUR POSITION, SO LISTEN UP--
DUTTSON
--AND STAY AWAKE!
FALK
CARVEY
DUTTSON
HEART RATE AND BLOOD PRESSURE READINGS LOOK LIKE SOMETHING OUT OF A HYPERTENSIVE'S HOW-TO MANUAL...
...THEY MAY DO A LOT OF THINGS, BUT SLEEPING WON'T BE ONE OF THEM.

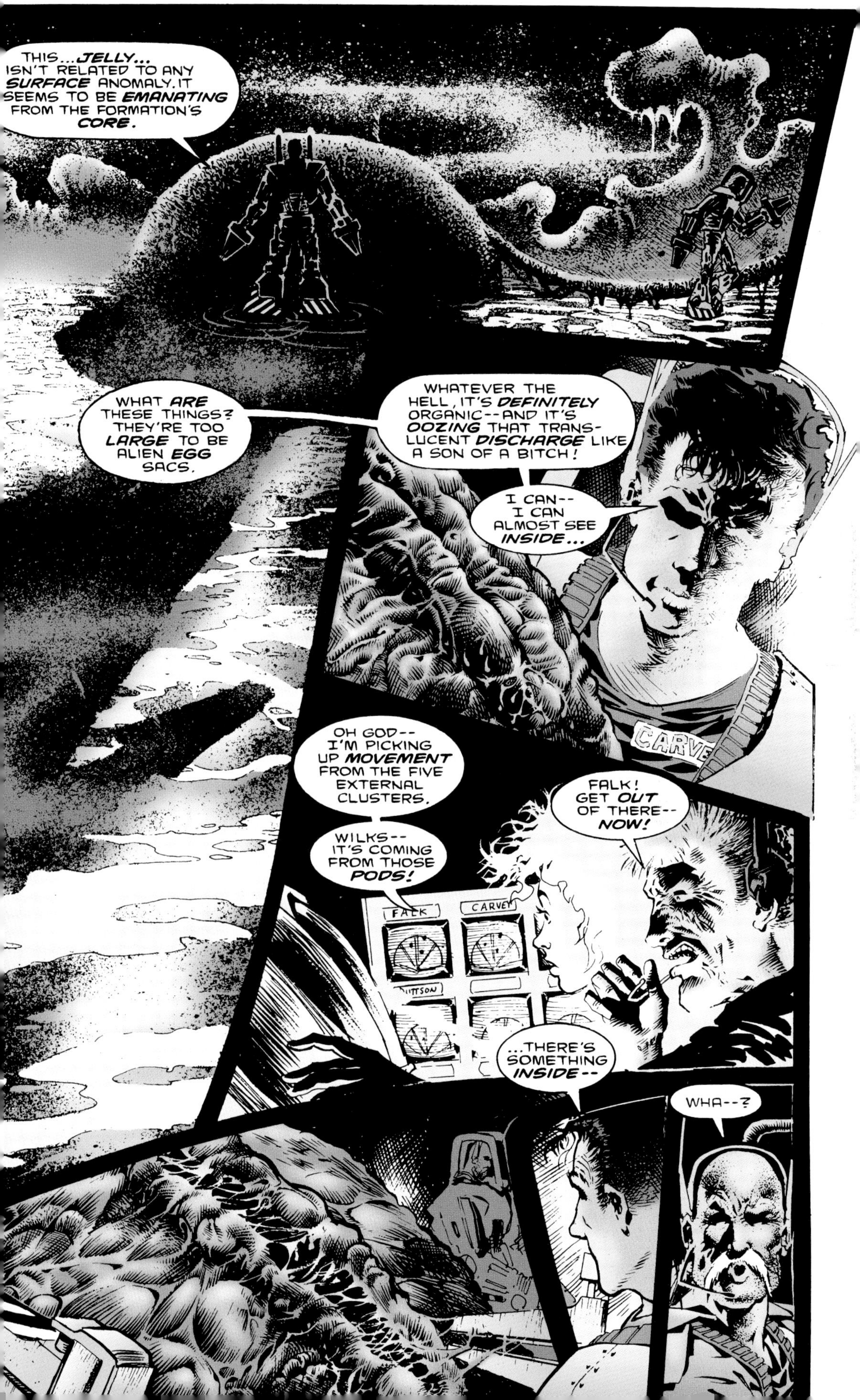
THIS...JELLY... ISN'T RELATED TO ANY SURFACE ANOMALY. IT SEEMS TO BE EMANATING FROM THE FORMATION'S CORE.
WHAT ARE THESE THINGS? THEY'RE TOO LARGE TO BE ALIEN EGG SACS.
WHATEVER THE HELL, IT'S DEFINITELY ORGANIC--AND IT'S OOZING THAT TRANS-LUCENT DISCHARGE LIKE A SON OF A BITCH!
I CAN-- I CAN ALMOST SEE INSIDE...
CARVE
OH GOD-- I'M PICKING UP MOVEMENT FROM THE FIVE EXTERNAL CLUSTERS.
FALK! GET OUT OF THERE-- NOW!
WILKS-- IT'S COMING FROM THOSE PODS!
FALK
CARVE
...THERE'S SOMETHING INSIDE--
WHA--?

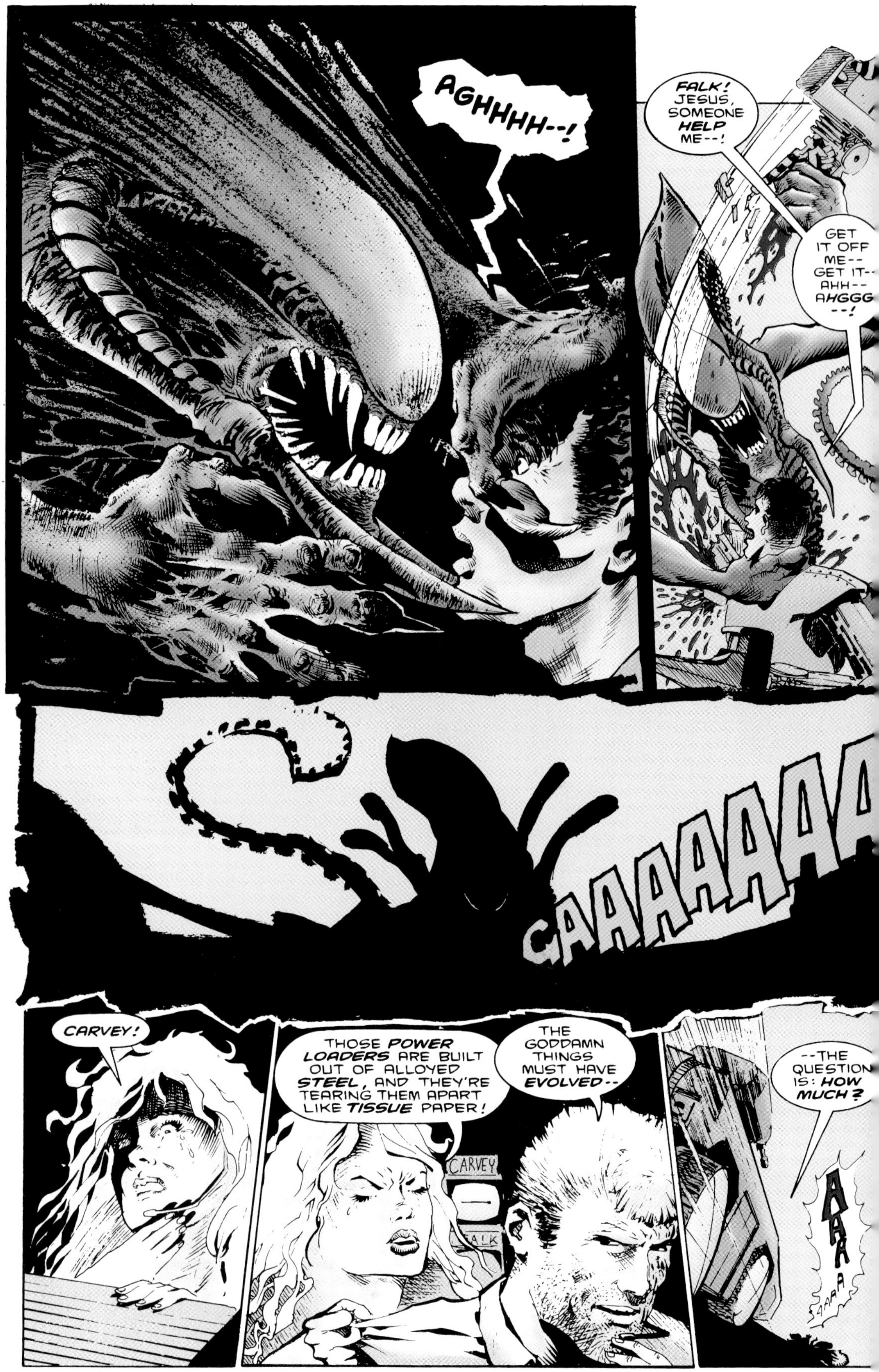
AGHHHH--!
FALK! JESUS, SOMEONE HELP ME--!
GET IT OFF ME-- GET IT-- AHH-- AHGGG --!
CAAAAAA
CARVEY!
THOSE POWER LOADERS ARE BUILT OUT OF ALLOYED STEEL, AND THEY'RE TEARING THEM APART LIKE TISSUE PAPER!
THE GODDAMN THINGS MUST HAVE EVOLVED--
--THE QUESTION IS: HOW MUCH?
CARVEY
FALK

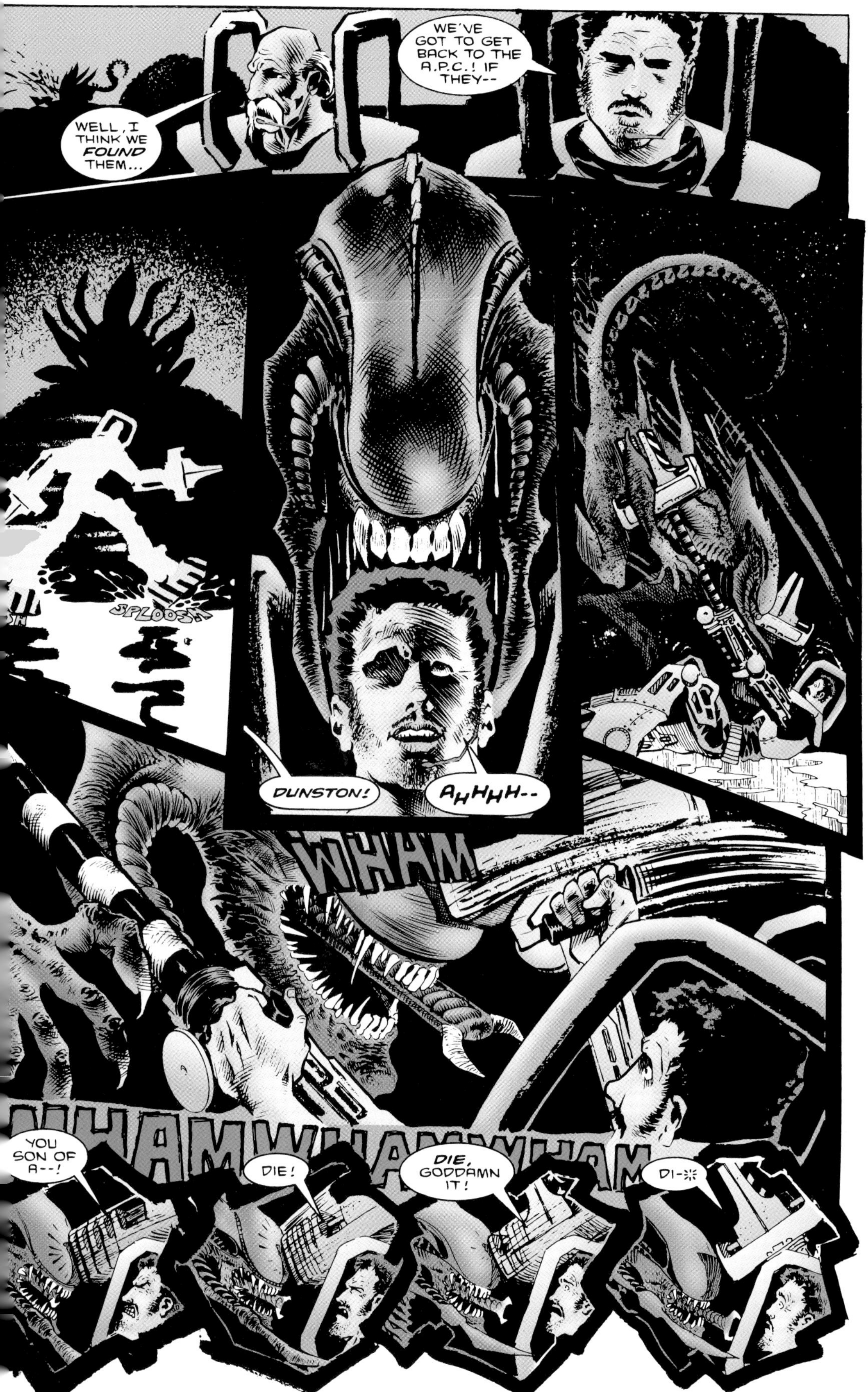
WELL, I THINK WE FOUND THEM...
WE'VE GOT TO GET BACK TO THE A.P.C.! IF THEY--
SPLOOSH
DUNSTON!
AHHHH--
WHAM
WHAMWHAMWHAM
YOU SON OF A--!
DIE!
DIE, GODDAMN IT!
DI-

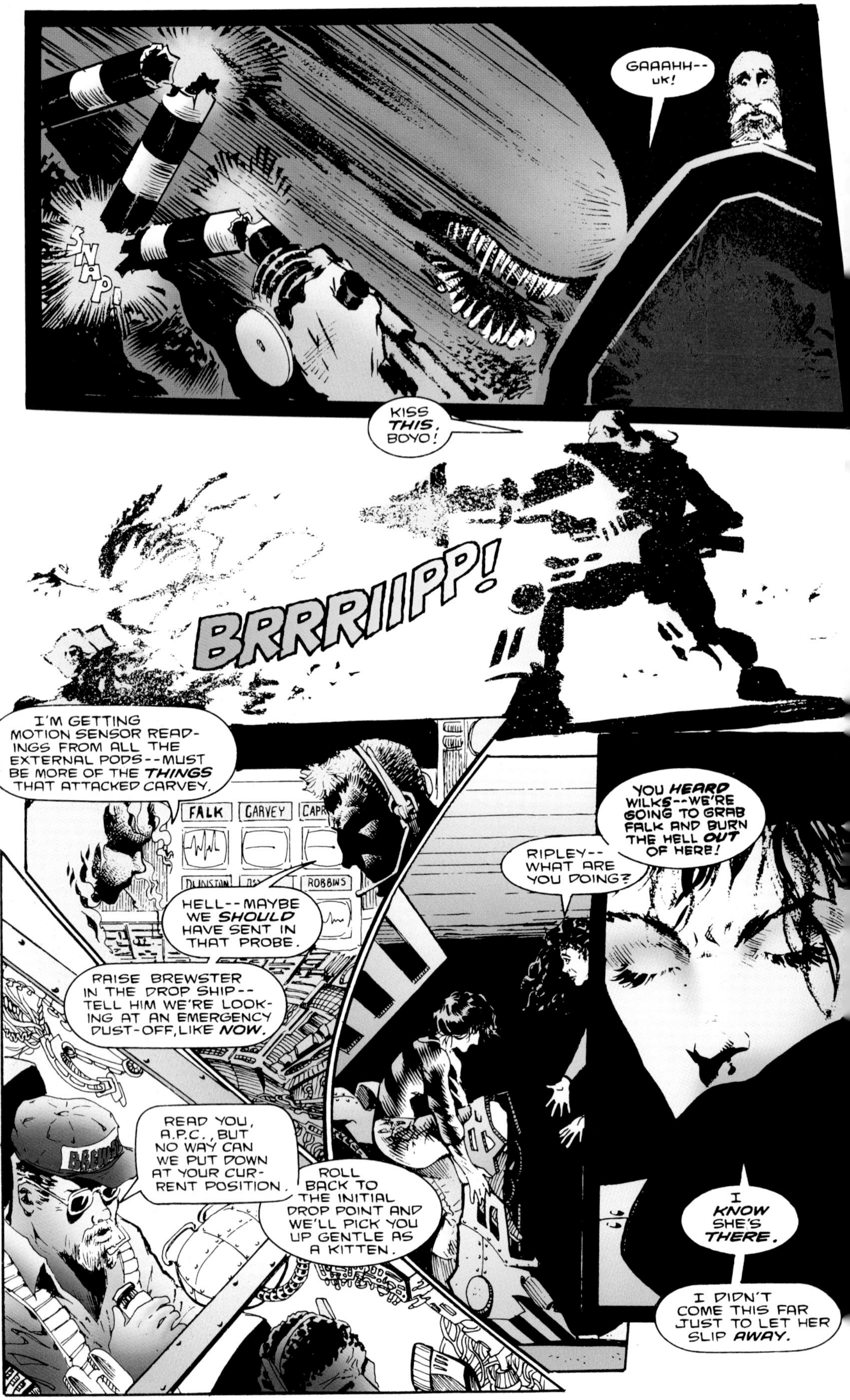
SNAP!
GAAAHH-- uk!
KISS THIS, BOYO!
BRRRIIPP!
I'M GETTING MOTION SENSOR READINGS FROM ALL THE EXTERNAL PODS--MUST BE MORE OF THE THINGS THAT ATTACKED CARVEY.
FALK
GARVEY
ROBBINS
HELL--MAYBE WE SHOULD HAVE SENT IN THAT PROBE.
RAISE BREWSTER IN THE DROP SHIP--TELL HIM WE'RE LOOKING AT AN EMERGENCY DUST-OFF, LIKE NOW.
RIPLEY--WHAT ARE YOU DOING?
YOU HEARD WILKS--WE'RE GOING TO GRAB FALK AND BURN THE HELL OUT OF HERE!
READ YOU, A.P.C., BUT NO WAY CAN WE PUT DOWN AT YOUR CURRENT POSITION.
ROLL BACK TO THE INITIAL DROP POINT AND WE'LL PICK YOU UP GENTLE AS A KITTEN.
I KNOW SHE'S THERE.
I DIDN'T COME THIS FAR JUST TO LET HER SLIP AWAY.

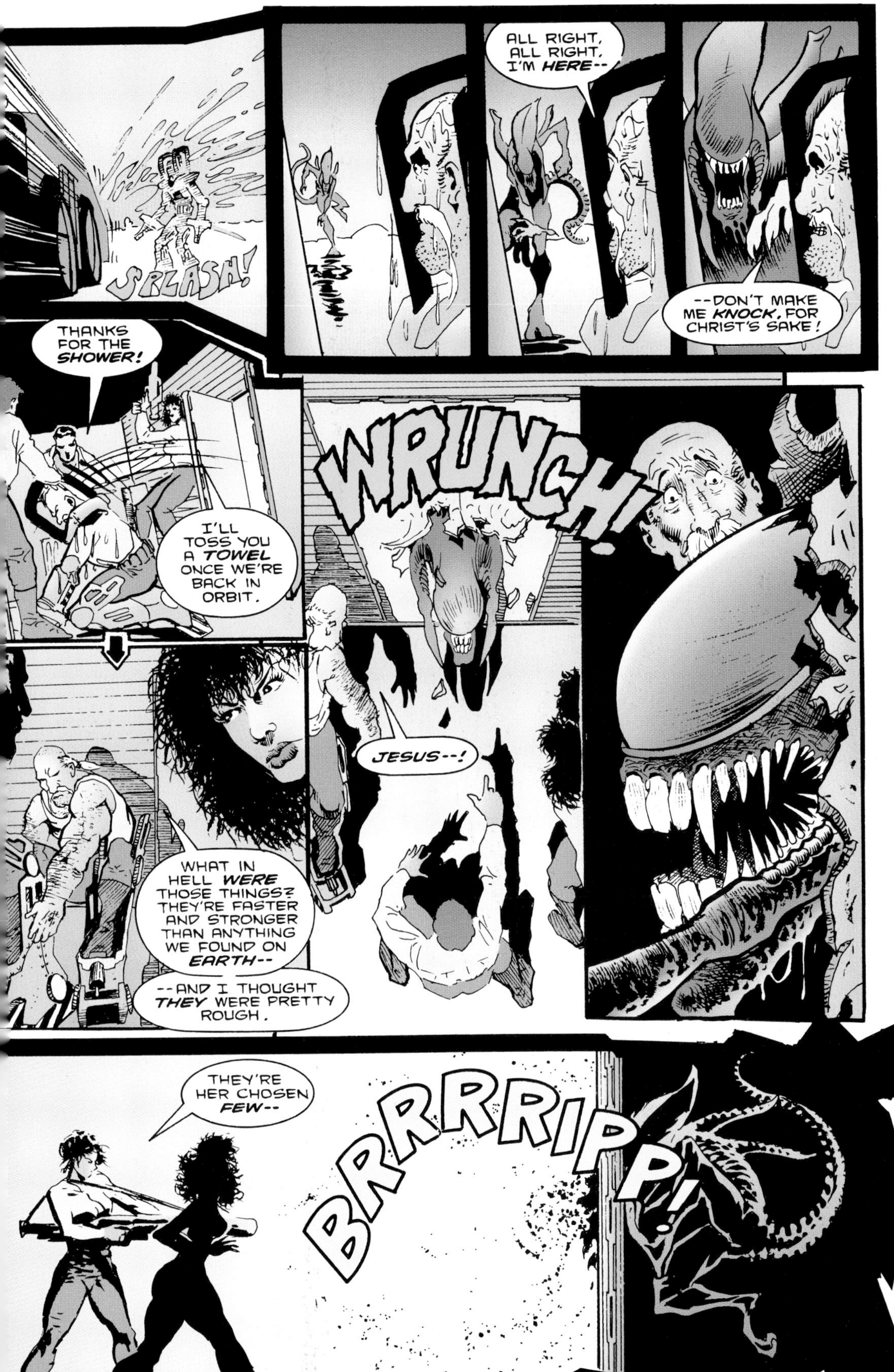
SPLASH!
ALL RIGHT, ALL RIGHT, I'M HERE--
--DON'T MAKE ME KNOCK, FOR CHRIST'S SAKE!
THANKS FOR THE SHOWER!
I'LL TOSS YOU A TOWEL ONCE WE'RE BACK IN ORBIT.
WRUNCH!
JESUS--!
WHAT IN HELL WERE THOSE THINGS? THEY'RE FASTER AND STRONGER THAN ANYTHING WE FOUND ON EARTH--
--AND I THOUGHT THEY WERE PRETTY ROUGH.
THEY'RE HER CHOSEN FEW--
BRRRRIPP!

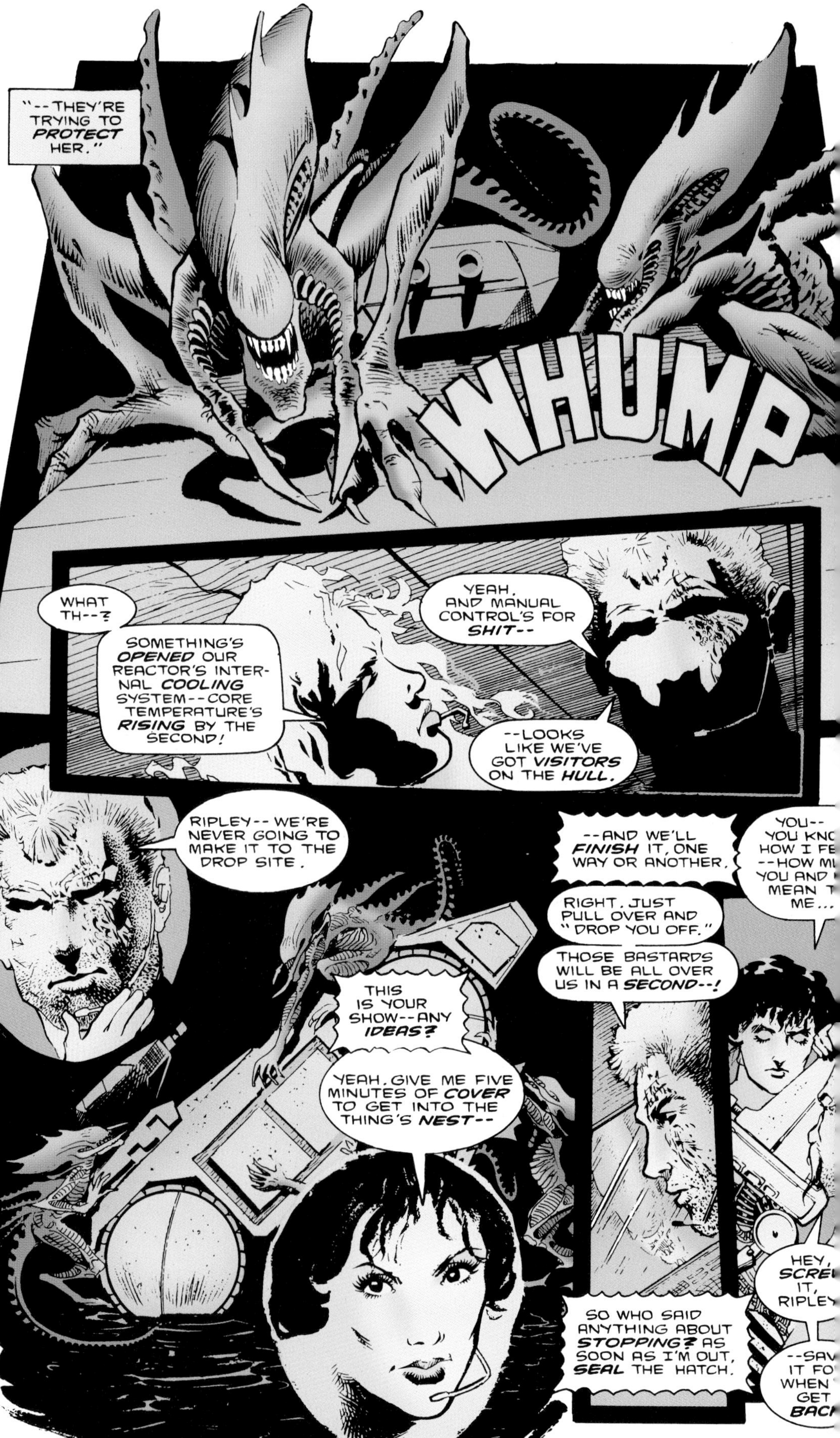
"--THEY'RE TRYING TO PROTECT HER."
WHUMP
WHAT TH--?
SOMETHING'S OPENED OUR REACTOR'S INTERNAL COOLING SYSTEM--CORE TEMPERATURE'S RISING BY THE SECOND!
YEAH, AND MANUAL CONTROL'S FOR SHIT--
--LOOKS LIKE WE'VE GOT VISITORS ON THE HULL.
RIPLEY--WE'RE NEVER GOING TO MAKE IT TO THE DROP SITE.
THIS IS YOUR SHOW--ANY IDEAS?
YEAH. GIVE ME FIVE MINUTES OF COVER TO GET INTO THE THING'S NEST--
--AND WE'LL FINISH IT, ONE WAY OR ANOTHER.
RIGHT. JUST PULL OVER AND "DROP YOU OFF."
THOSE BASTARDS WILL BE ALL OVER US IN A SECOND--!
SO WHO SAID ANYTHING ABOUT STOPPING? AS SOON AS I'M OUT, SEAL THE HATCH.

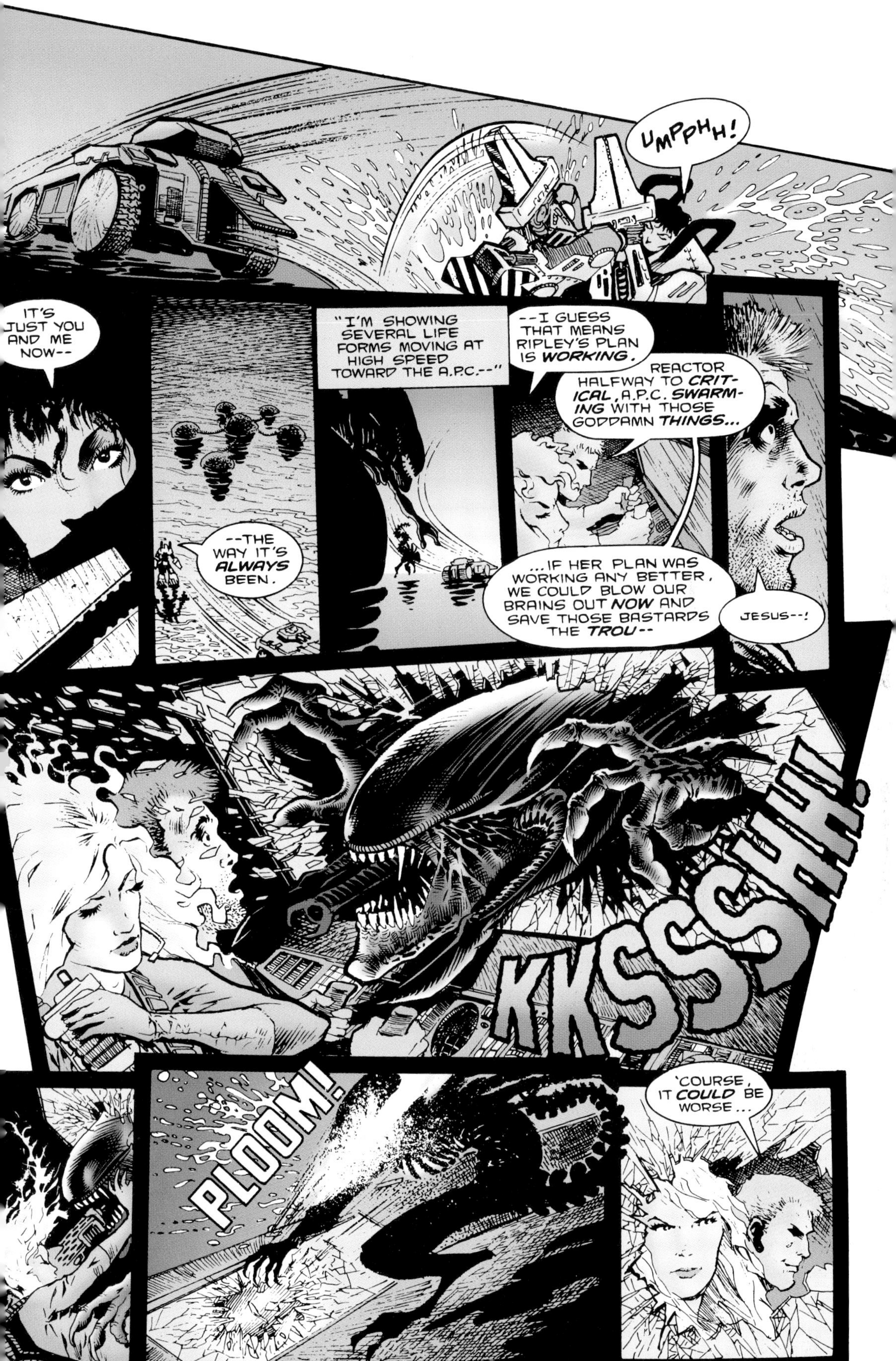
UMPHH!
IT'S JUST YOU AND ME NOW--
--THE WAY IT'S ALWAYS BEEN.
"I'M SHOWING SEVERAL LIFE FORMS MOVING AT HIGH SPEED TOWARD THE A.P.C.--"
--I GUESS THAT MEANS RIPLEY'S PLAN IS WORKING.
REACTOR HALFWAY TO CRITICAL, A.P.C. SWARMING WITH THOSE GODDAMN THINGS...
...IF HER PLAN WAS WORKING ANY BETTER, WE COULD BLOW OUR BRAINS OUT NOW AND SAVE THOSE BASTARDS THE TROU--
JESUS--!
KKSSSHH!!
PLOOM!
'COURSE, IT COULD BE WORSE...

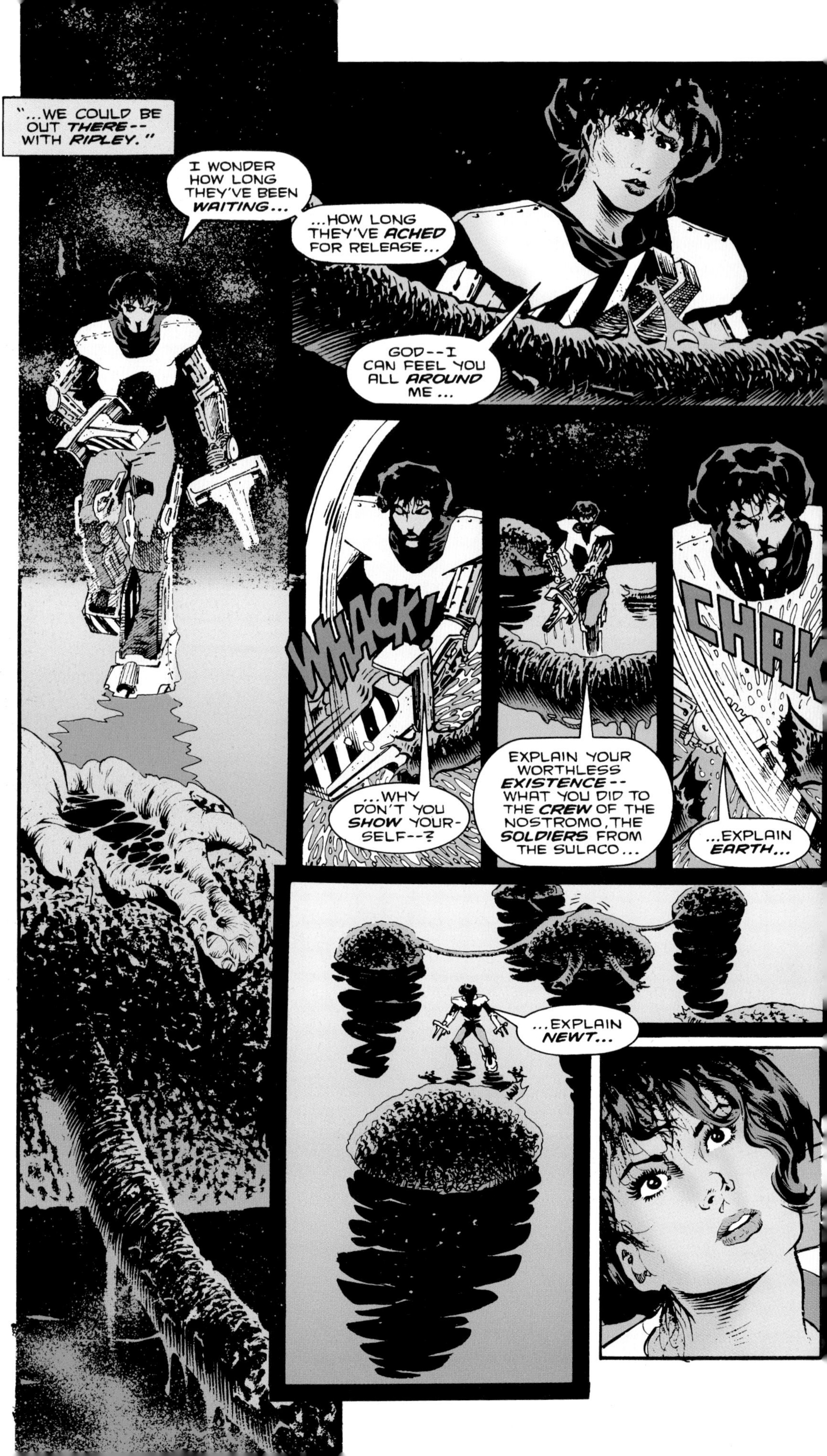
"...WE COULD BE OUT THERE-- WITH RIPLEY."
I WONDER HOW LONG THEY'VE BEEN WAITING...
...HOW LONG THEY'VE ACHED FOR RELEASE...
GOD--I CAN FEEL YOU ALL AROUND ME...
WHACK!
...WHY DON'T YOU SHOW YOURSELF--?
EXPLAIN YOUR WORTHLESS EXISTENCE-- WHAT YOU DID TO THE CREW OF THE NOSTROMO, THE SOLDIERS FROM THE SULACO...
CHAK
...EXPLAIN EARTH...
...EXPLAIN NEWT...

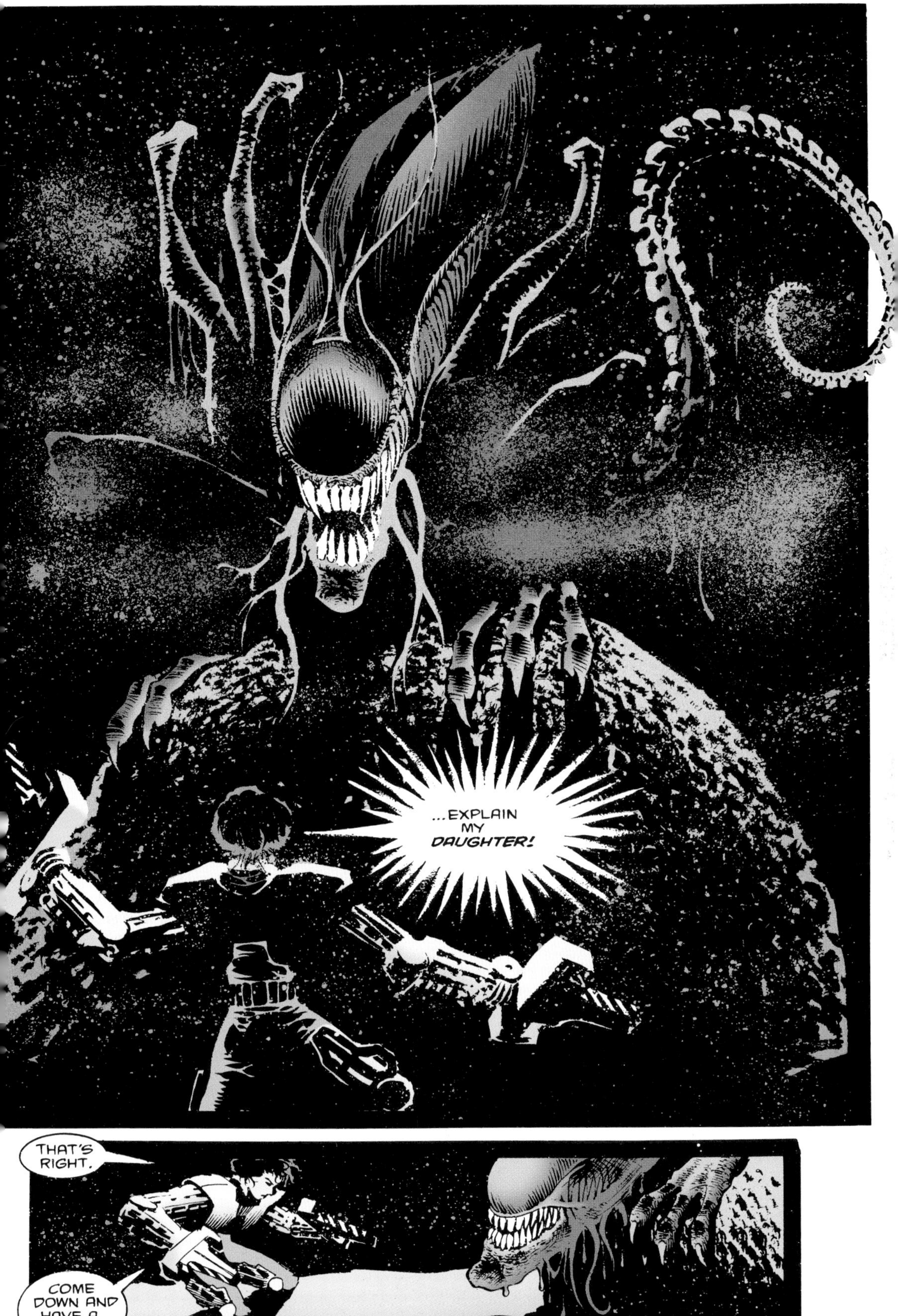
...EXPLAIN MY DAUGHTER!

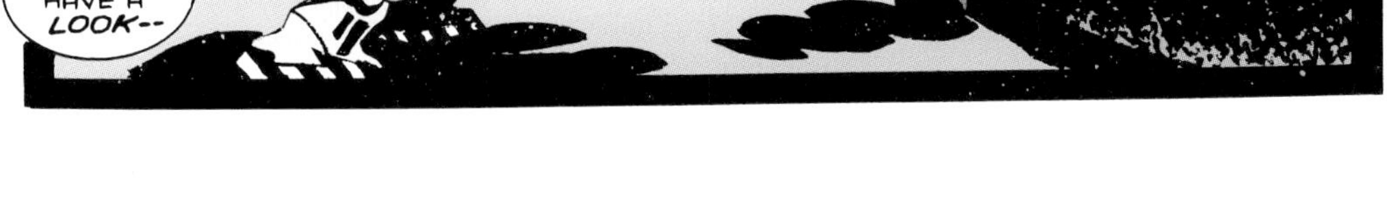
THAT'S RIGHT.
COME DOWN AND HAVE A LOOK--

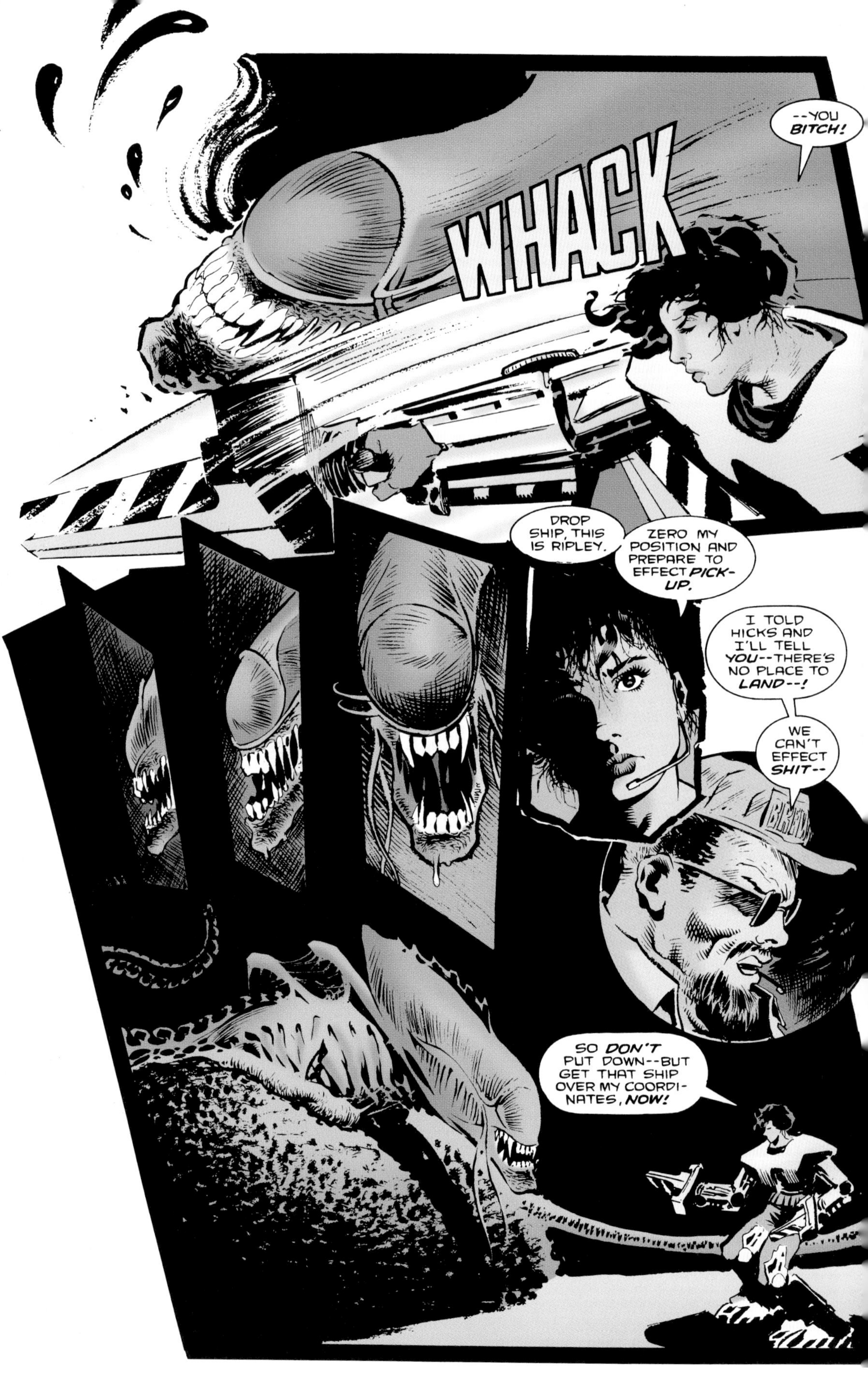
WHACK
--YOU BITCH!
DROP SHIP, THIS IS RIPLEY.
ZERO MY POSITION AND PREPARE TO EFFECT PICK-UP.
I TOLD HICKS AND I'LL TELL YOU--THERE'S NO PLACE TO LAND--!
WE CAN'T EFFECT SHIT--
SO DON'T PUT DOWN--BUT GET THAT SHIP OVER MY COORDINATES, NOW!

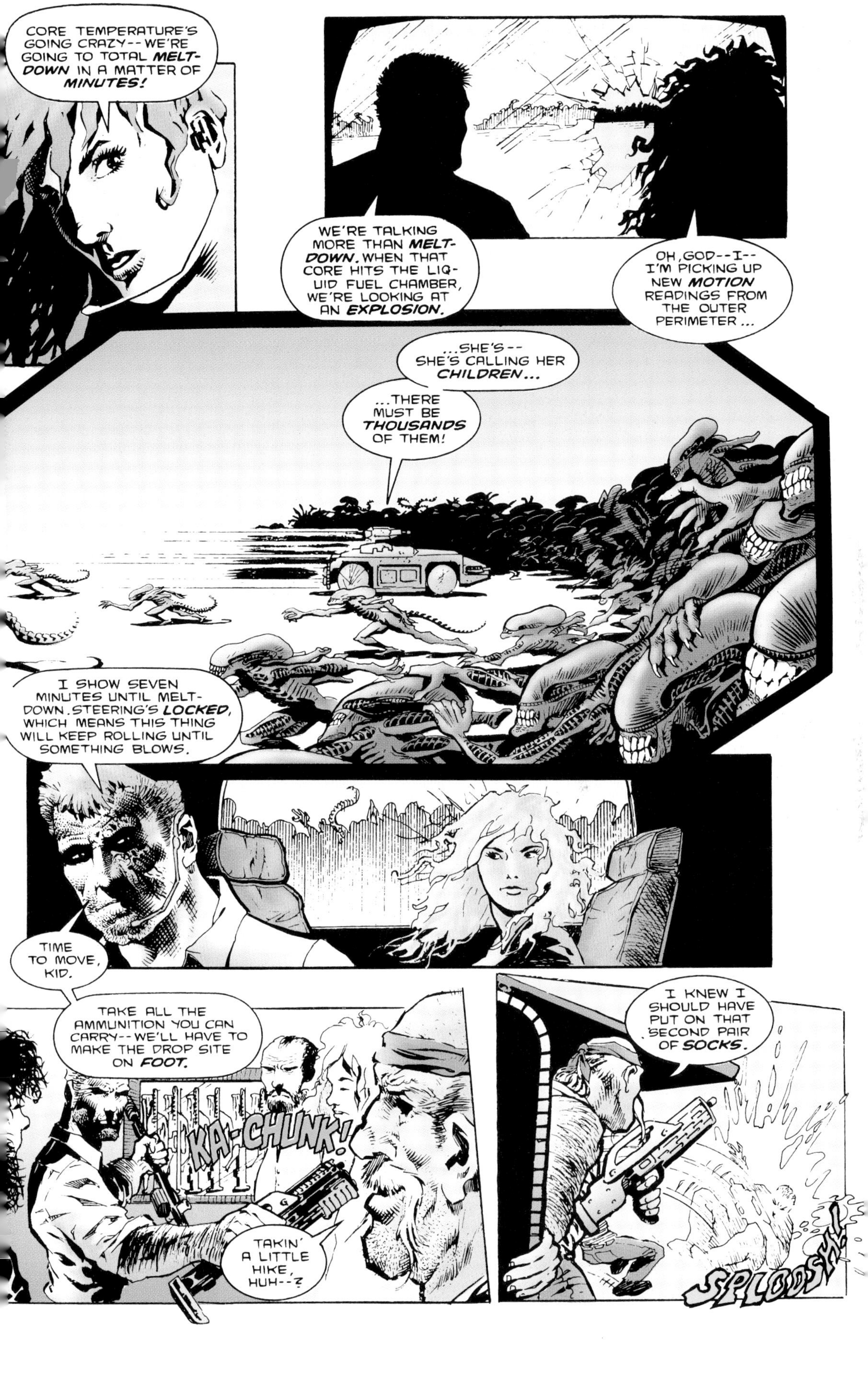
CORE TEMPERATURE'S GOING CRAZY--WE'RE GOING TO TOTAL MELT-DOWN IN A MATTER OF MINUTES!
WE'RE TALKING MORE THAN MELT-DOWN. WHEN THAT CORE HITS THE LIQ-UID FUEL CHAMBER, WE'RE LOOKING AT AN EXPLOSION.
OH, GOD--I--I'M PICKING UP NEW MOTION READINGS FROM THE OUTER PERIMETER...
...SHE'S--SHE'S CALLING HER CHILDREN...
...THERE MUST BE THOUSANDS OF THEM!
I SHOW SEVEN MINUTES UNTIL MELT-DOWN. STEERING'S LOCKED, WHICH MEANS THIS THING WILL KEEP ROLLING UNTIL SOMETHING BLOWS.
TIME TO MOVE, KID.
TAKE ALL THE AMMUNITION YOU CAN CARRY--WE'LL HAVE TO MAKE THE DROP SITE ON FOOT.
KA-CHUNK!
TAKIN' A LITTLE HIKE, HUH--?
I KNEW I SHOULD HAVE PUT ON THAT SECOND PAIR OF SOCKS.
SPLOOSH!

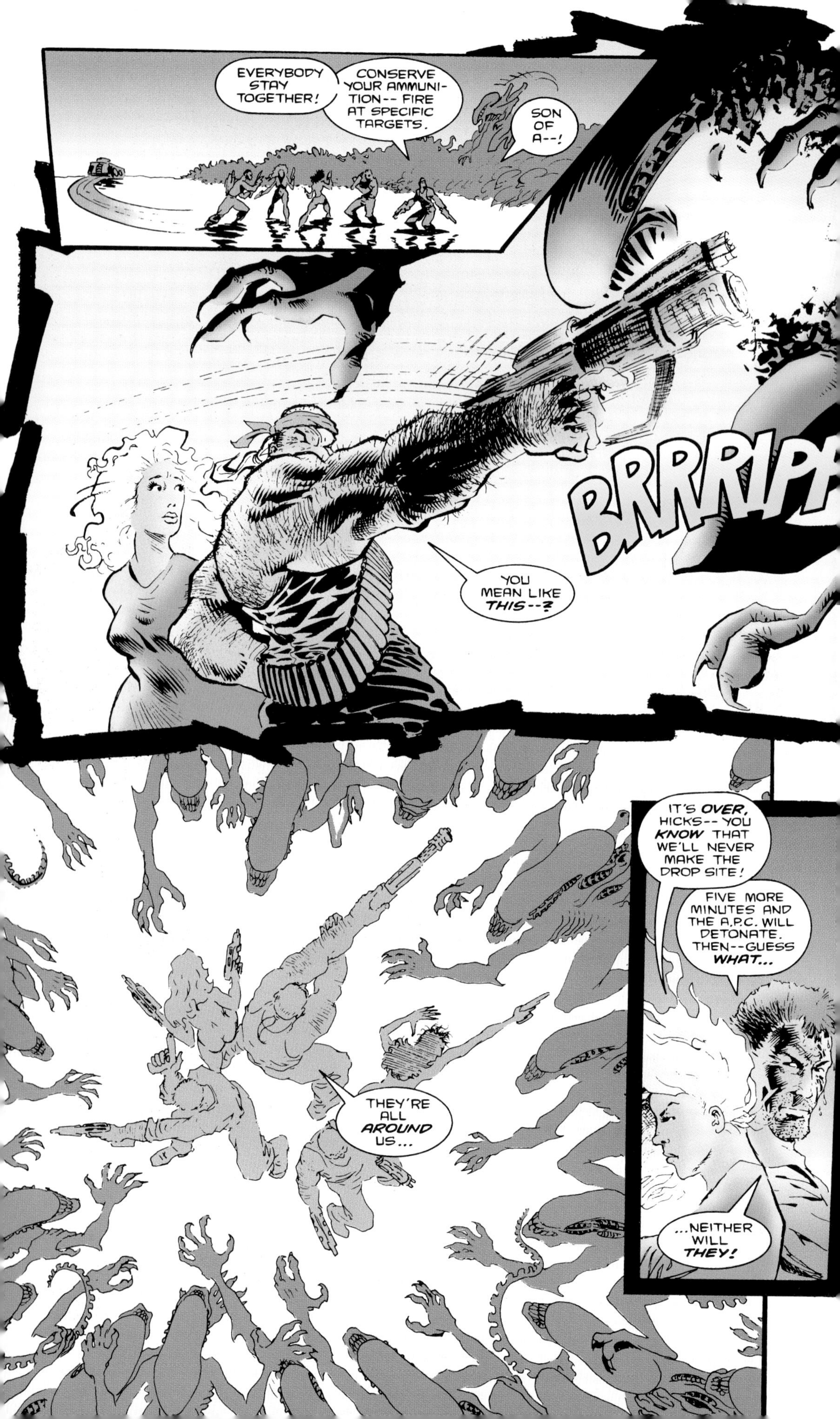
EVERYBODY STAY TOGETHER!
CONSERVE YOUR AMMUNITION-- FIRE AT SPECIFIC TARGETS.
SON OF A--!
BRRRIPP
YOU MEAN LIKE THIS--?
IT'S OVER, HICKS-- YOU KNOW THAT WE'LL NEVER MAKE THE DROP SITE!
FIVE MORE MINUTES AND THE A.P.C. WILL DETONATE. THEN--GUESS WHAT...
...NEITHER WILL THEY!
THEY'RE ALL AROUND US...

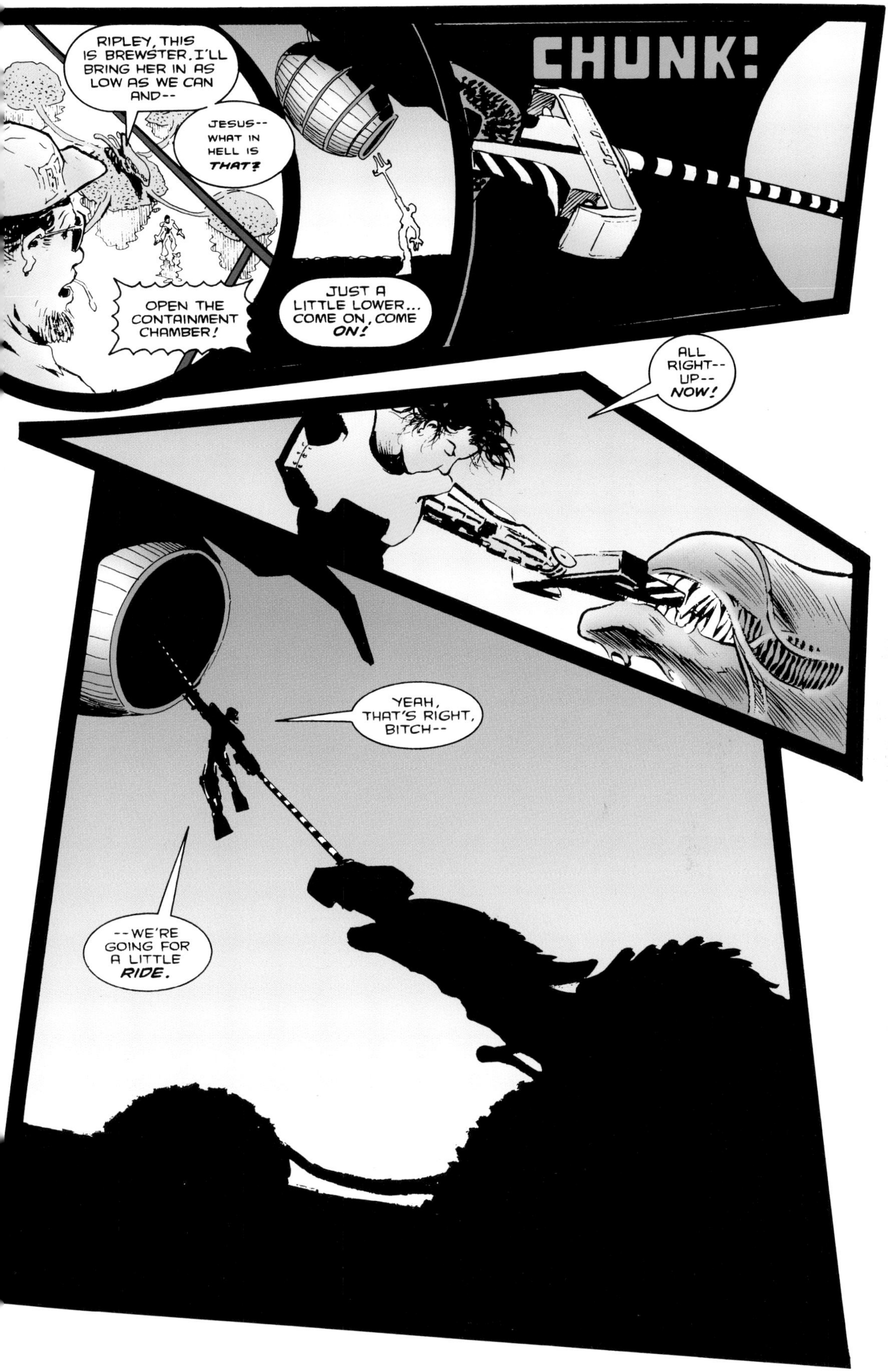
RIPLEY, THIS IS BREWSTER. I'LL BRING HER IN AS LOW AS WE CAN AND--
JESUS-- WHAT IN HELL IS THAT?
OPEN THE CONTAINMENT CHAMBER!
JUST A LITTLE LOWER... COME ON, COME ON!
CHUNK!
ALL RIGHT-- UP-- NOW!
YEAH, THAT'S RIGHT, BITCH--
--WE'RE GOING FOR A LITTLE RIDE.

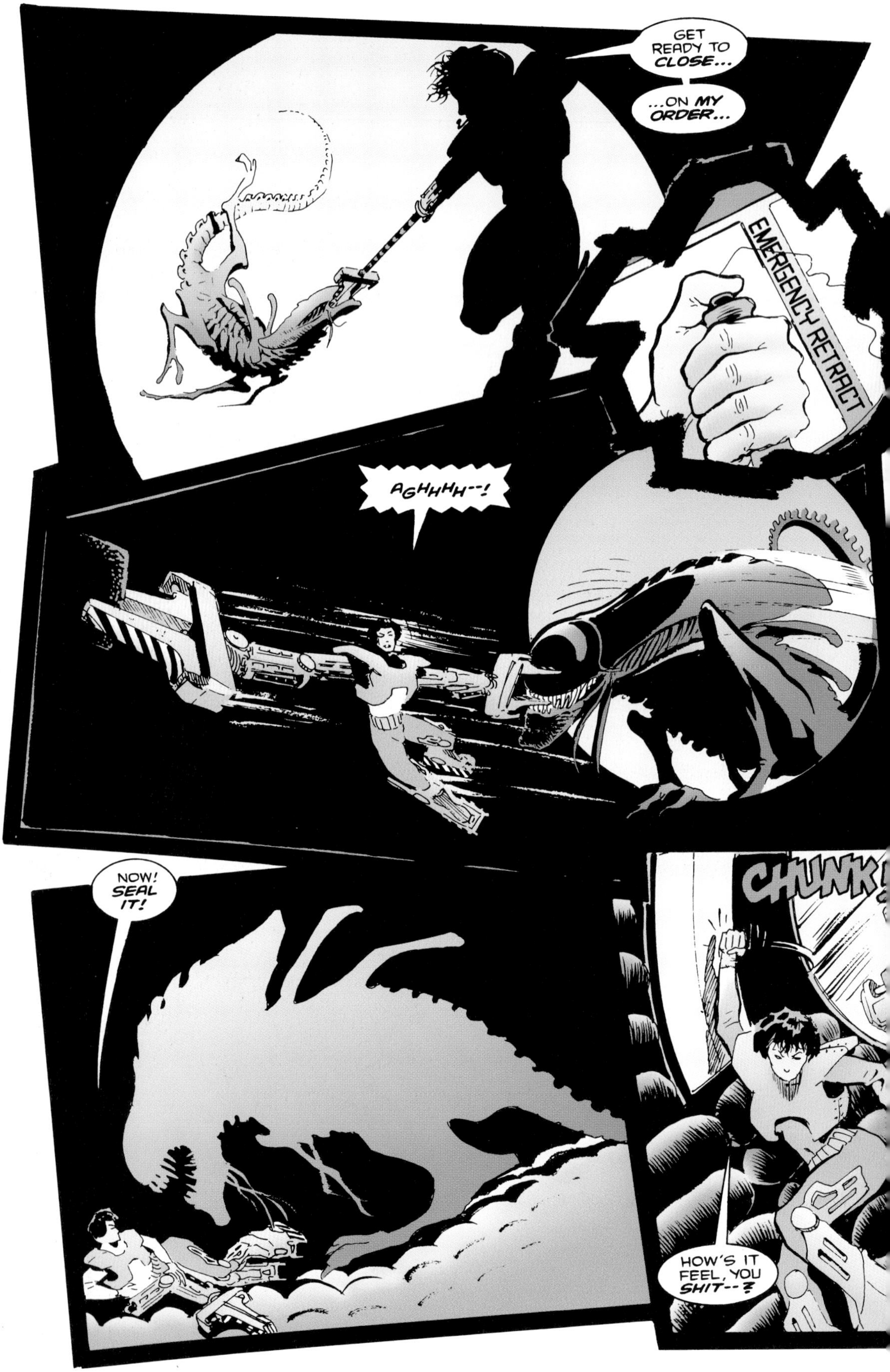
GET READY TO CLOSE...
...ON MY ORDER...
EMERGENCY RETRACT
AGHHHH--!
NOW! SEAL IT!
CHUNK
HOW'S IT FEEL, YOU SHIT--?

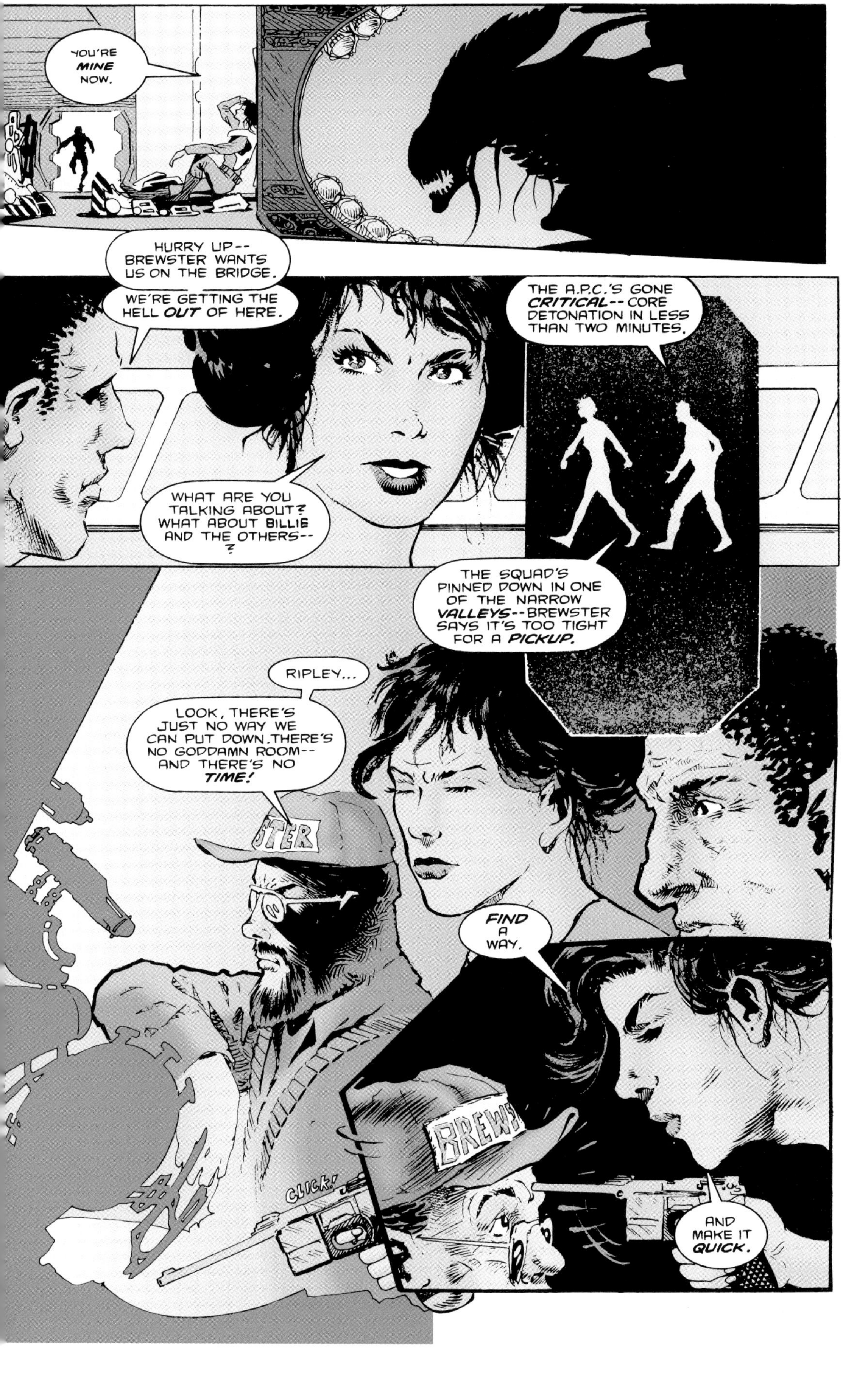
YOU'RE MINE NOW.
HURRY UP-- BREWSTER WANTS US ON THE BRIDGE.
WE'RE GETTING THE HELL OUT OF HERE.
WHAT ARE YOU TALKING ABOUT? WHAT ABOUT BILLIE AND THE OTHERS--?
THE A.P.C.'S GONE CRITICAL-- CORE DETONATION IN LESS THAN TWO MINUTES.
THE SQUAD'S PINNED DOWN IN ONE OF THE NARROW VALLEYS--BREWSTER SAYS IT'S TOO TIGHT FOR A PICKUP.
RIPLEY...
LOOK, THERE'S JUST NO WAY WE CAN PUT DOWN. THERE'S NO GODDAMN ROOM-- AND THERE'S NO TIME!
FIND A WAY.
CLICK!
AND MAKE IT QUICK.

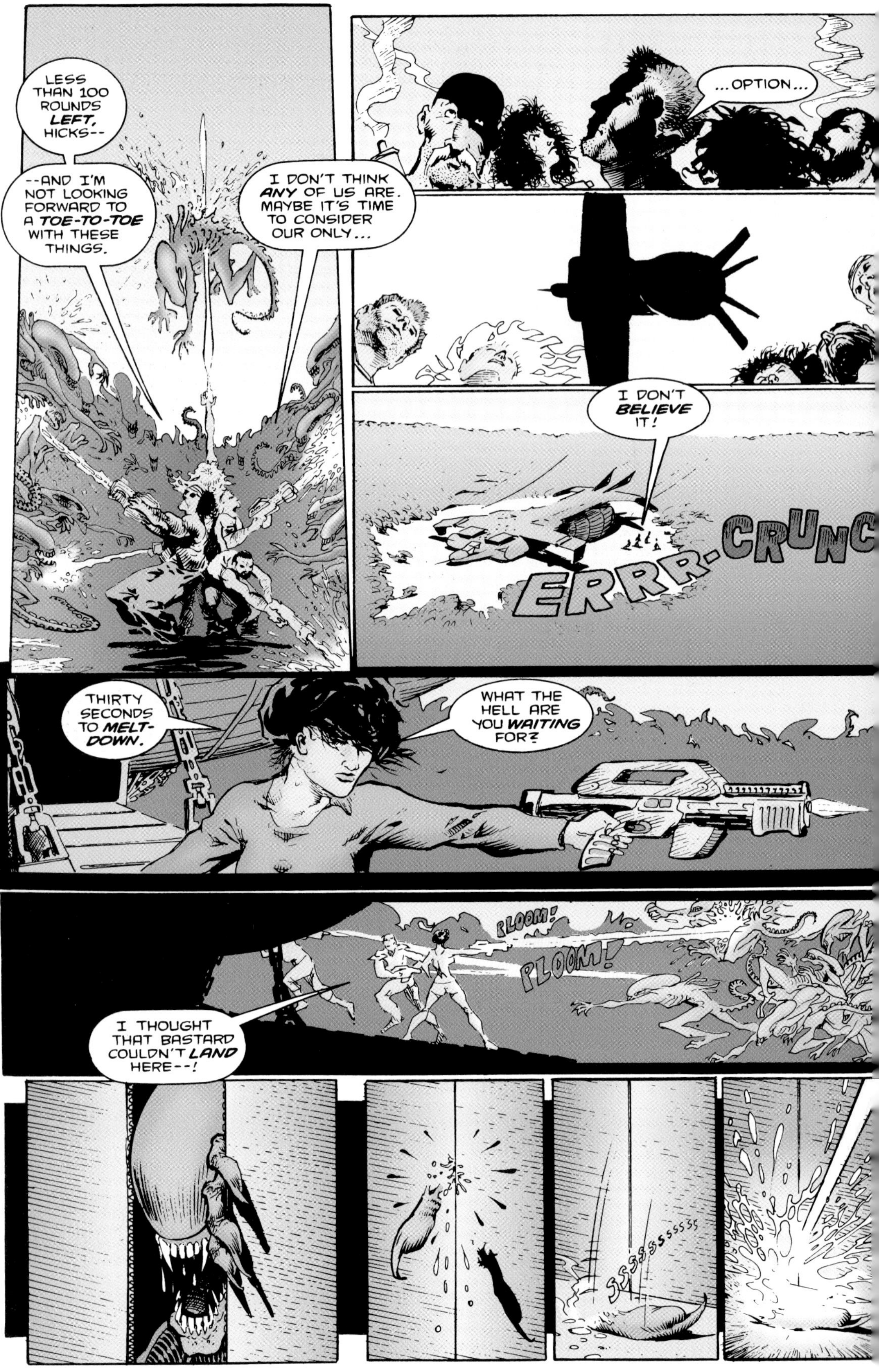
LESS THAN 100 ROUNDS **LEFT,** HICKS--
--AND I'M NOT LOOKING FORWARD TO A **TOE-TO-TOE** WITH THESE THINGS.
I DON'T THINK **ANY** OF US ARE. MAYBE IT'S TIME TO CONSIDER OUR ONLY...
...OPTION...
I DON'T **BELIEVE** IT!
ERRR-CRUNC
THIRTY SECONDS TO **MELT-DOWN.**
WHAT THE HELL ARE YOU **WAITING** FOR?
BLOOM!
PLOOM!
I THOUGHT THAT BASTARD COULDN'T **LAND** HERE--!
SSSSSSSSSSS

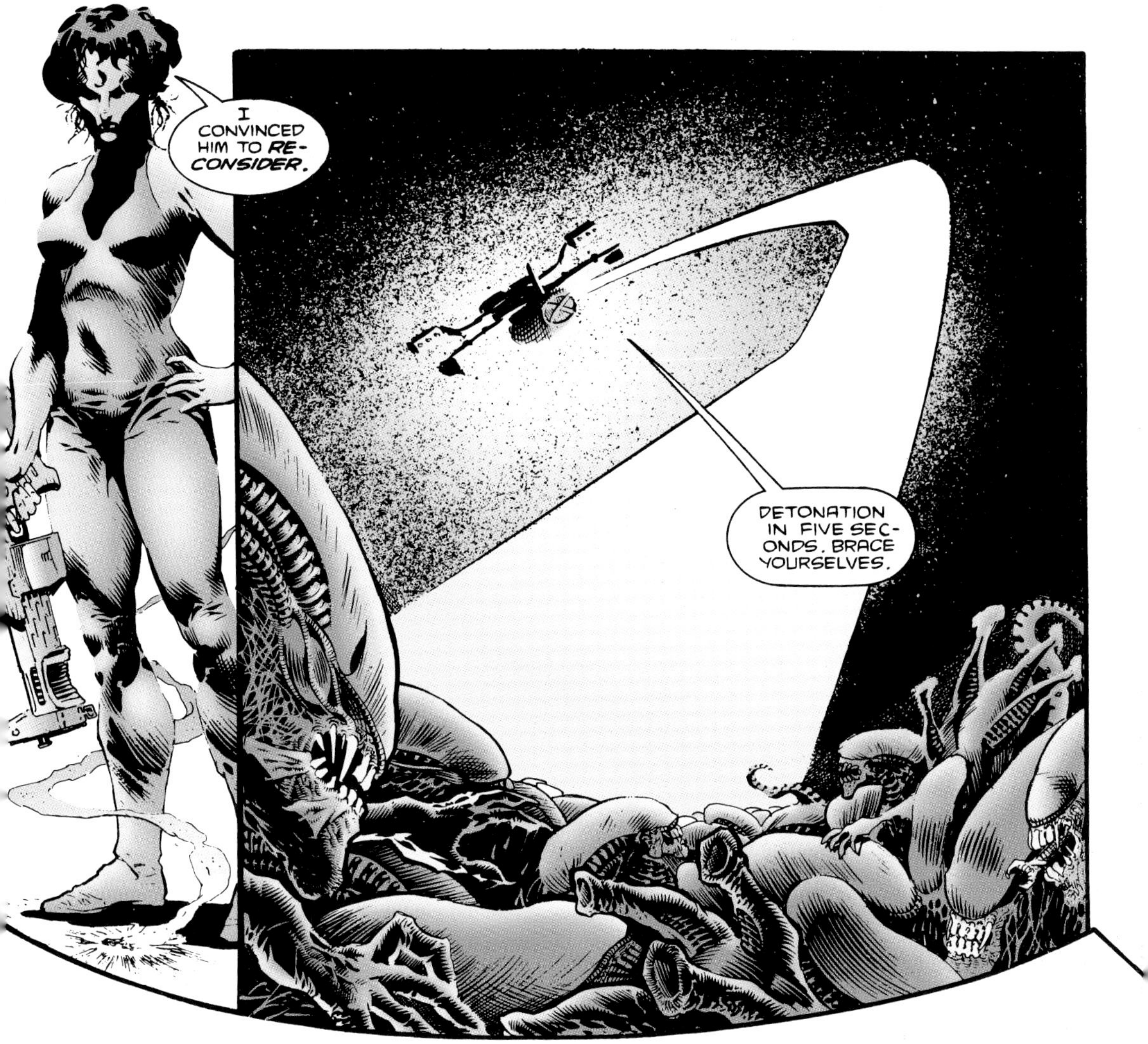
I CONVINCED HIM TO RE-CONSIDER.
DETONATION IN FIVE SEC-ONDS. BRACE YOURSELVES.

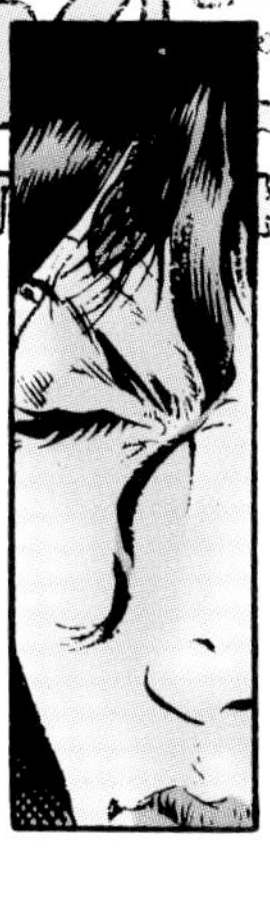

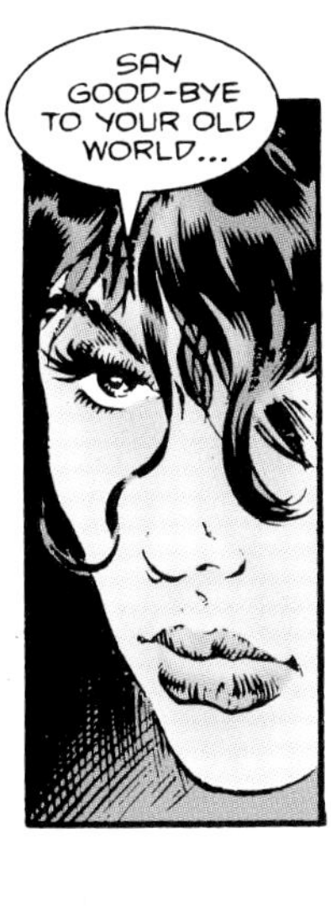
SAY GOOD-BYE TO YOUR OLD WORLD...

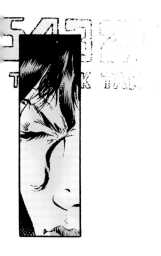

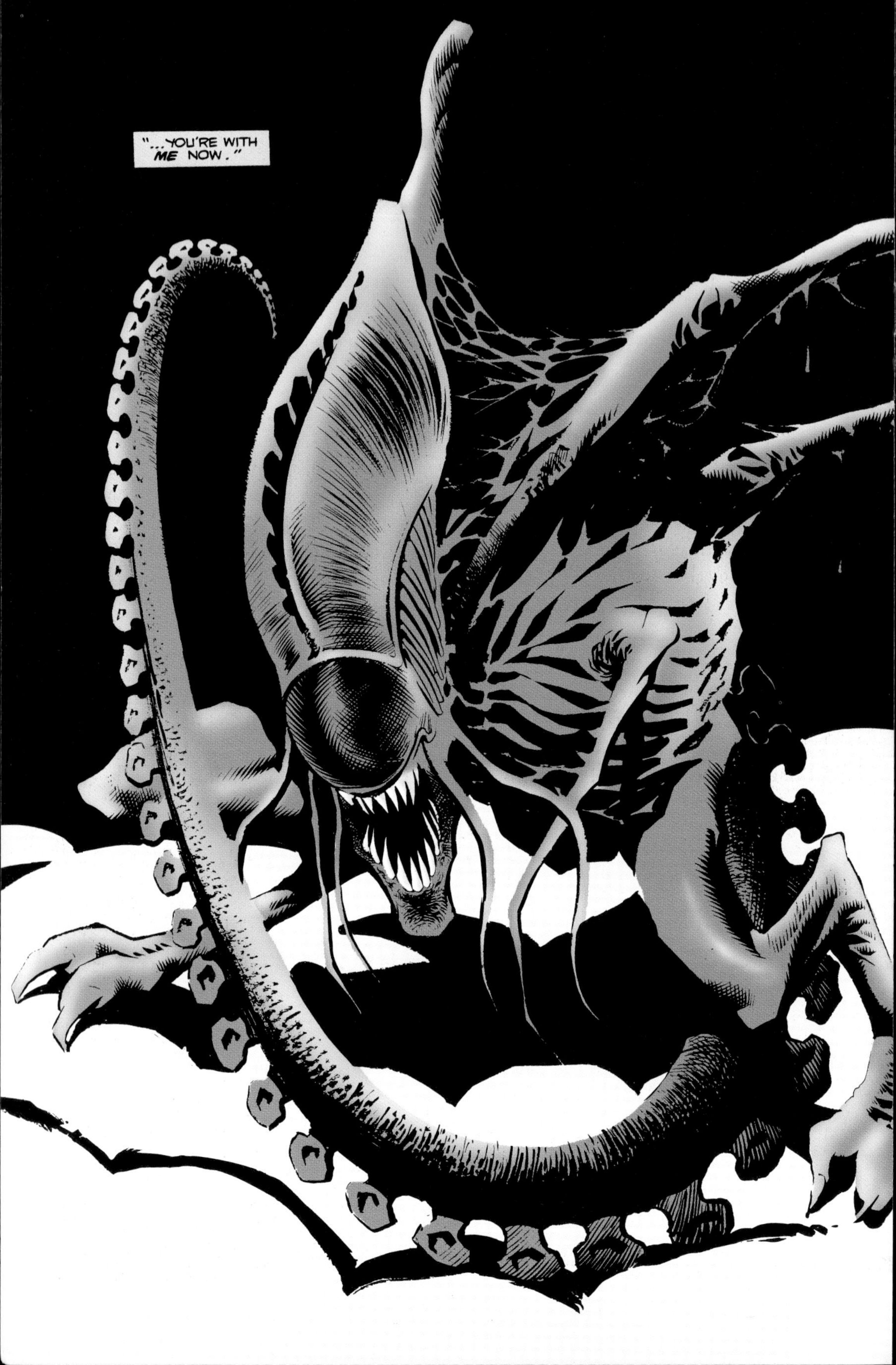
"...YOU'RE WITH ME NOW."

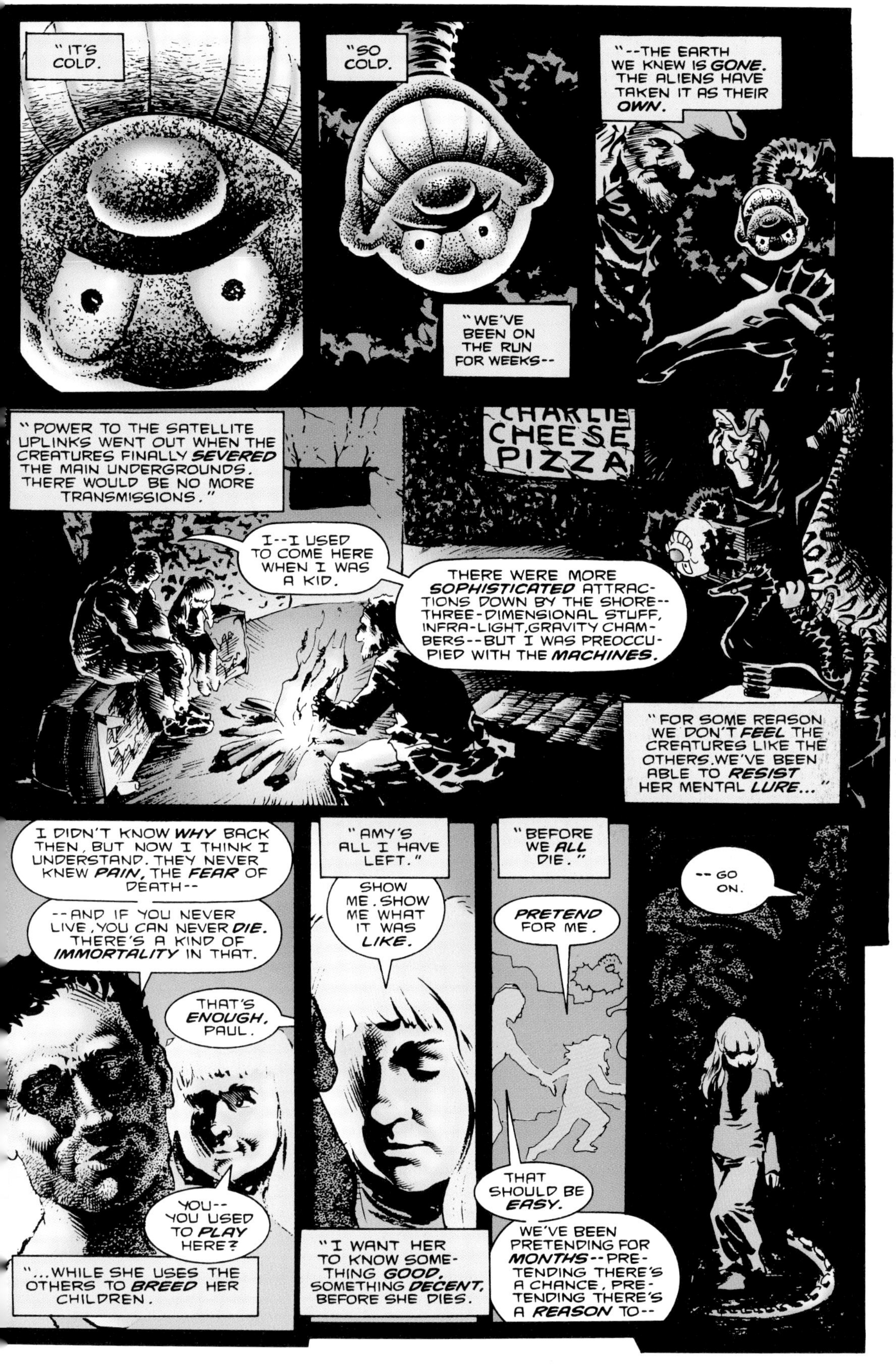
"IT'S COLD.
"SO COLD.
"WE'VE BEEN ON THE RUN FOR WEEKS--
"--THE EARTH WE KNEW IS GONE. THE ALIENS HAVE TAKEN IT AS THEIR OWN.
"POWER TO THE SATELLITE UPLINKS WENT OUT WHEN THE CREATURES FINALLY SEVERED THE MAIN UNDERGROUNDS. THERE WOULD BE NO MORE TRANSMISSIONS."
CHARLIE CHEESE PIZZA
I--I USED TO COME HERE WHEN I WAS A KID.
THERE WERE MORE SOPHISTICATED ATTRACTIONS DOWN BY THE SHORE--THREE-DIMENSIONAL STUFF, INFRA-LIGHT, GRAVITY CHAMBERS--BUT I WAS PREOCCUPIED WITH THE MACHINES.
"FOR SOME REASON WE DON'T FEEL THE CREATURES LIKE THE OTHERS. WE'VE BEEN ABLE TO RESIST HER MENTAL LURE..."
I DIDN'T KNOW WHY BACK THEN, BUT NOW I THINK I UNDERSTAND. THEY NEVER KNEW PAIN, THE FEAR OF DEATH--
--AND IF YOU NEVER LIVE, YOU CAN NEVER DIE. THERE'S A KIND OF IMMORTALITY IN THAT.
THAT'S ENOUGH, PAUL.
YOU--YOU USED TO PLAY HERE?
"...WHILE SHE USES THE OTHERS TO BREED HER CHILDREN.
"AMY'S ALL I HAVE LEFT."
SHOW ME. SHOW ME WHAT IT WAS LIKE.
"I WANT HER TO KNOW SOMETHING GOOD, SOMETHING DECENT, BEFORE SHE DIES.
"BEFORE WE ALL DIE."
PRETEND FOR ME.
THAT SHOULD BE EASY.
WE'VE BEEN PRETENDING FOR MONTHS--PRETENDING THERE'S A CHANCE, PRETENDING THERE'S A REASON TO--
--GO ON.

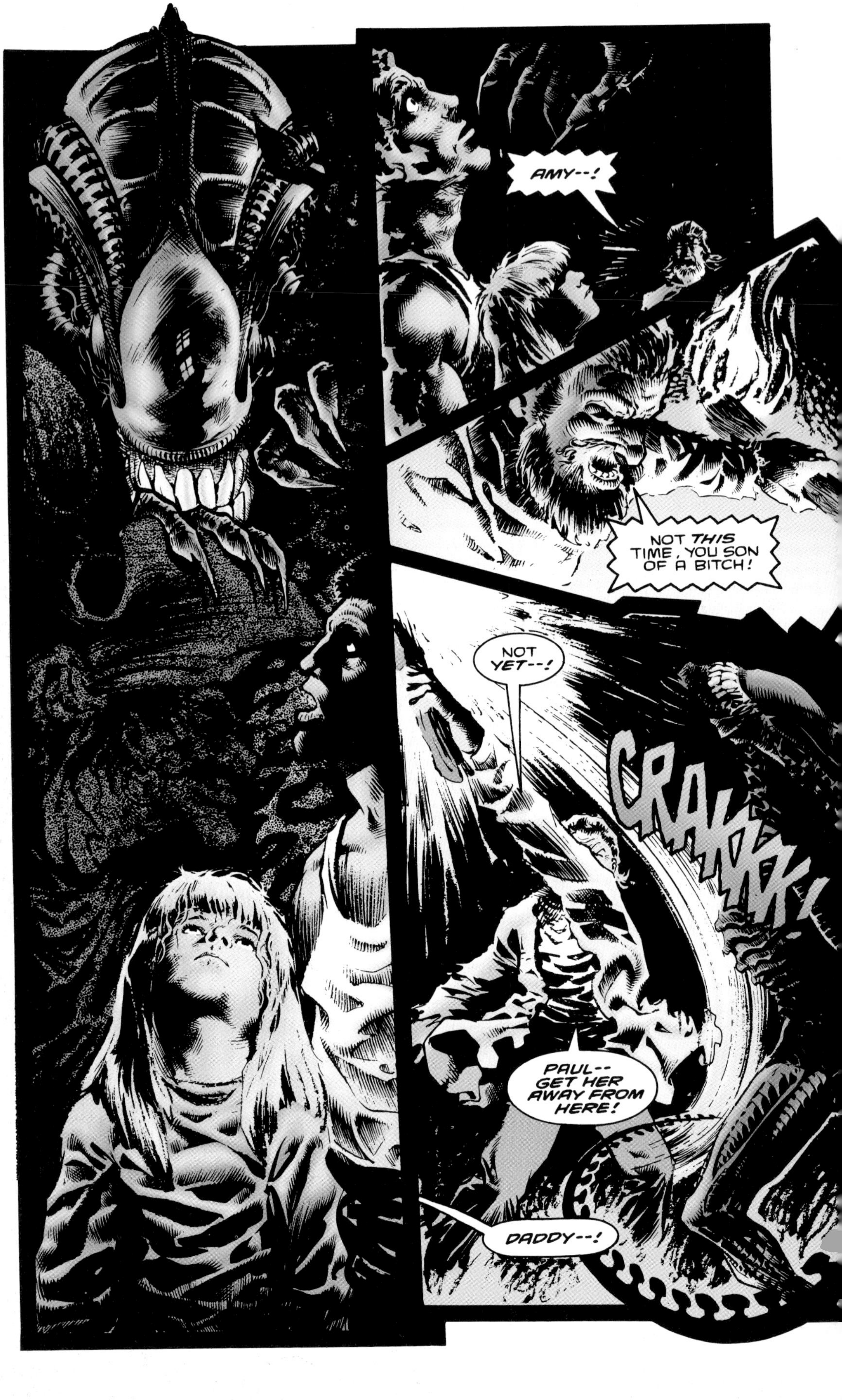
AMY--!
NOT THIS TIME, YOU SON OF A BITCH!
NOT YET--!
CRAKKKK!
PAUL-- GET HER AWAY FROM HERE!
DADDY--!

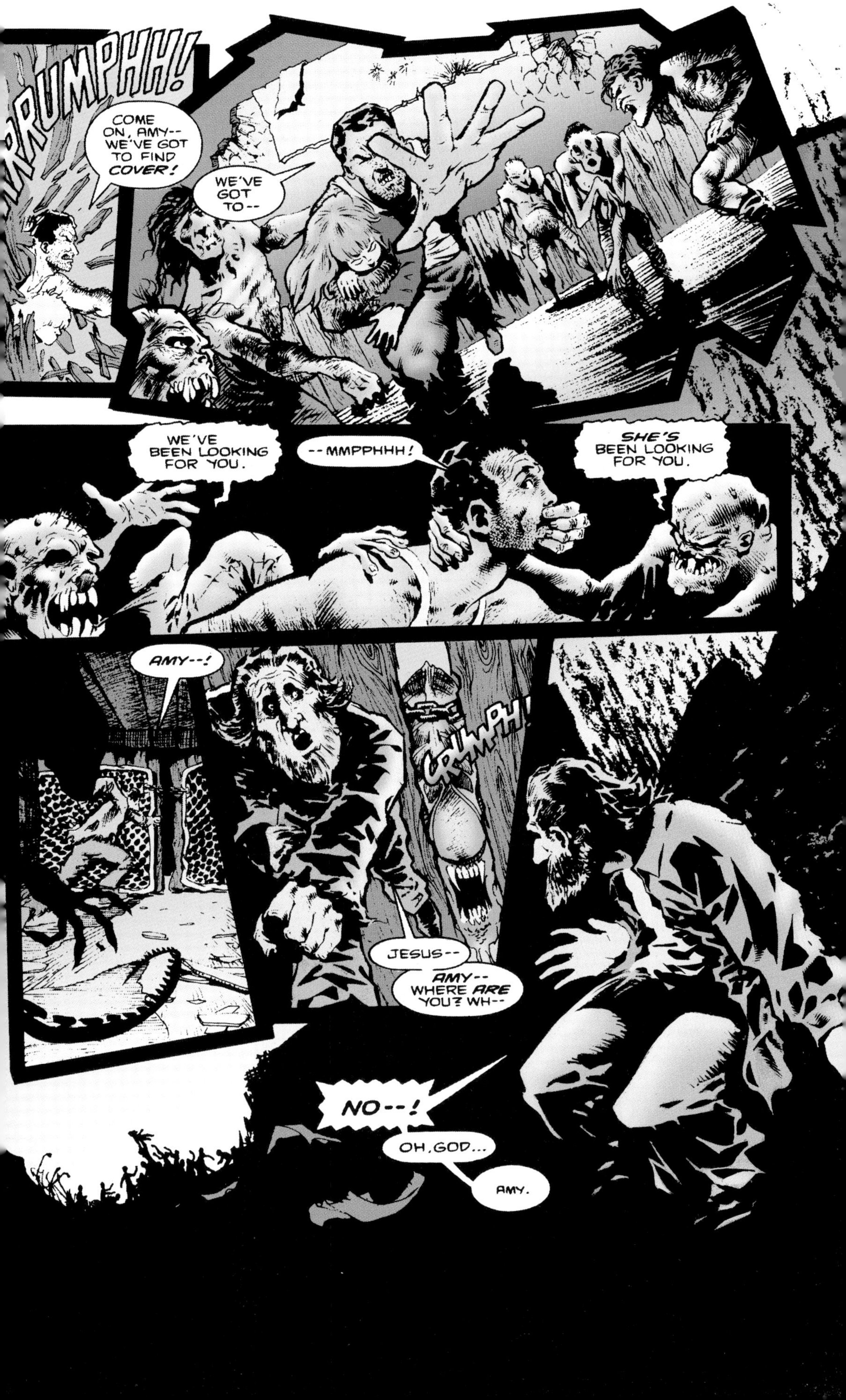
RRUMPHH!
COME ON, AMY-- WE'VE GOT TO FIND COVER!
WE'VE GOT TO--
WE'VE BEEN LOOKING FOR YOU.
--MMPPHHH!
SHE'S BEEN LOOKING FOR YOU.
AMY--!
CRUMPH!
JESUS--
AMY-- WHERE ARE YOU? WH--
NO--!
OH, GOD...
AMY.

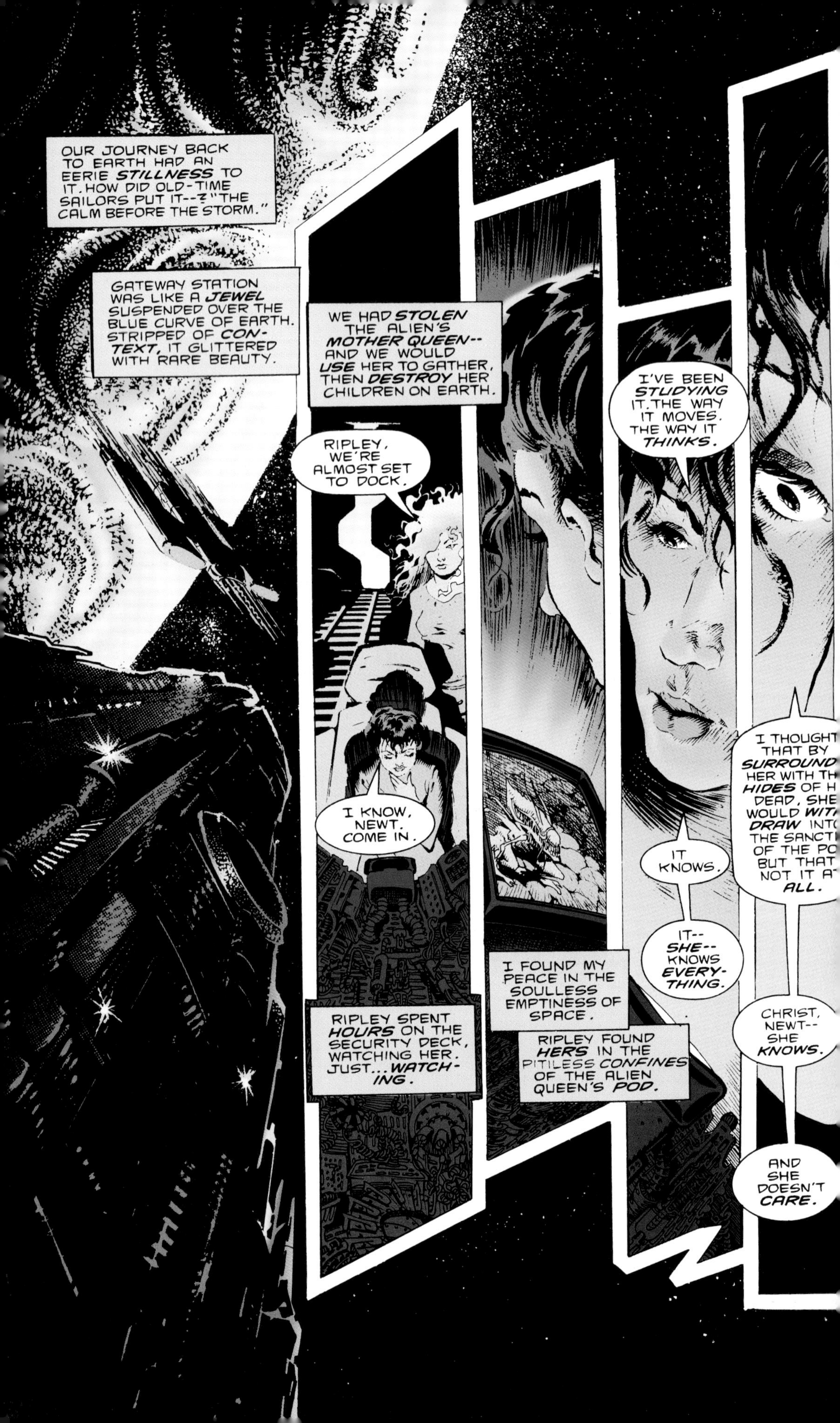
OUR JOURNEY BACK TO EARTH HAD AN EERIE STILLNESS TO IT. HOW DID OLD-TIME SAILORS PUT IT--? "THE CALM BEFORE THE STORM."
GATEWAY STATION WAS LIKE A JEWEL SUSPENDED OVER THE BLUE CURVE OF EARTH. STRIPPED OF CONTEXT, IT GLITTERED WITH RARE BEAUTY.
WE HAD STOLEN THE ALIEN'S MOTHER QUEEN-- AND WE WOULD USE HER TO GATHER, THEN DESTROY HER CHILDREN ON EARTH.
RIPLEY, WE'RE ALMOST SET TO DOCK.
I KNOW, NEWT. COME IN.
RIPLEY SPENT HOURS ON THE SECURITY DECK, WATCHING HER. JUST...WATCHING.
I FOUND MY PEACE IN THE SOULLESS EMPTINESS OF SPACE.
RIPLEY FOUND HERS IN THE PITILESS CONFINES OF THE ALIEN QUEEN'S POD.
I'VE BEEN STUDYING IT. THE WAY IT MOVES. THE WAY IT THINKS.
IT KNOWS.
IT-- SHE-- KNOWS EVERYTHING.
I THOUGHT THAT BY SURROUND HER WITH TH HIDES OF H DEAD, SHE WOULD WIT DRAW INTO THE SANCT OF THE PO BUT THAT NOT IT A ALL.
CHRIST, NEWT-- SHE KNOWS.
AND SHE DOESN'T CARE.

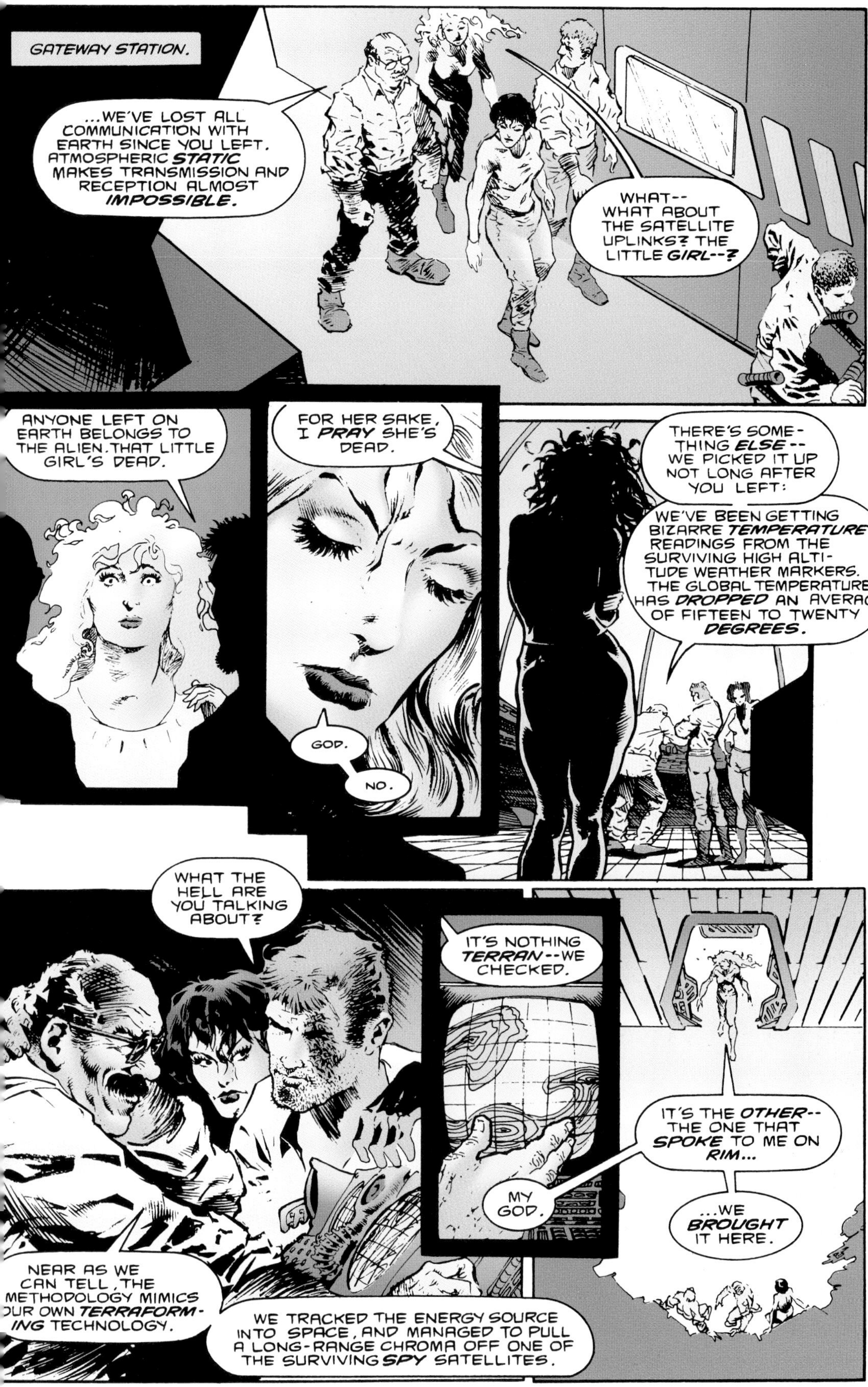
GATEWAY STATION.
...WE'VE LOST ALL COMMUNICATION WITH EARTH SINCE YOU LEFT. ATMOSPHERIC STATIC MAKES TRANSMISSION AND RECEPTION ALMOST IMPOSSIBLE.
WHAT-- WHAT ABOUT THE SATELLITE UPLINKS? THE LITTLE GIRL--?
ANYONE LEFT ON EARTH BELONGS TO THE ALIEN. THAT LITTLE GIRL'S DEAD.
FOR HER SAKE, I PRAY SHE'S DEAD.
GOD.
NO.
THERE'S SOME-THING ELSE-- WE PICKED IT UP NOT LONG AFTER YOU LEFT:
WE'VE BEEN GETTING BIZARRE TEMPERATURE READINGS FROM THE SURVIVING HIGH ALTI-TUDE WEATHER MARKERS. THE GLOBAL TEMPERATURE HAS DROPPED AN AVERAGE OF FIFTEEN TO TWENTY DEGREES.
WHAT THE HELL ARE YOU TALKING ABOUT?
IT'S NOTHING TERRAN--WE CHECKED.
MY GOD.
IT'S THE OTHER-- THE ONE THAT SPOKE TO ME ON RIM...
...WE BROUGHT IT HERE.
NEAR AS WE CAN TELL, THE METHODOLOGY MIMICS OUR OWN TERRAFORM-ING TECHNOLOGY.
WE TRACKED THE ENERGY SOURCE INTO SPACE, AND MANAGED TO PULL A LONG-RANGE CHROMA OFF ONE OF THE SURVIVING SPY SATELLITES.

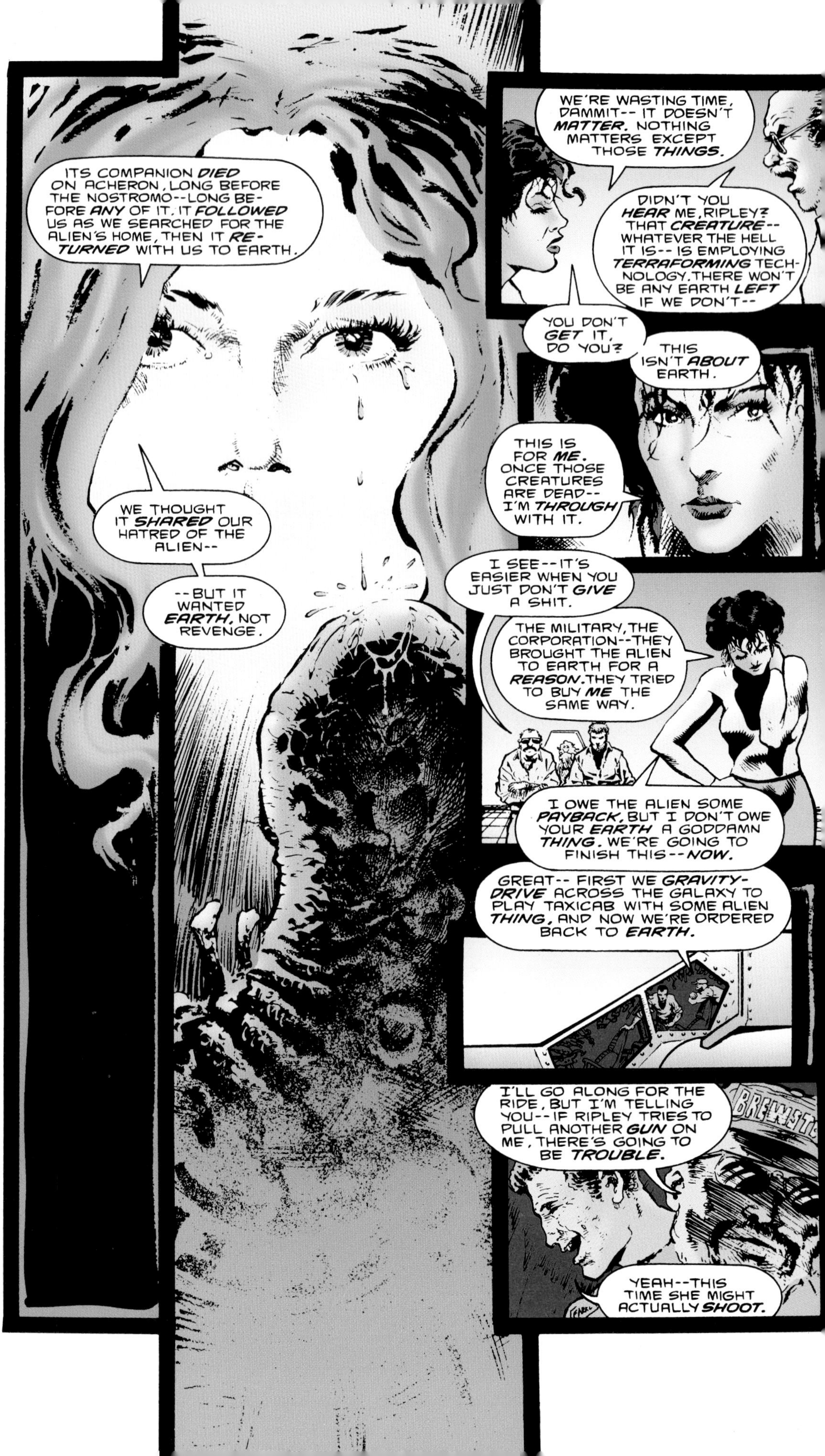

ITS COMPANION DIED ON ACHERON, LONG BEFORE THE NOSTROMO--LONG BEFORE ANY OF IT. IT FOLLOWED US AS WE SEARCHED FOR THE ALIEN'S HOME, THEN IT RETURNED WITH US TO EARTH.
WE THOUGHT IT SHARED OUR HATRED OF THE ALIEN--
--BUT IT WANTED EARTH, NOT REVENGE.
WE'RE WASTING TIME, DAMMIT-- IT DOESN'T MATTER. NOTHING MATTERS EXCEPT THOSE THINGS.
DIDN'T YOU HEAR ME, RIPLEY? THAT CREATURE--WHATEVER THE HELL IT IS-- IS EMPLOYING TERRAFORMING TECHNOLOGY. THERE WON'T BE ANY EARTH LEFT IF WE DON'T--
YOU DON'T GET IT, DO YOU?
THIS ISN'T ABOUT EARTH.
THIS IS FOR ME. ONCE THOSE CREATURES ARE DEAD-- I'M THROUGH WITH IT.
I SEE--IT'S EASIER WHEN YOU JUST DON'T GIVE A SHIT.
THE MILITARY, THE CORPORATION--THEY BROUGHT THE ALIEN TO EARTH FOR A REASON. THEY TRIED TO BUY ME THE SAME WAY.
I OWE THE ALIEN SOME PAYBACK, BUT I DON'T OWE YOUR EARTH A GODDAMN THING. WE'RE GOING TO FINISH THIS--NOW.
GREAT-- FIRST WE GRAVITY-DRIVE ACROSS THE GALAXY TO PLAY TAXICAB WITH SOME ALIEN THING, AND NOW WE'RE ORDERED BACK TO EARTH.
I'LL GO ALONG FOR THE RIDE, BUT I'M TELLING YOU--IF RIPLEY TRIES TO PULL ANOTHER GUN ON ME, THERE'S GOING TO BE TROUBLE.
YEAH--THIS TIME SHE MIGHT ACTUALLY SHOOT.

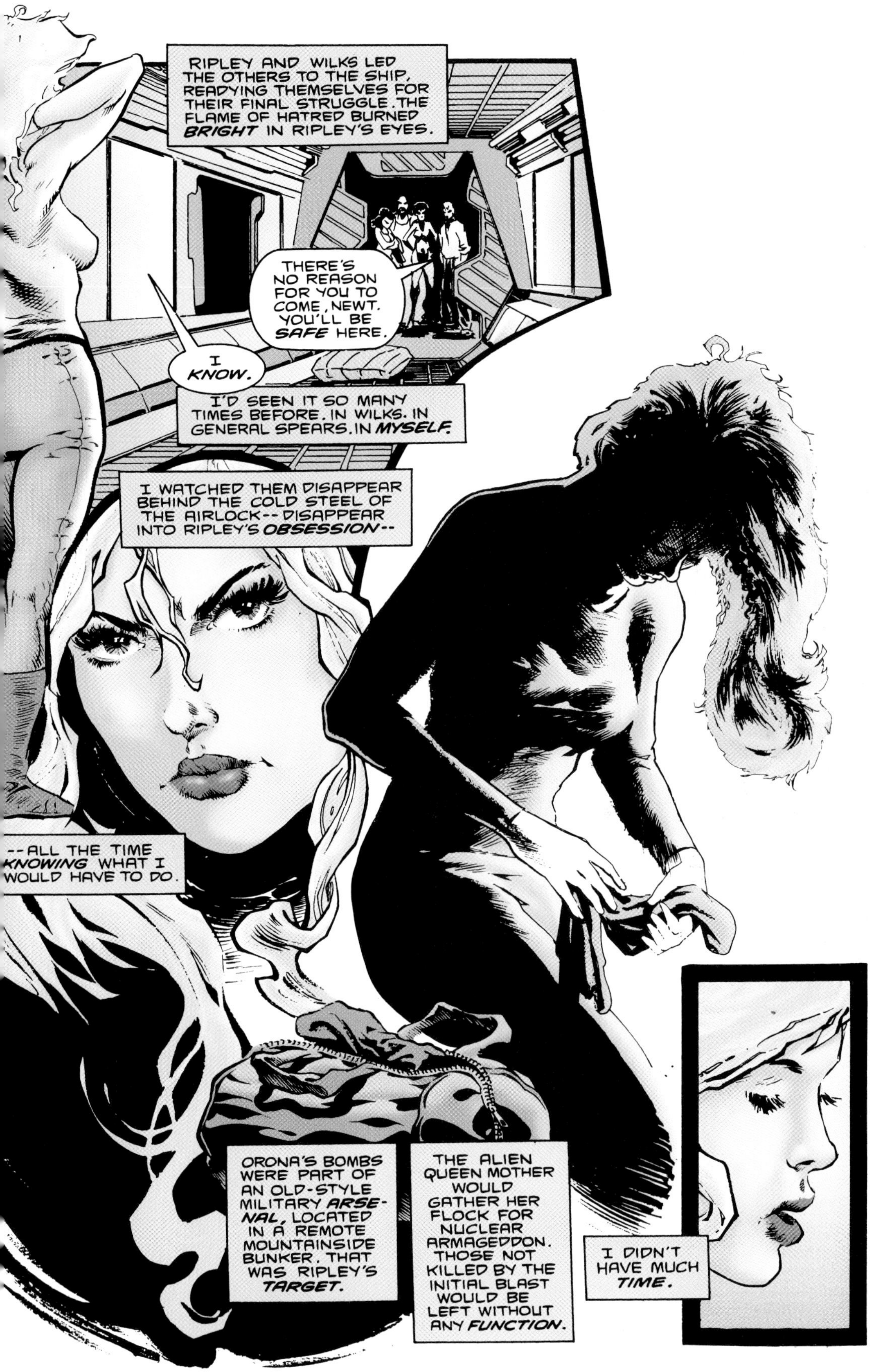
RIPLEY AND WILKS LED THE OTHERS TO THE SHIP, READYING THEMSELVES FOR THEIR FINAL STRUGGLE. THE FLAME OF HATRED BURNED BRIGHT IN RIPLEY'S EYES.
THERE'S NO REASON FOR YOU TO COME, NEWT. YOU'LL BE SAFE HERE.
I KNOW.
I'D SEEN IT SO MANY TIMES BEFORE. IN WILKS. IN GENERAL SPEARS. IN MYSELF.
I WATCHED THEM DISAPPEAR BEHIND THE COLD STEEL OF THE AIRLOCK--DISAPPEAR INTO RIPLEY'S OBSESSION--
--ALL THE TIME KNOWING WHAT I WOULD HAVE TO DO.
ORONA'S BOMBS WERE PART OF AN OLD-STYLE MILITARY ARSENAL, LOCATED IN A REMOTE MOUNTAINSIDE BUNKER. THAT WAS RIPLEY'S TARGET.
THE ALIEN QUEEN MOTHER WOULD GATHER HER FLOCK FOR NUCLEAR ARMAGEDDON. THOSE NOT KILLED BY THE INITIAL BLAST WOULD BE LEFT WITHOUT ANY FUNCTION.
I DIDN'T HAVE MUCH TIME.

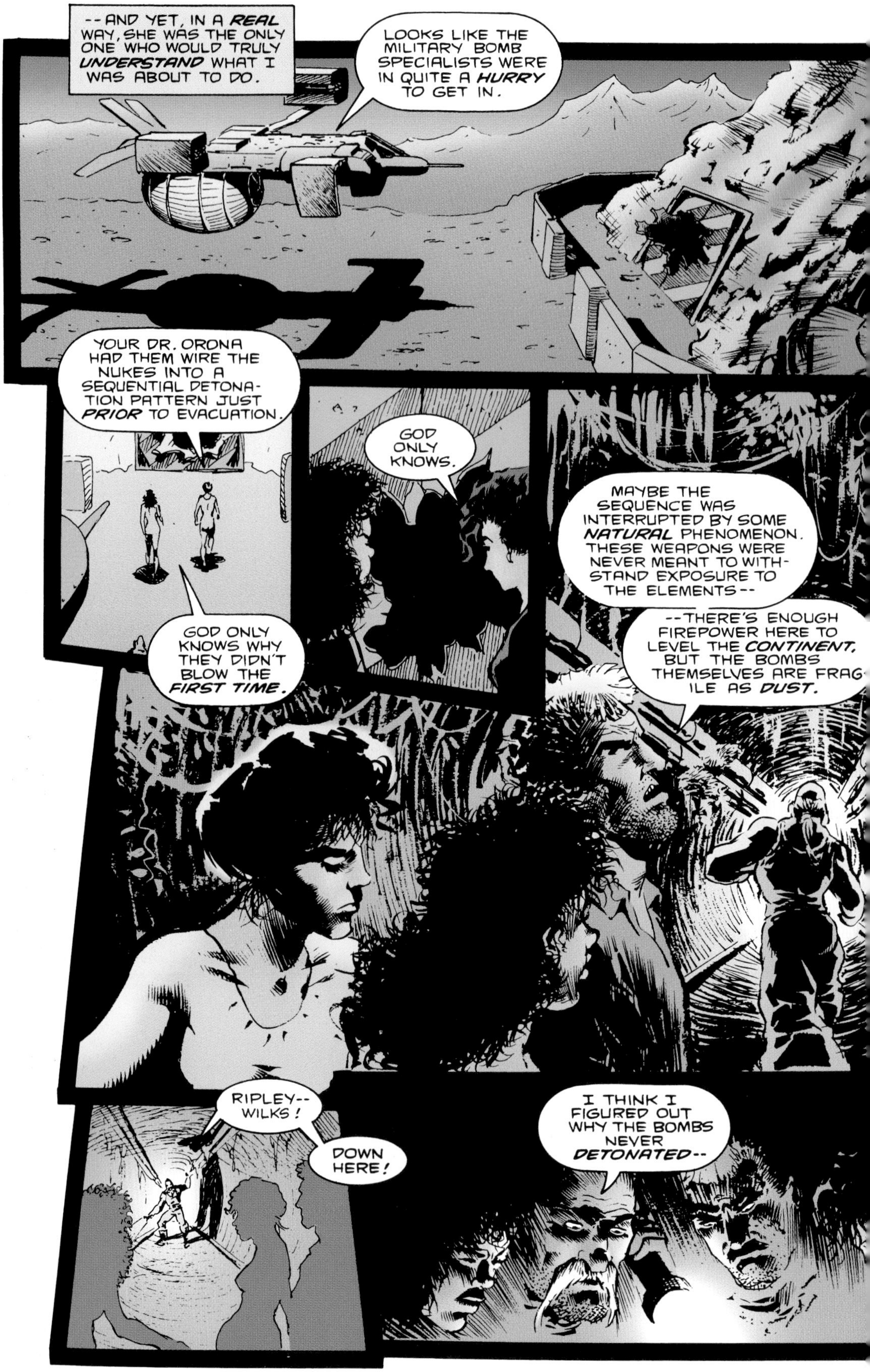
--AND YET, IN A REAL WAY, SHE WAS THE ONLY ONE WHO WOULD TRULY UNDERSTAND WHAT I WAS ABOUT TO DO.
LOOKS LIKE THE MILITARY BOMB SPECIALISTS WERE IN QUITE A HURRY TO GET IN.
YOUR DR. ORONA HAD THEM WIRE THE NUKES INTO A SEQUENTIAL DETONATION PATTERN JUST PRIOR TO EVACUATION.
GOD ONLY KNOWS WHY THEY DIDN'T BLOW THE FIRST TIME.
GOD ONLY KNOWS.
MAYBE THE SEQUENCE WAS INTERRUPTED BY SOME NATURAL PHENOMENON. THESE WEAPONS WERE NEVER MEANT TO WITHSTAND EXPOSURE TO THE ELEMENTS--
--THERE'S ENOUGH FIREPOWER HERE TO LEVEL THE CONTINENT, BUT THE BOMBS THEMSELVES ARE FRAGILE AS DUST.
RIPLEY-- WILKS!
DOWN HERE!
I THINK I FIGURED OUT WHY THE BOMBS NEVER DETONATED--

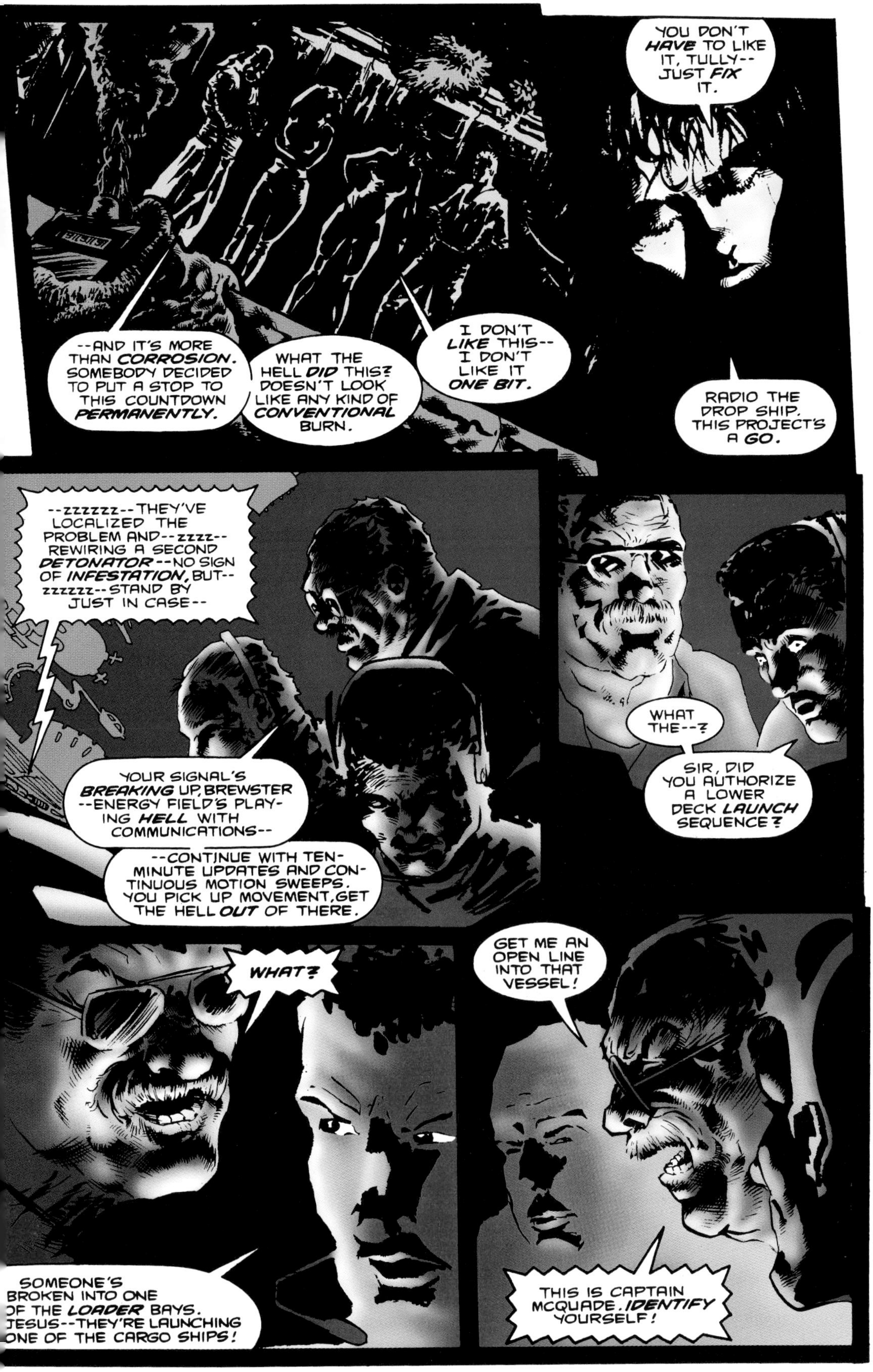
YOU DON'T HAVE TO LIKE IT, TULLY-- JUST FIX IT.
--AND IT'S MORE THAN CORROSION. SOMEBODY DECIDED TO PUT A STOP TO THIS COUNTDOWN PERMANENTLY.
WHAT THE HELL DID THIS? DOESN'T LOOK LIKE ANY KIND OF CONVENTIONAL BURN.
I DON'T LIKE THIS-- I DON'T LIKE IT ONE BIT.
RADIO THE DROP SHIP. THIS PROJECT'S A GO.
--zzzzzz--THEY'VE LOCALIZED THE PROBLEM AND--zzzz-- REWIRING A SECOND DETONATOR--NO SIGN OF INFESTATION, BUT-- zzzzzz--STAND BY JUST IN CASE--
YOUR SIGNAL'S BREAKING UP, BREWSTER --ENERGY FIELD'S PLAYING HELL WITH COMMUNICATIONS--
--CONTINUE WITH TEN-MINUTE UPDATES AND CONTINUOUS MOTION SWEEPS. YOU PICK UP MOVEMENT, GET THE HELL OUT OF THERE.
WHAT THE--?
SIR, DID YOU AUTHORIZE A LOWER DECK LAUNCH SEQUENCE?
WHAT?
SOMEONE'S BROKEN INTO ONE OF THE LOADER BAYS. JESUS--THEY'RE LAUNCHING ONE OF THE CARGO SHIPS!
GET ME AN OPEN LINE INTO THAT VESSEL!
THIS IS CAPTAIN MCQUADE. IDENTIFY YOURSELF!

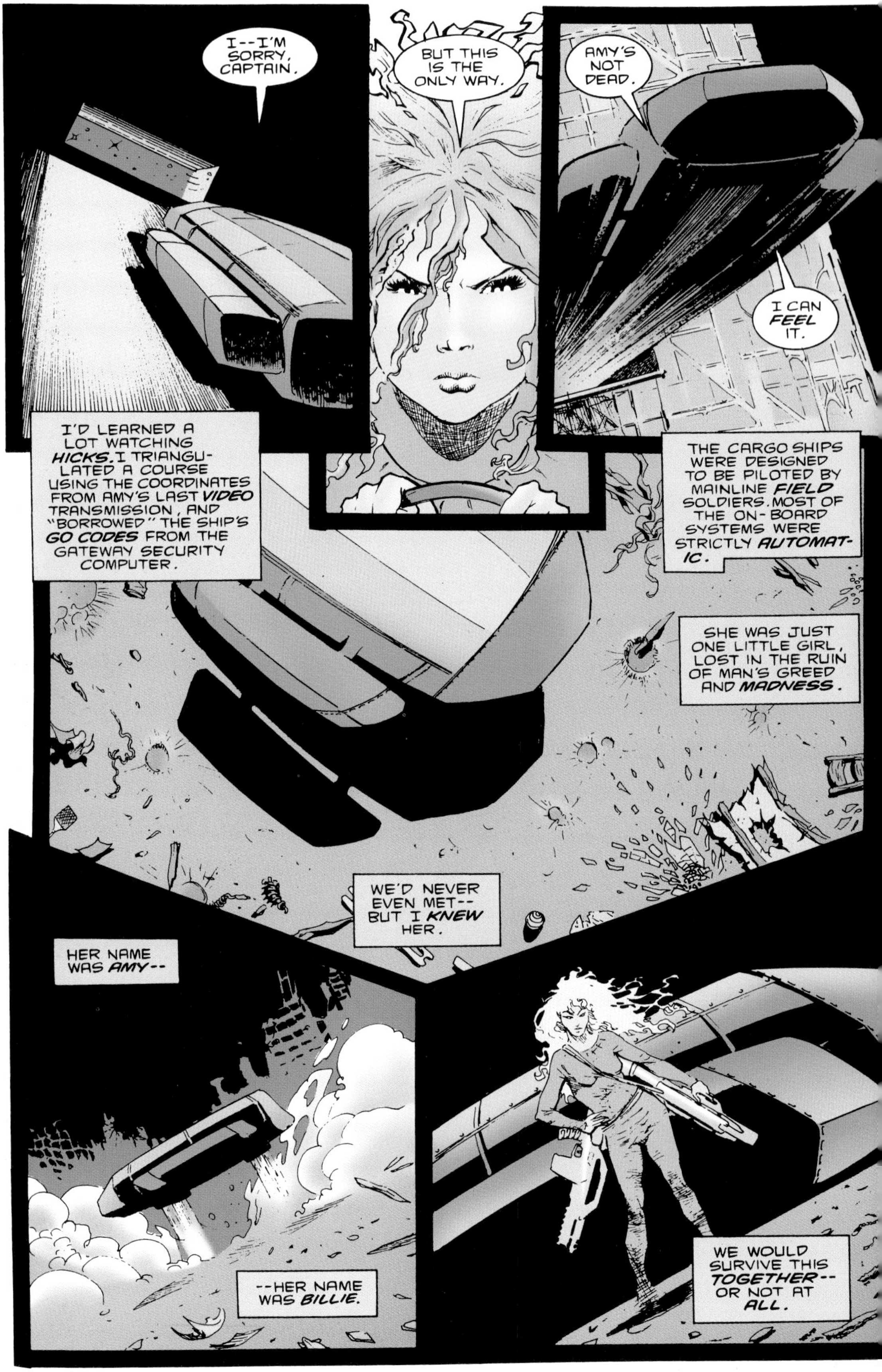

I--I'M SORRY, CAPTAIN.
BUT THIS IS THE ONLY WAY.
AMY'S NOT DEAD.
I CAN FEEL IT.
I'D LEARNED A LOT WATCHING HICKS. I TRIANGULATED A COURSE USING THE COORDINATES FROM AMY'S LAST VIDEO TRANSMISSION, AND "BORROWED" THE SHIP'S GO CODES FROM THE GATEWAY SECURITY COMPUTER.
THE CARGO SHIPS WERE DESIGNED TO BE PILOTED BY MAINLINE FIELD SOLDIERS. MOST OF THE ON-BOARD SYSTEMS WERE STRICTLY AUTOMATIC.
SHE WAS JUST ONE LITTLE GIRL, LOST IN THE RUIN OF MAN'S GREED AND MADNESS.
WE'D NEVER EVEN MET-- BUT I KNEW HER.
HER NAME WAS AMY--
--HER NAME WAS BILLIE.
WE WOULD SURVIVE THIS TOGETHER-- OR NOT AT ALL.

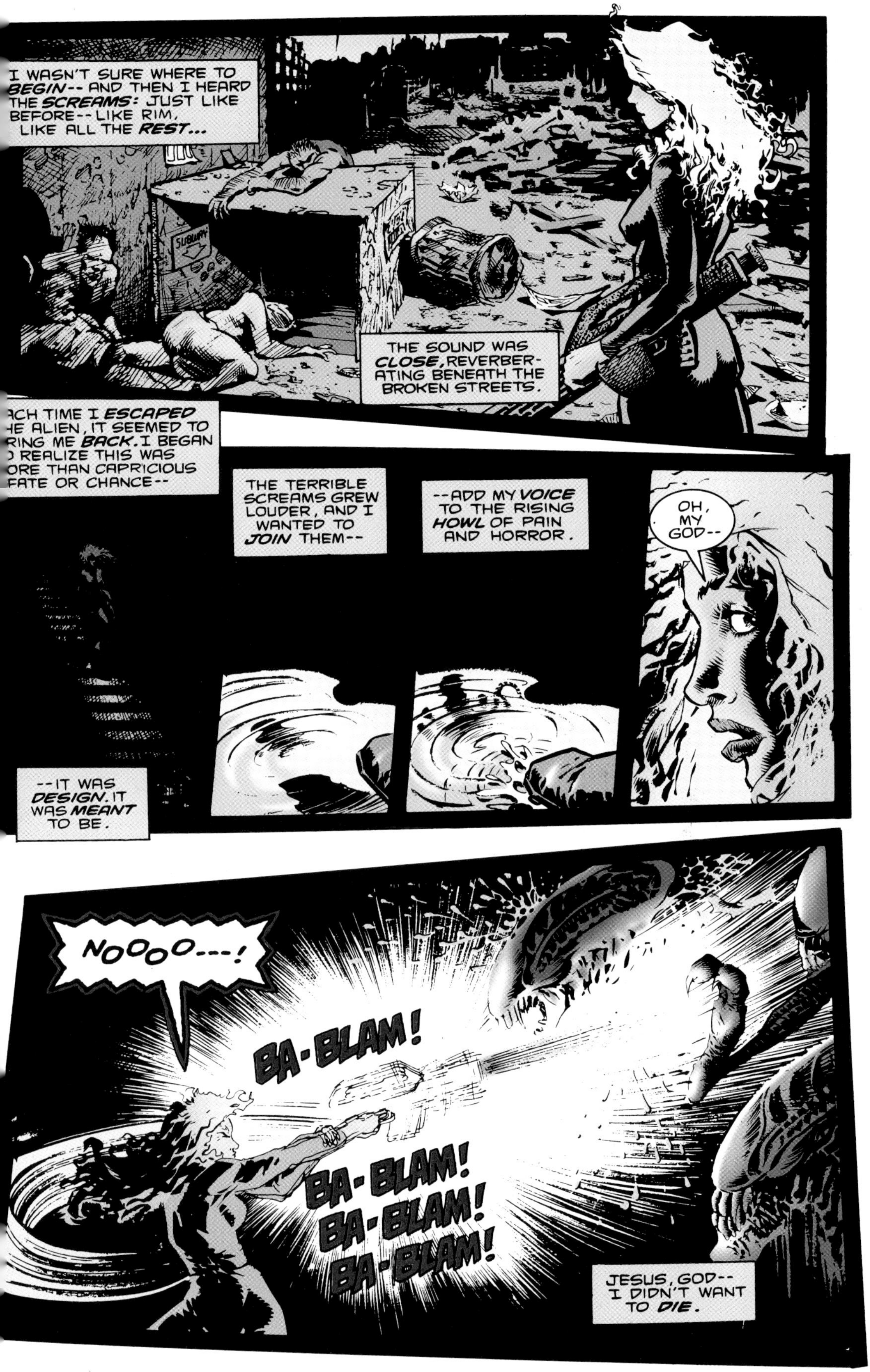
I WASN'T SURE WHERE TO BEGIN-- AND THEN I HEARD THE SCREAMS: JUST LIKE BEFORE--LIKE RIM, LIKE ALL THE REST...
SUBWAY
THE SOUND WAS CLOSE, REVERBERATING BENEATH THE BROKEN STREETS.
ACH TIME I ESCAPED HE ALIEN, IT SEEMED TO RING ME BACK. I BEGAN O REALIZE THIS WAS ORE THAN CAPRICIOUS FATE OR CHANCE--
--IT WAS DESIGN. IT WAS MEANT TO BE.
THE TERRIBLE SCREAMS GREW LOUDER, AND I WANTED TO JOIN THEM--
--ADD MY VOICE TO THE RISING HOWL OF PAIN AND HORROR.
OH, MY GOD--
NOOOO---!
BA-BLAM!
BA-BLAM! BA-BLAM! BA-BLAM!
JESUS, GOD-- I DIDN'T WANT TO DIE.

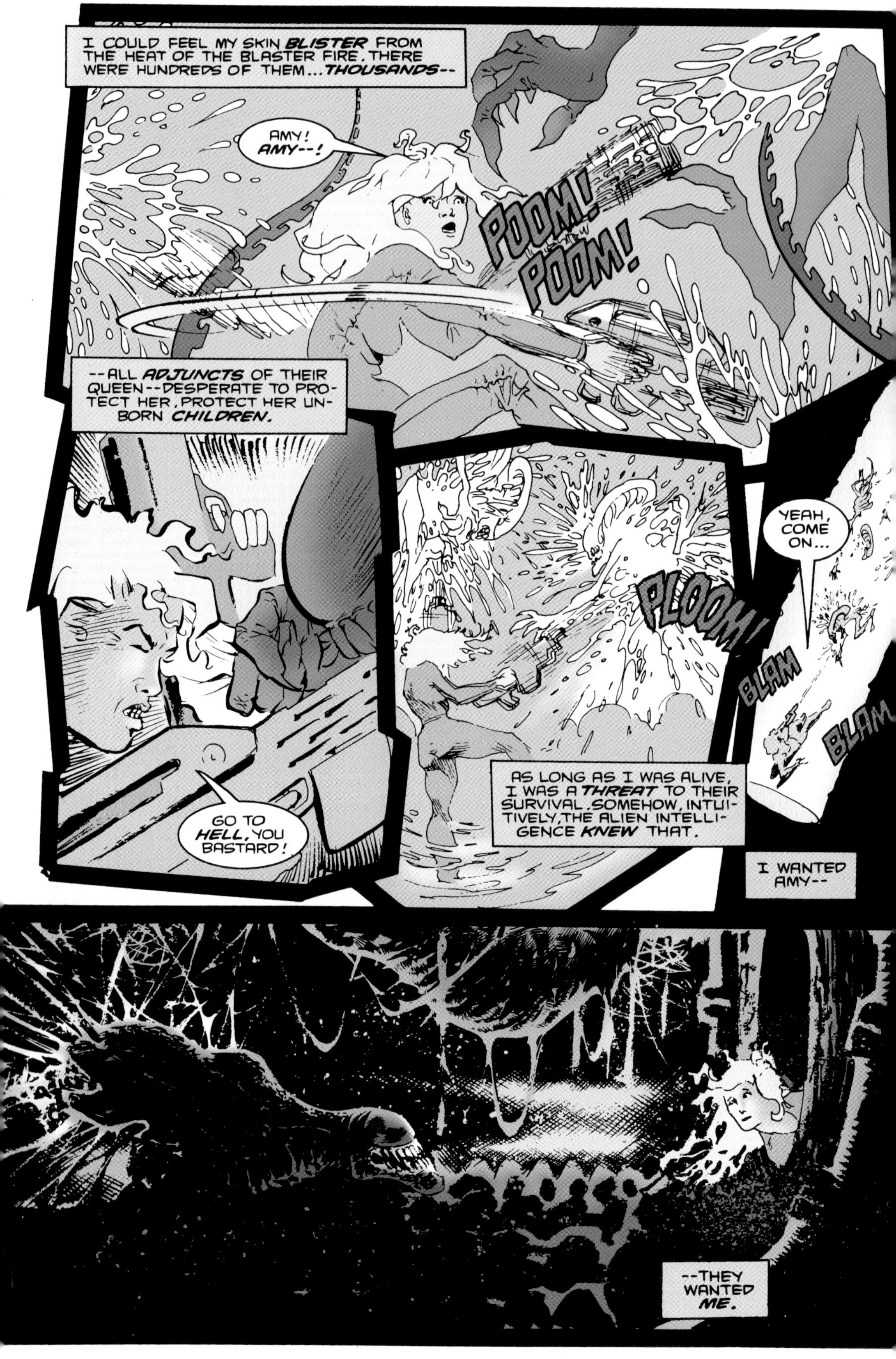
I COULD FEEL MY SKIN BLISTER FROM THE HEAT OF THE BLASTER FIRE. THERE WERE HUNDREDS OF THEM... THOUSANDS--
AMY! AMY--!
POOM! POOM!
--ALL ADJUNCTS OF THEIR QUEEN--DESPERATE TO PROTECT HER, PROTECT HER UNBORN CHILDREN.
GO TO HELL, YOU BASTARD!
PLOOM!
AS LONG AS I WAS ALIVE, I WAS A THREAT TO THEIR SURVIVAL. SOMEHOW, INTUITIVELY, THE ALIEN INTELLIGENCE KNEW THAT.
YEAH, COME ON...
BLAM
BLAM
I WANTED AMY--
--THEY WANTED ME.

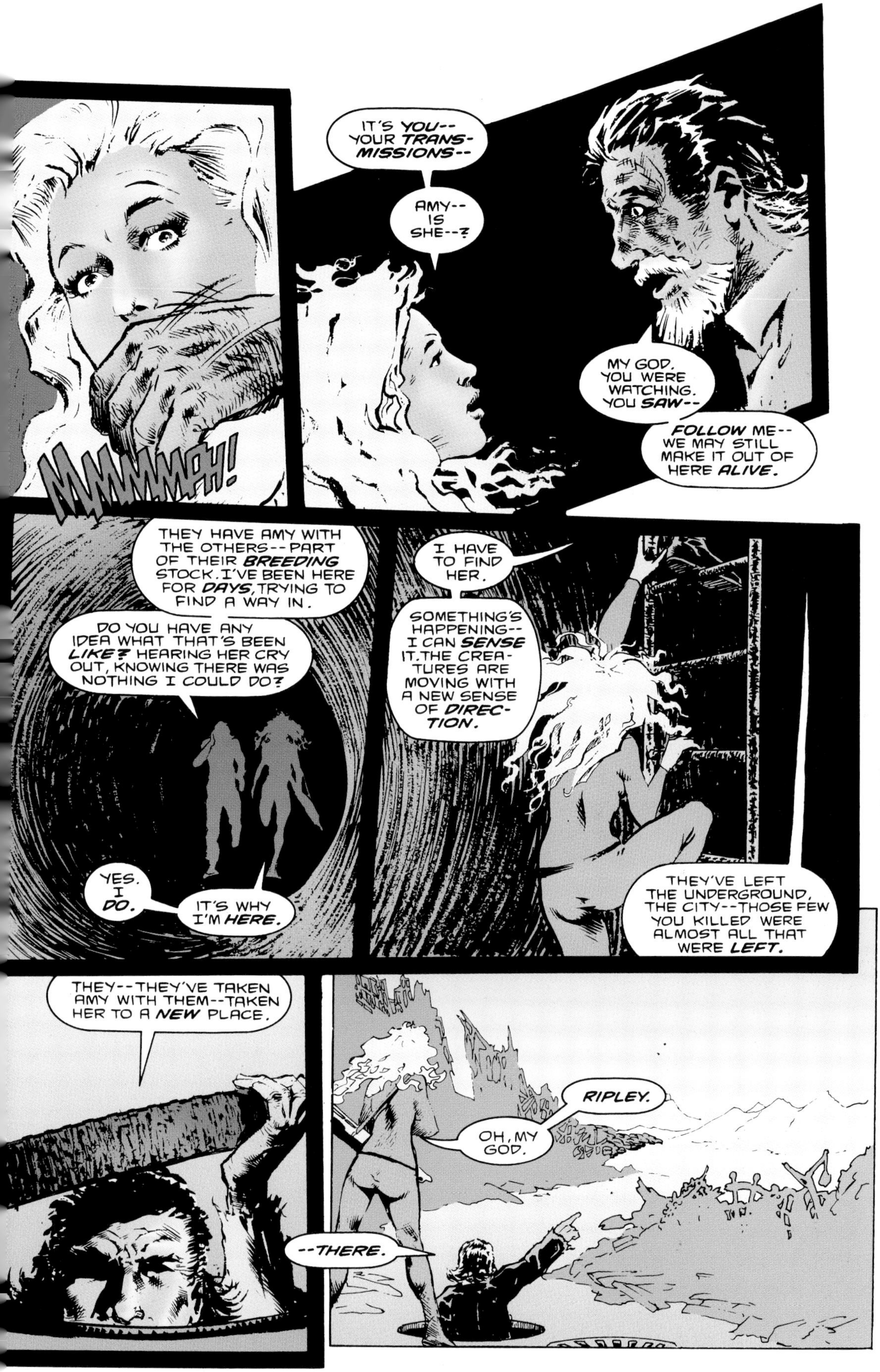
MMMMMPH!
IT'S YOU-- YOUR TRANSMISSIONS--
AMY-- IS SHE--?
MY GOD. YOU WERE WATCHING. YOU SAW--
FOLLOW ME-- WE MAY STILL MAKE IT OUT OF HERE ALIVE.
THEY HAVE AMY WITH THE OTHERS--PART OF THEIR BREEDING STOCK. I'VE BEEN HERE FOR DAYS, TRYING TO FIND A WAY IN.
DO YOU HAVE ANY IDEA WHAT THAT'S BEEN LIKE? HEARING HER CRY OUT, KNOWING THERE WAS NOTHING I COULD DO?
YES. I DO.
IT'S WHY I'M HERE.
I HAVE TO FIND HER.
SOMETHING'S HAPPENING-- I CAN SENSE IT. THE CREATURES ARE MOVING WITH A NEW SENSE OF DIRECTION.
THEY'VE LEFT THE UNDERGROUND, THE CITY--THOSE FEW YOU KILLED WERE ALMOST ALL THAT WERE LEFT.
THEY--THEY'VE TAKEN AMY WITH THEM--TAKEN HER TO A NEW PLACE.
RIPLEY.
OH, MY GOD.
--THERE.

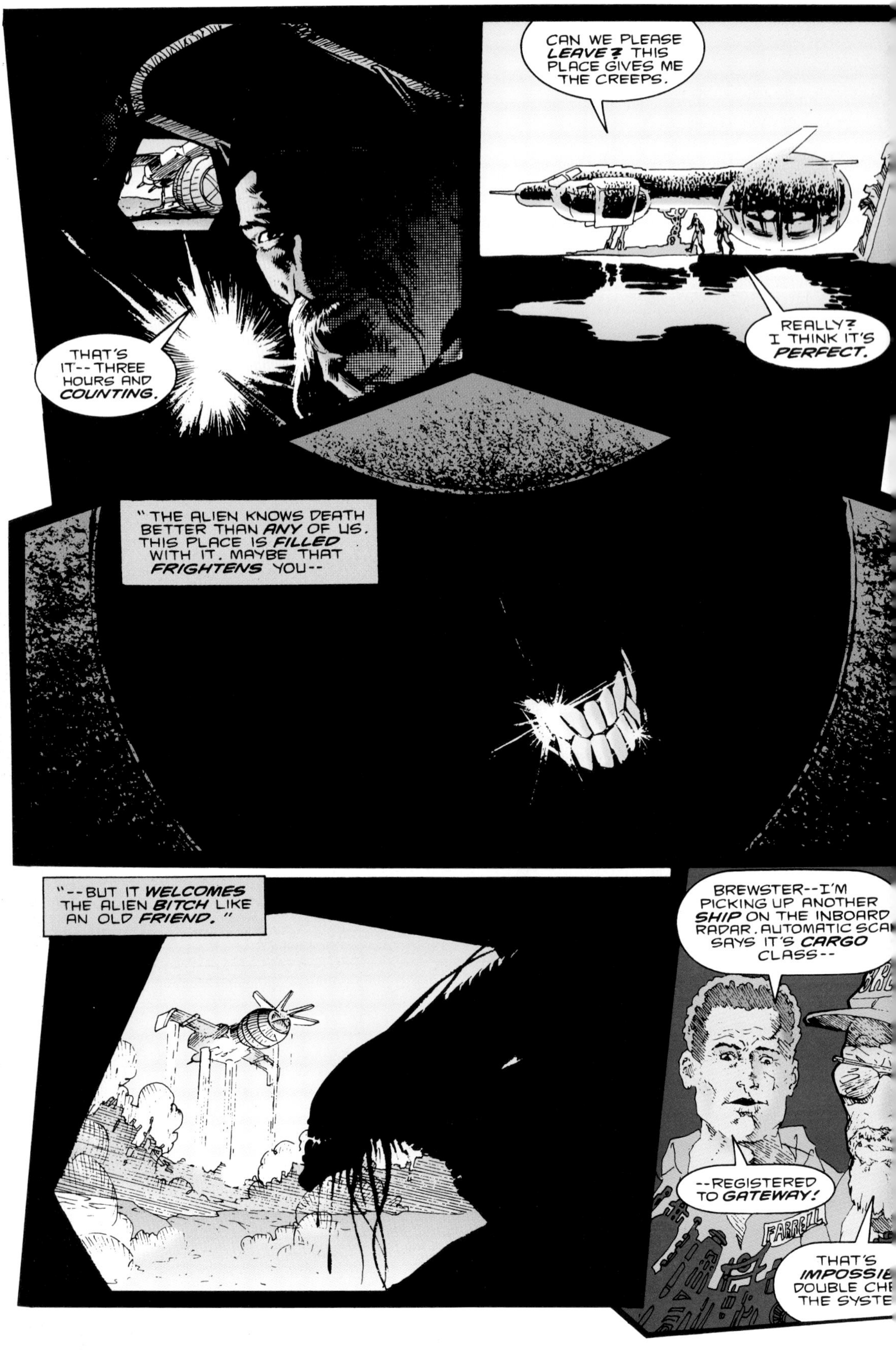
THAT'S IT--THREE HOURS AND COUNTING.
CAN WE PLEASE LEAVE? THIS PLACE GIVES ME THE CREEPS.
REALLY? I THINK IT'S PERFECT.
"THE ALIEN KNOWS DEATH BETTER THAN ANY OF US. THIS PLACE IS FILLED WITH IT. MAYBE THAT FRIGHTENS YOU--
"--BUT IT WELCOMES THE ALIEN BITCH LIKE AN OLD FRIEND."
BREWSTER--I'M PICKING UP ANOTHER SHIP ON THE INBOARD RADAR. AUTOMATIC SCA
SAYS IT'S CARGO CLASS--
--REGISTERED TO GATEWAY!
FARRELL
THAT'S IMPOSSIB
DOUBLE CH
THE SYSTE

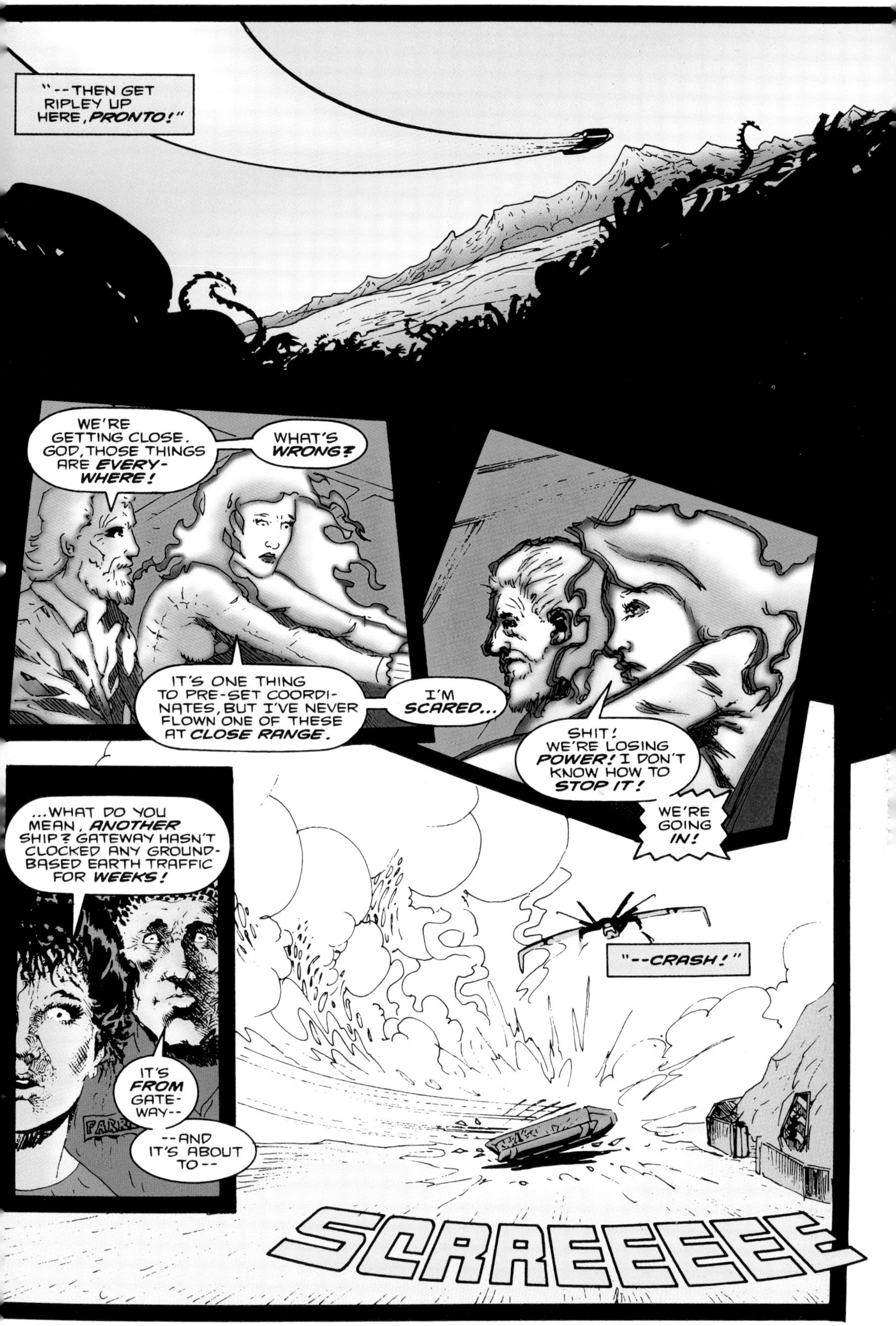
"--THEN GET RIPLEY UP HERE, PRONTO!"
WE'RE GETTING CLOSE. GOD, THOSE THINGS ARE EVERY-WHERE!
WHAT'S WRONG?
IT'S ONE THING TO PRE-SET COORDI-NATES, BUT I'VE NEVER FLOWN ONE OF THESE AT CLOSE RANGE.
I'M SCARED...
SHIT! WE'RE LOSING POWER! I DON'T KNOW HOW TO STOP IT!
WE'RE GOING IN!
...WHAT DO YOU MEAN, ANOTHER SHIP? GATEWAY HASN'T CLOCKED ANY GROUND-BASED EARTH TRAFFIC FOR WEEKS!
IT'S FROM GATE-WAY--
--AND IT'S ABOUT TO--
"--CRASH!"
SCREEEEEE

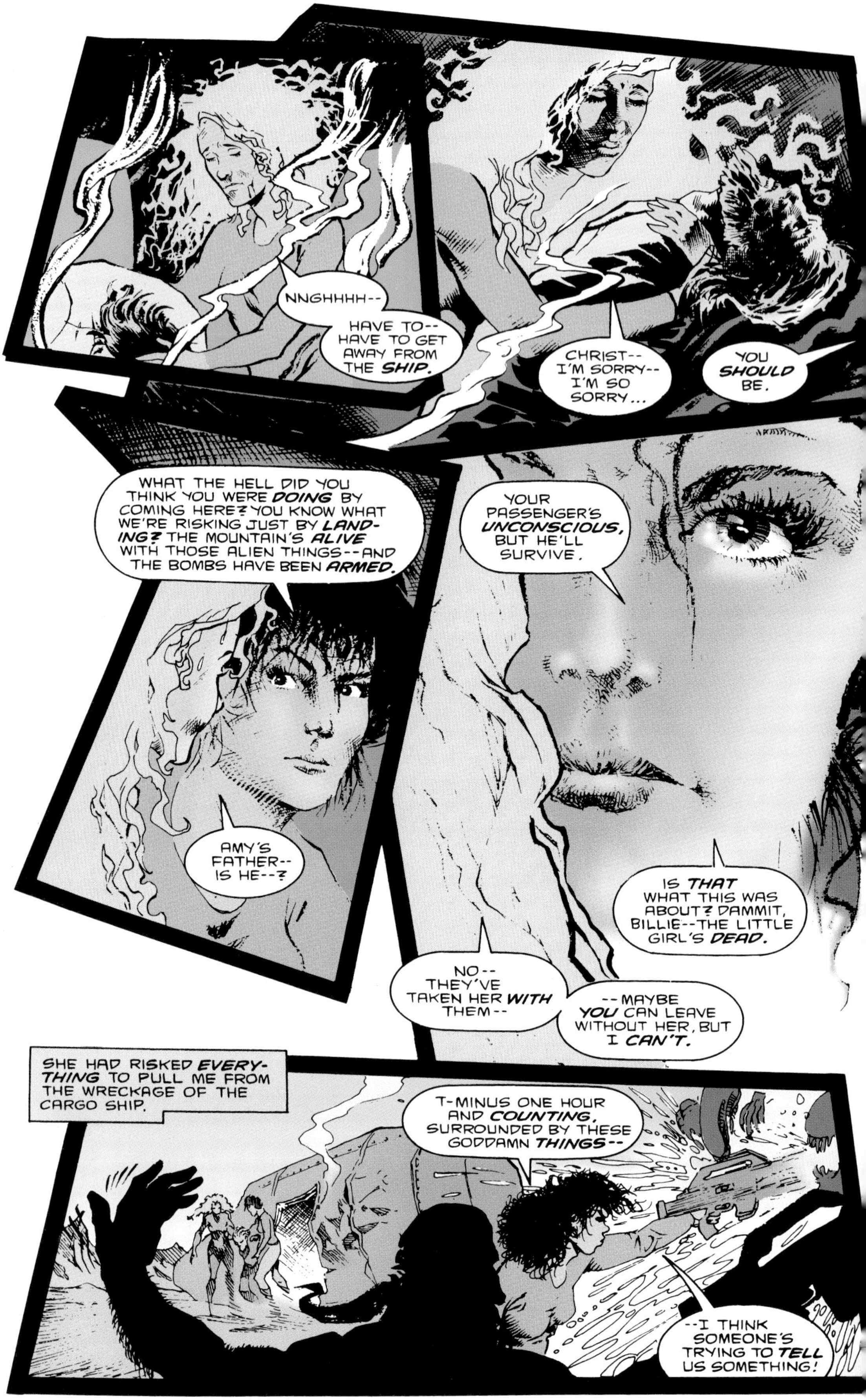
NNGHHHH--
HAVE TO-- HAVE TO GET AWAY FROM THE SHIP.
CHRIST-- I'M SORRY-- I'M SO SORRY...
YOU SHOULD BE.
WHAT THE HELL DID YOU THINK YOU WERE DOING BY COMING HERE? YOU KNOW WHAT WE'RE RISKING JUST BY LANDING? THE MOUNTAIN'S ALIVE WITH THOSE ALIEN THINGS--AND THE BOMBS HAVE BEEN ARMED.
YOUR PASSENGER'S UNCONSCIOUS, BUT HE'LL SURVIVE.
AMY'S FATHER-- IS HE--?
IS THAT WHAT THIS WAS ABOUT? DAMMIT, BILLIE--THE LITTLE GIRL'S DEAD.
NO-- THEY'VE TAKEN HER WITH THEM--
--MAYBE YOU CAN LEAVE WITHOUT HER, BUT I CAN'T.
SHE HAD RISKED EVERYTHING TO PULL ME FROM THE WRECKAGE OF THE CARGO SHIP.
T-MINUS ONE HOUR AND COUNTING, SURROUNDED BY THESE GODDAMN THINGS--
--I THINK SOMEONE'S TRYING TO TELL US SOMETHING!

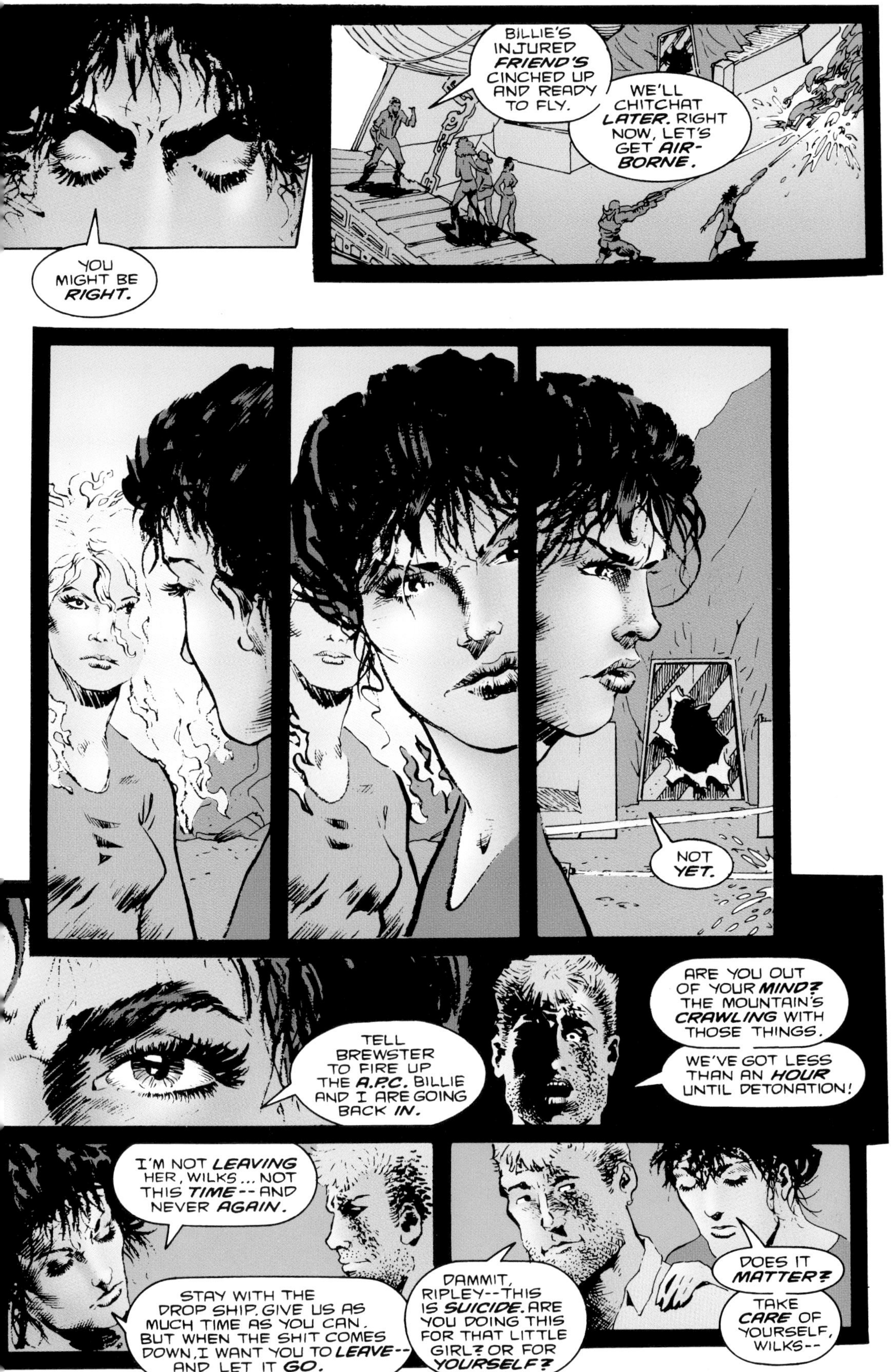
YOU MIGHT BE RIGHT.
BILLIE'S INJURED FRIEND'S CINCHED UP AND READY TO FLY.
WE'LL CHITCHAT LATER. RIGHT NOW, LET'S GET AIR-BORNE.
NOT YET.
TELL BREWSTER TO FIRE UP THE A.P.C. BILLIE AND I ARE GOING BACK IN.
ARE YOU OUT OF YOUR MIND? THE MOUNTAIN'S CRAWLING WITH THOSE THINGS.
WE'VE GOT LESS THAN AN HOUR UNTIL DETONATION!
I'M NOT LEAVING HER, WILKS... NOT THIS TIME--AND NEVER AGAIN.
STAY WITH THE DROP SHIP. GIVE US AS MUCH TIME AS YOU CAN. BUT WHEN THE SHIT COMES DOWN, I WANT YOU TO LEAVE--AND LET IT GO.
DAMMIT, RIPLEY--THIS IS SUICIDE. ARE YOU DOING THIS FOR THAT LITTLE GIRL? OR FOR YOURSELF?
DOES IT MATTER?
TAKE CARE OF YOURSELF, WILKS--

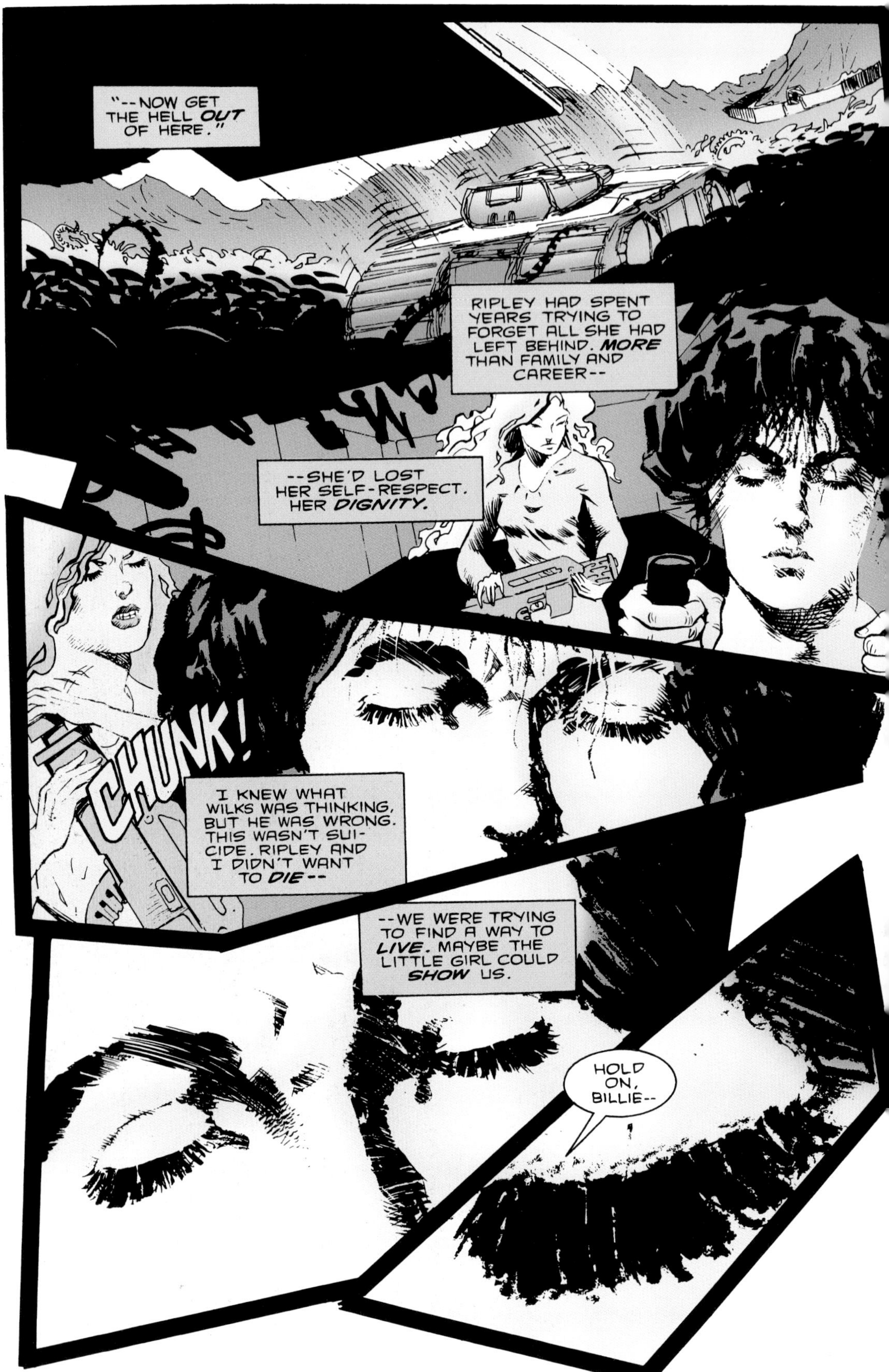
"--NOW GET THE HELL OUT OF HERE."
RIPLEY HAD SPENT YEARS TRYING TO FORGET ALL SHE HAD LEFT BEHIND. MORE THAN FAMILY AND CAREER--
--SHE'D LOST HER SELF-RESPECT. HER DIGNITY.
CHUNK!
I KNEW WHAT WILKS WAS THINKING, BUT HE WAS WRONG. THIS WASN'T SUICIDE. RIPLEY AND I DIDN'T WANT TO DIE--
--WE WERE TRYING TO FIND A WAY TO LIVE. MAYBE THE LITTLE GIRL COULD SHOW US.
HOLD ON, BILLIE--

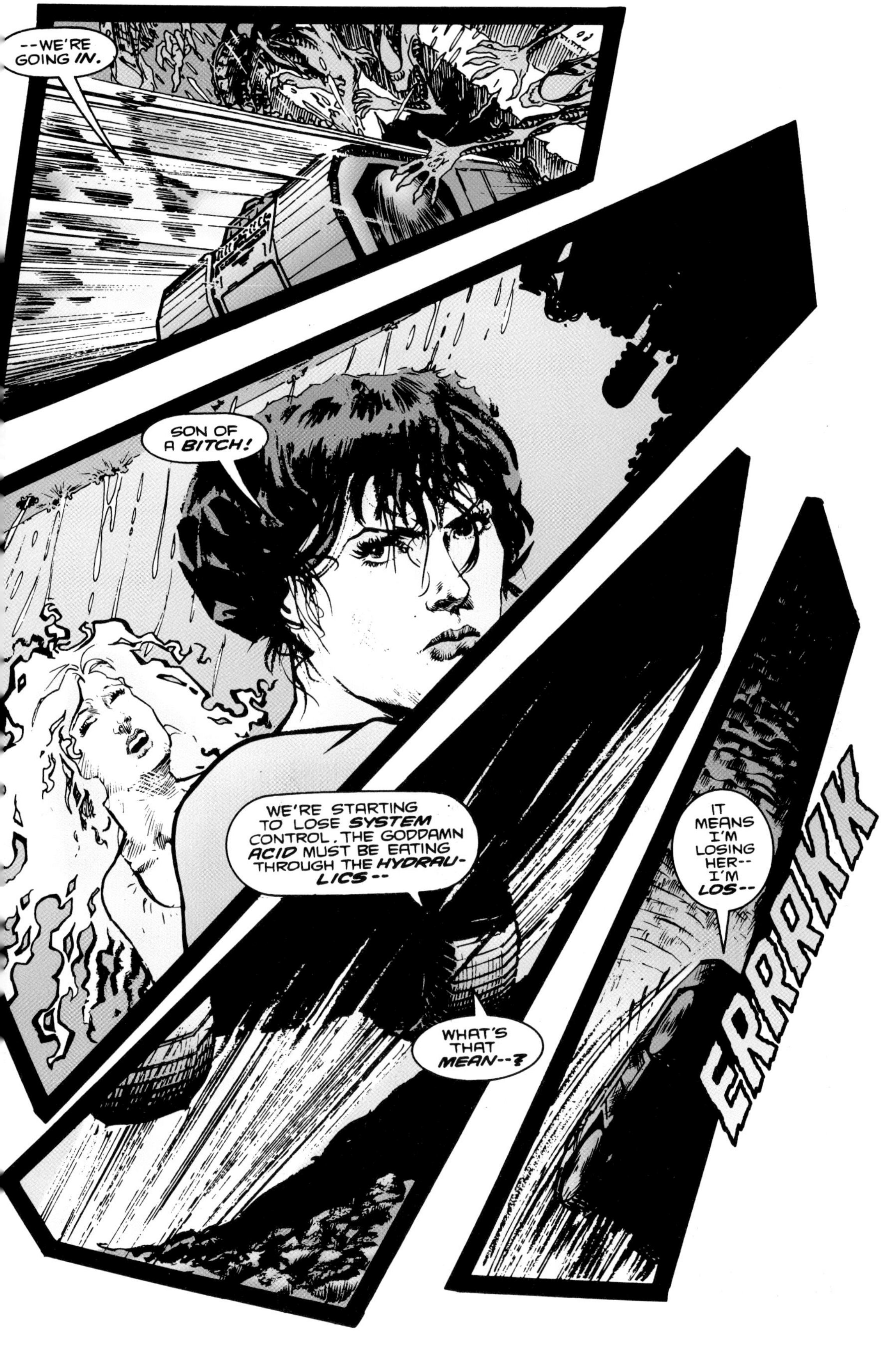
--WE'RE GOING IN.
SON OF A BITCH!
WE'RE STARTING TO LOSE SYSTEM CONTROL. THE GODDAMN ACID MUST BE EATING THROUGH THE HYDRAU-LICS--
WHAT'S THAT MEAN--?
IT MEANS I'M LOSING HER--I'M LOS--
GRRRKK

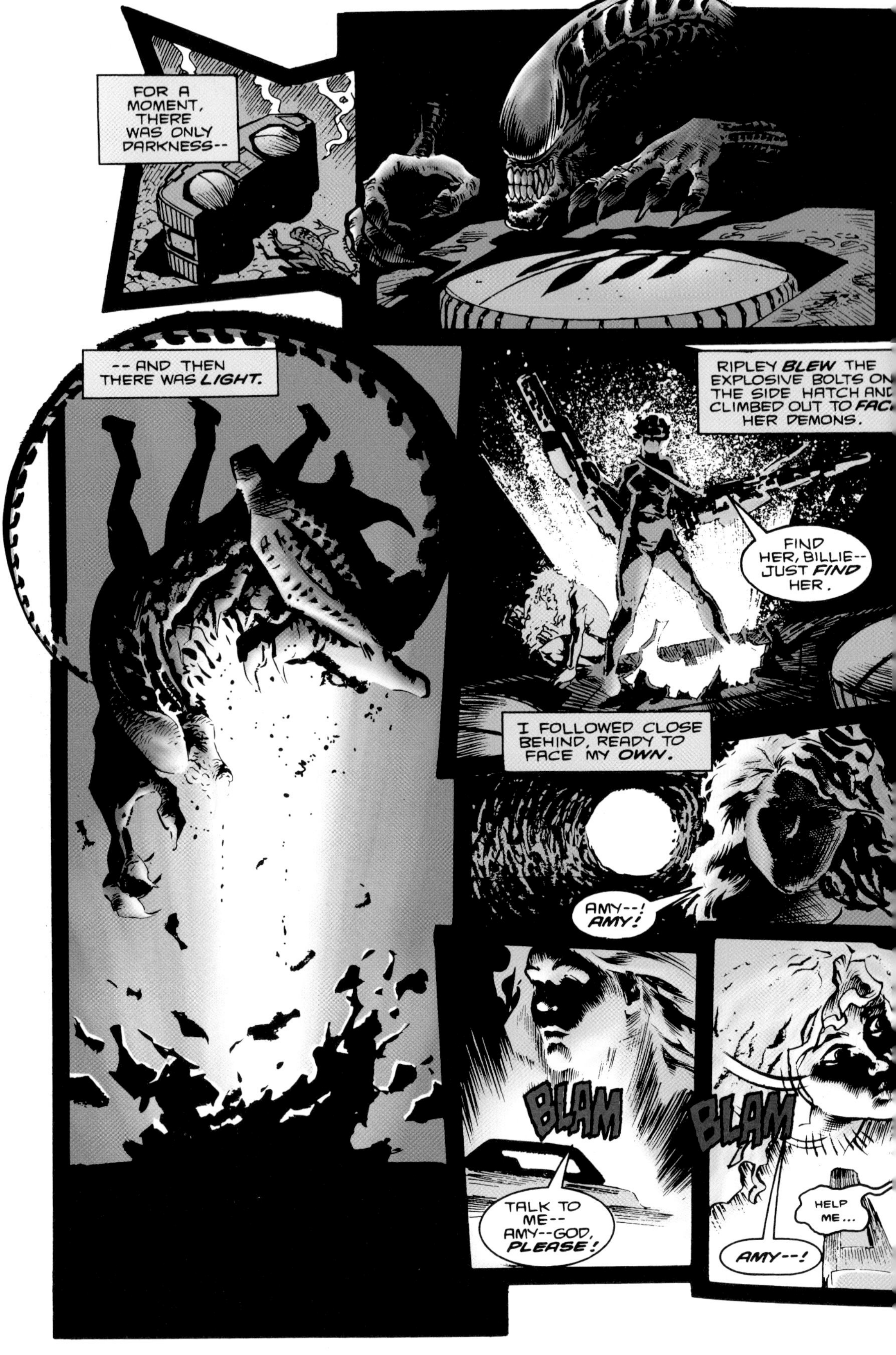
FOR A MOMENT, THERE WAS ONLY DARKNESS--
-- AND THEN THERE WAS LIGHT.
RIPLEY BLEW THE EXPLOSIVE BOLTS ON THE SIDE HATCH AND CLIMBED OUT TO FACE HER DEMONS.
FIND HER, BILLIE-- JUST FIND HER.
I FOLLOWED CLOSE BEHIND, READY TO FACE MY OWN.
AMY--! AMY!
BLAM
TALK TO ME-- AMY--GOD, PLEASE!
BLAM
HELP ME...
AMY--!

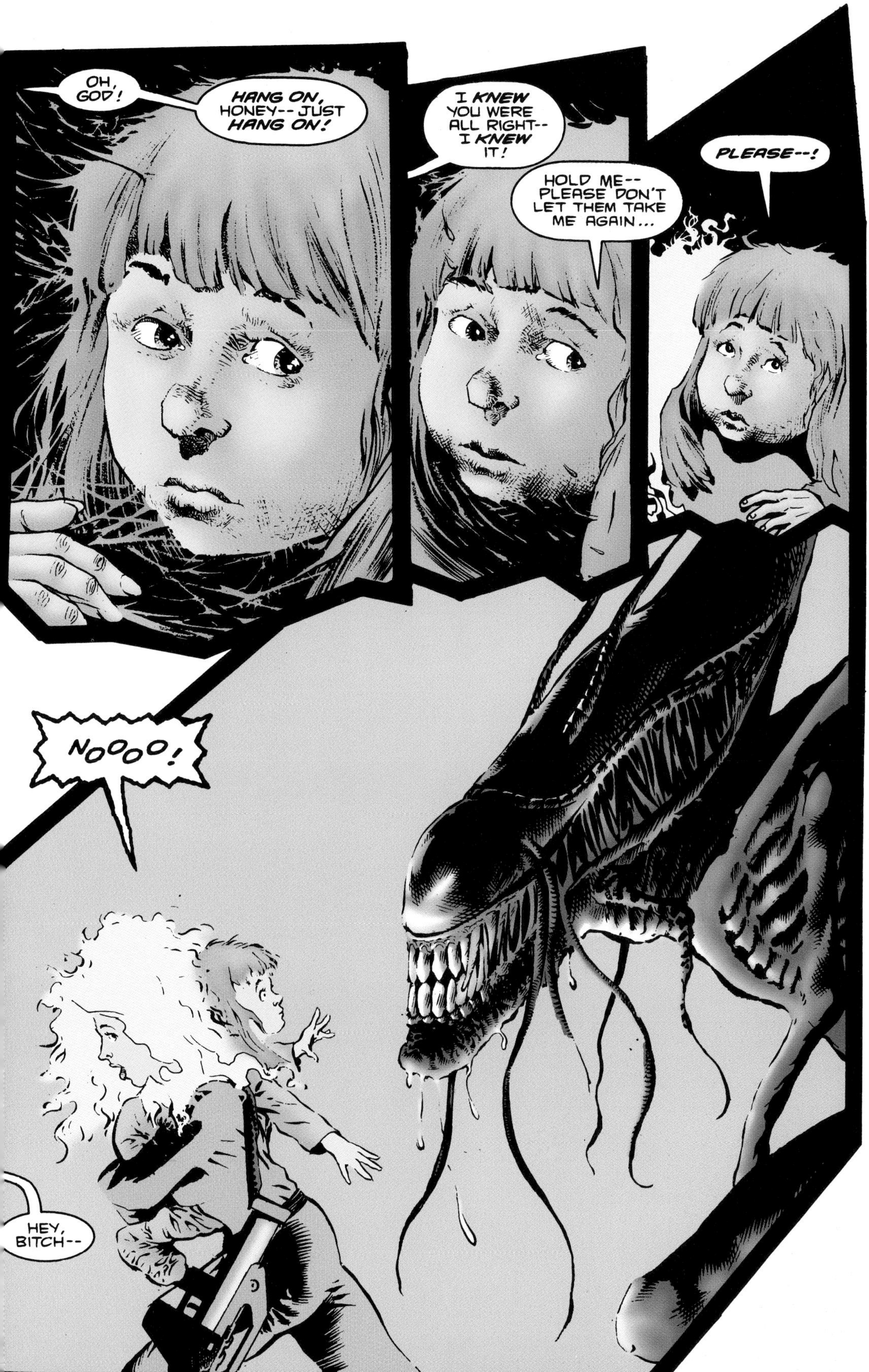
OH, GOD!
HANG ON, HONEY-- JUST HANG ON!
I KNEW YOU WERE ALL RIGHT-- I KNEW IT!
HOLD ME-- PLEASE DON'T LET THEM TAKE ME AGAIN...
PLEASE--!
NOOOO!
HEY, BITCH--

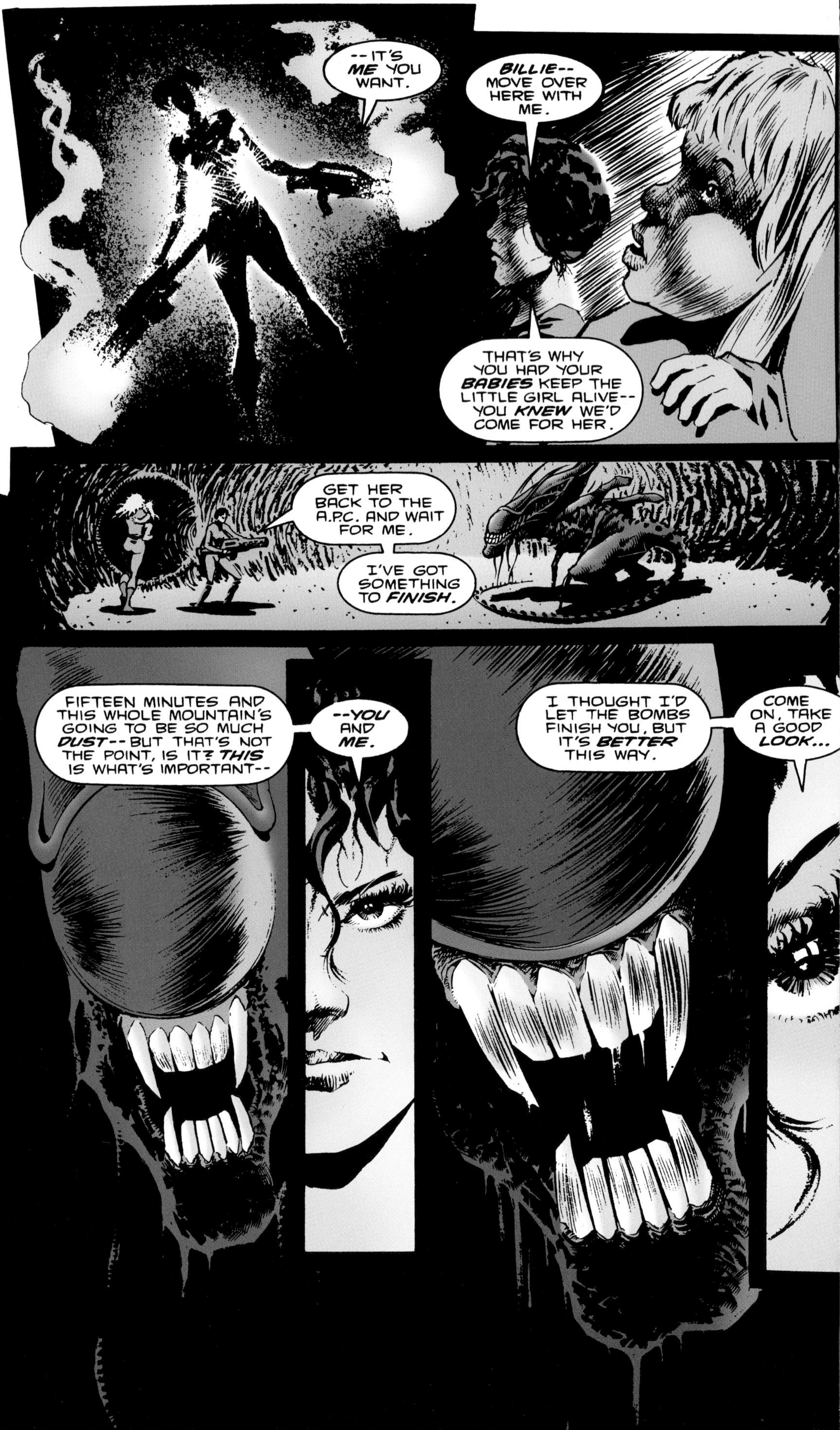
--IT'S ME YOU WANT.
BILLIE--MOVE OVER HERE WITH ME.
THAT'S WHY YOU HAD YOUR BABIES KEEP THE LITTLE GIRL ALIVE--YOU KNEW WE'D COME FOR HER.
GET HER BACK TO THE A.P.C. AND WAIT FOR ME.
I'VE GOT SOMETHING TO FINISH.
FIFTEEN MINUTES AND THIS WHOLE MOUNTAIN'S GOING TO BE SO MUCH DUST--BUT THAT'S NOT THE POINT, IS IT? THIS IS WHAT'S IMPORTANT--
--YOU AND ME.
I THOUGHT I'D LET THE BOMBS FINISH YOU, BUT IT'S BETTER THIS WAY.
COME ON, TAKE A GOOD LOOK...

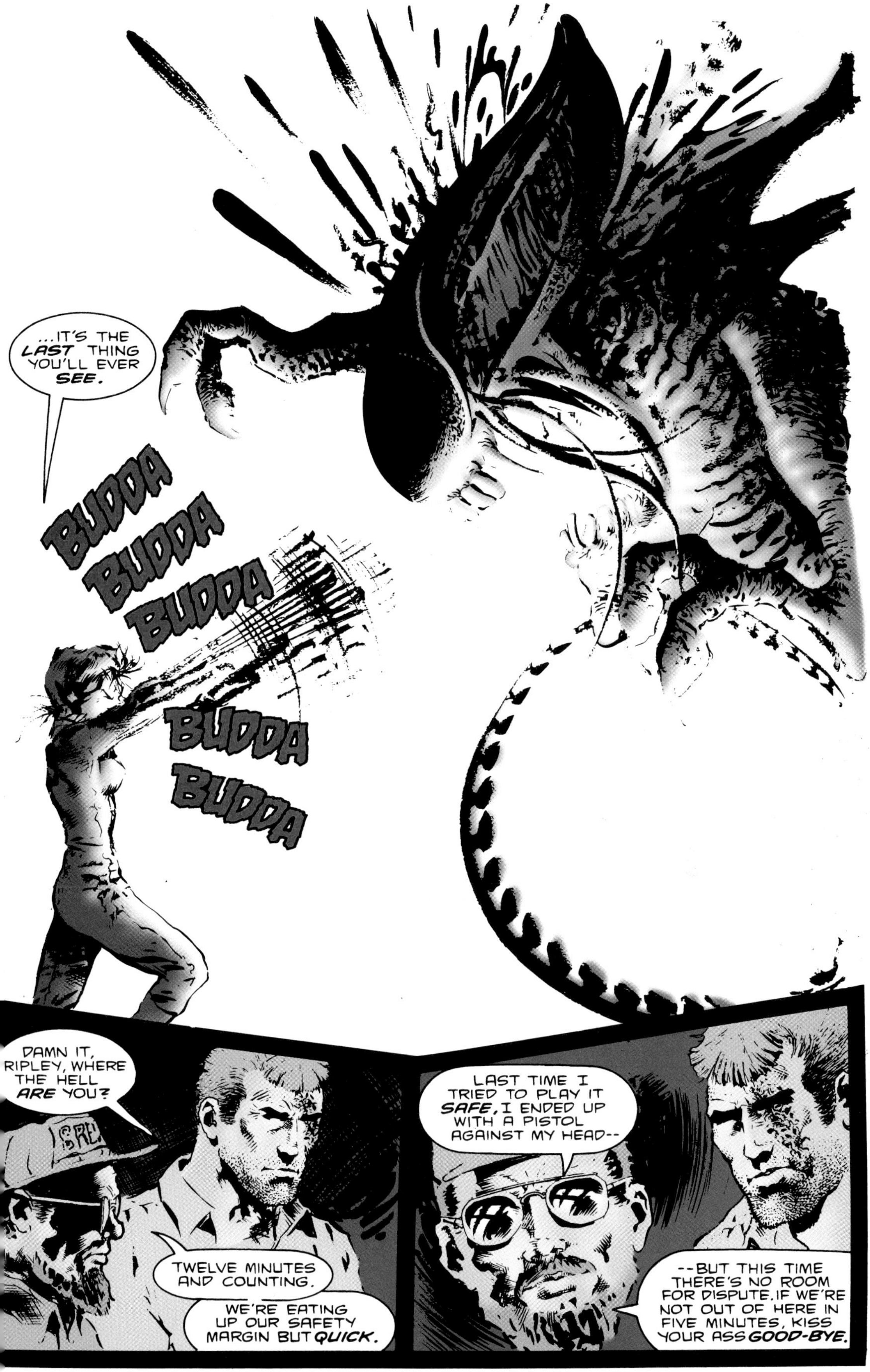

...IT'S THE LAST THING YOU'LL EVER SEE.
BUDDA BUDDA BUDDA
BUDDA BUDDA
DAMN IT, RIPLEY, WHERE THE HELL ARE YOU?
TWELVE MINUTES AND COUNTING.
WE'RE EATING UP OUR SAFETY MARGIN BUT QUICK.
LAST TIME I TRIED TO PLAY IT SAFE, I ENDED UP WITH A PISTOL AGAINST MY HEAD--
--BUT THIS TIME THERE'S NO ROOM FOR DISPUTE. IF WE'RE NOT OUT OF HERE IN FIVE MINUTES, KISS YOUR ASS GOOD-BYE.

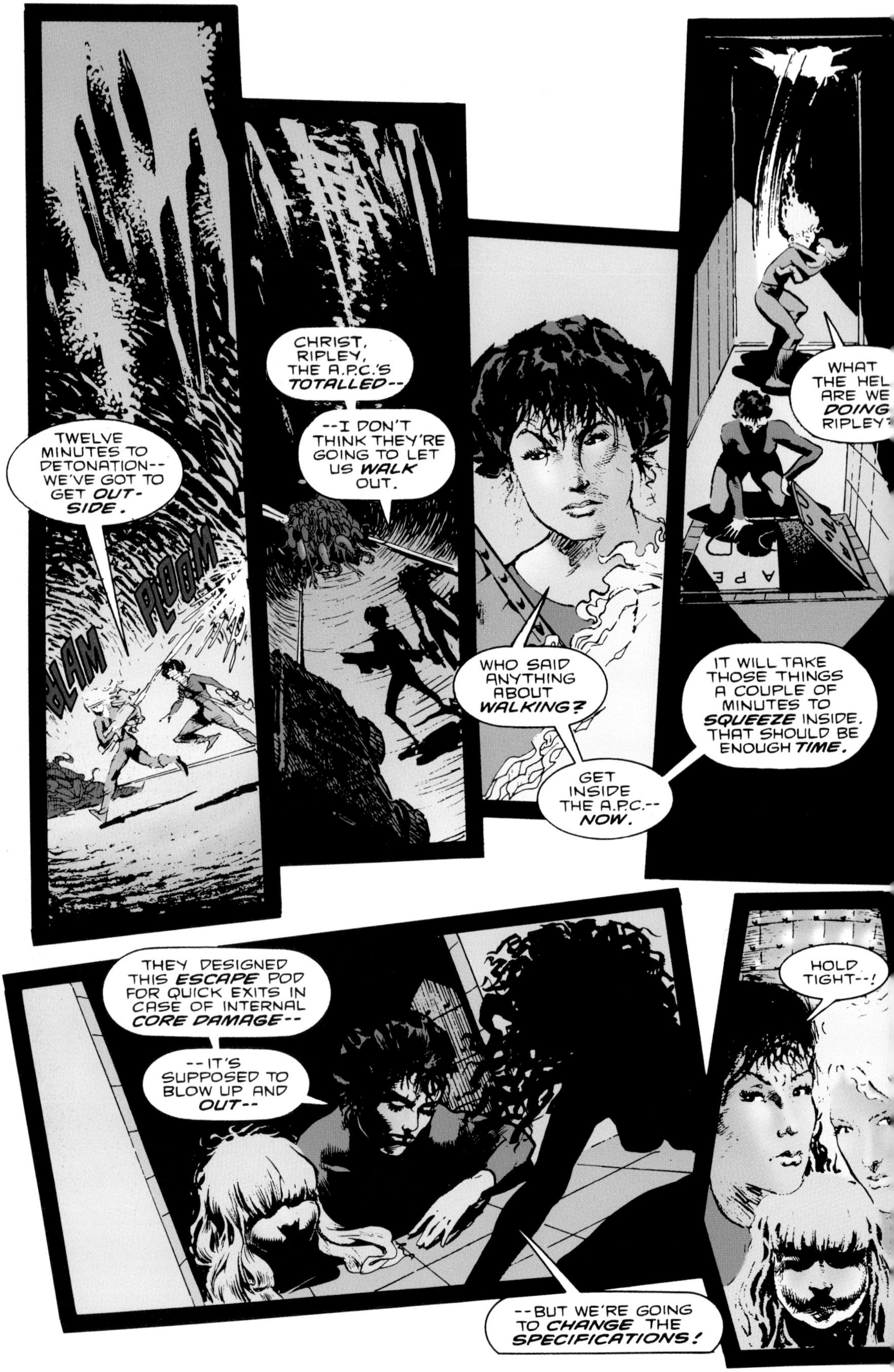
TWELVE MINUTES TO DETONATION-- WE'VE GOT TO GET OUT-SIDE.
BLAM
BLOOM
CHRIST, RIPLEY, THE A.P.C.'S TOTALLED--
--I DON'T THINK THEY'RE GOING TO LET US WALK OUT.
WHO SAID ANYTHING ABOUT WALKING?
GET INSIDE THE A.P.C.-- NOW.
IT WILL TAKE THOSE THINGS A COUPLE OF MINUTES TO SQUEEZE INSIDE. THAT SHOULD BE ENOUGH TIME.
THEY DESIGNED THIS ESCAPE POD FOR QUICK EXITS IN CASE OF INTERNAL CORE DAMAGE--
--IT'S SUPPOSED TO BLOW UP AND OUT--
--BUT WE'RE GOING TO CHANGE THE SPECIFICATIONS!
HOLD TIGHT--!

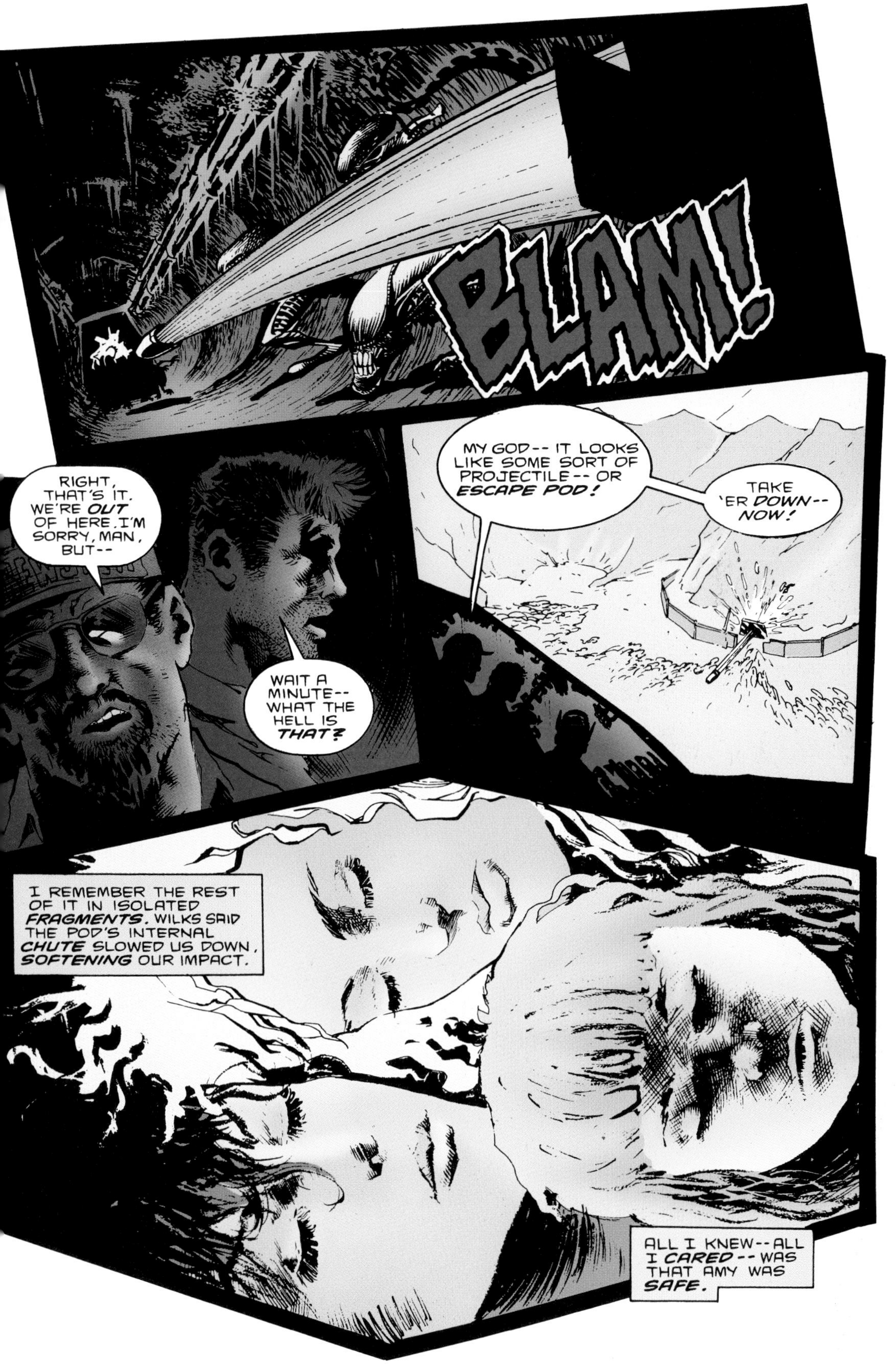
BLAM!
RIGHT, THAT'S IT. WE'RE OUT OF HERE. I'M SORRY, MAN, BUT--
WAIT A MINUTE-- WHAT THE HELL IS THAT?
MY GOD-- IT LOOKS LIKE SOME SORT OF PROJECTILE-- OR ESCAPE POD!
TAKE 'ER DOWN-- NOW!
I REMEMBER THE REST OF IT IN ISOLATED FRAGMENTS. WILKS SAID THE POD'S INTERNAL CHUTE SLOWED US DOWN, SOFTENING OUR IMPACT.
ALL I KNEW--ALL I CARED--WAS THAT AMY WAS SAFE.

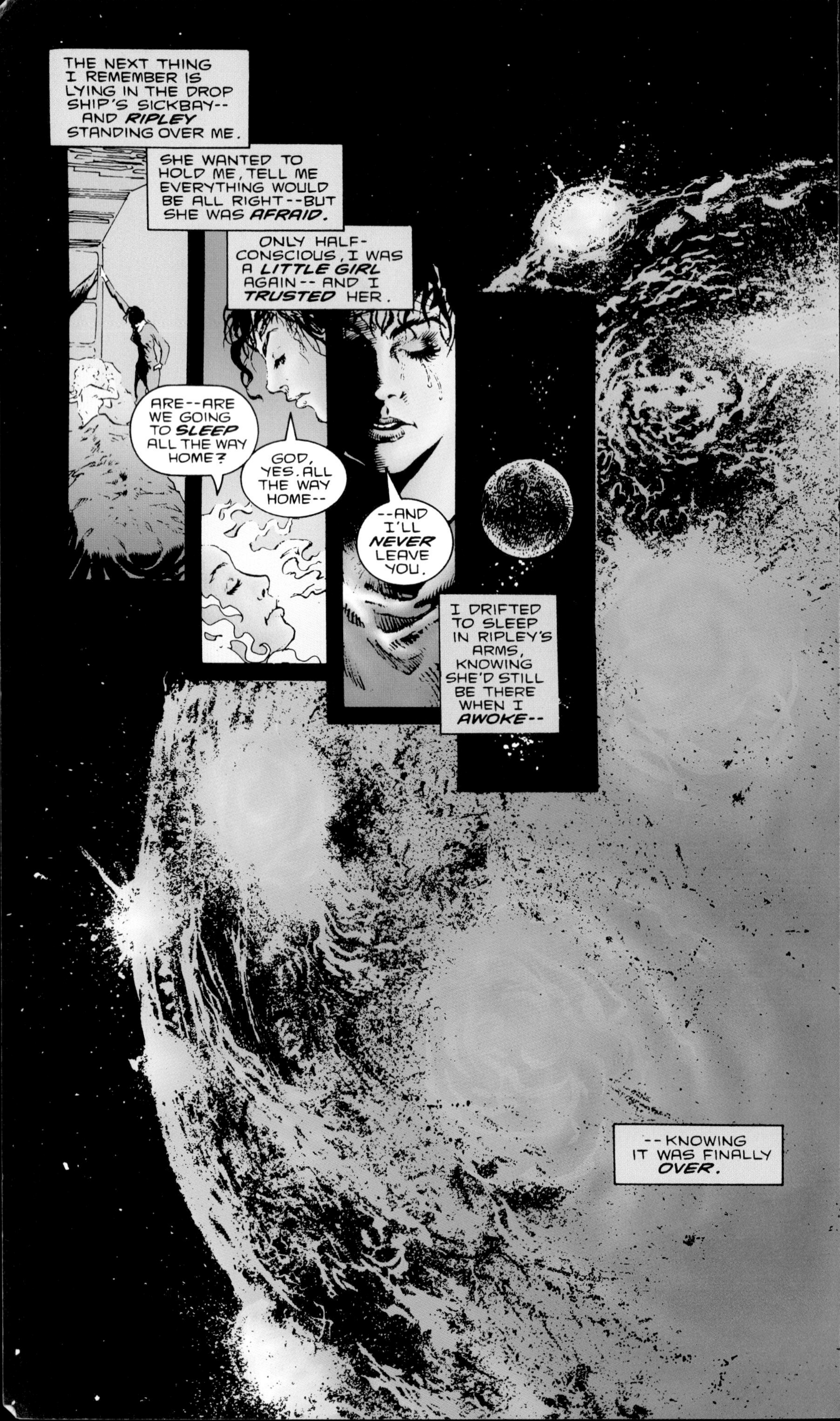
THE NEXT THING I REMEMBER IS LYING IN THE DROP SHIP'S SICKBAY-- AND RIPLEY STANDING OVER ME.
SHE WANTED TO HOLD ME, TELL ME EVERYTHING WOULD BE ALL RIGHT--BUT SHE WAS AFRAID.
ONLY HALF-CONSCIOUS, I WAS A LITTLE GIRL AGAIN-- AND I TRUSTED HER.
ARE--ARE WE GOING TO SLEEP ALL THE WAY HOME?
GOD, YES. ALL THE WAY HOME--
--AND I'LL NEVER LEAVE YOU.
I DRIFTED TO SLEEP IN RIPLEY'S ARMS, KNOWING SHE'D STILL BE THERE WHEN I AWOKE--
--KNOWING IT WAS FINALLY OVER.

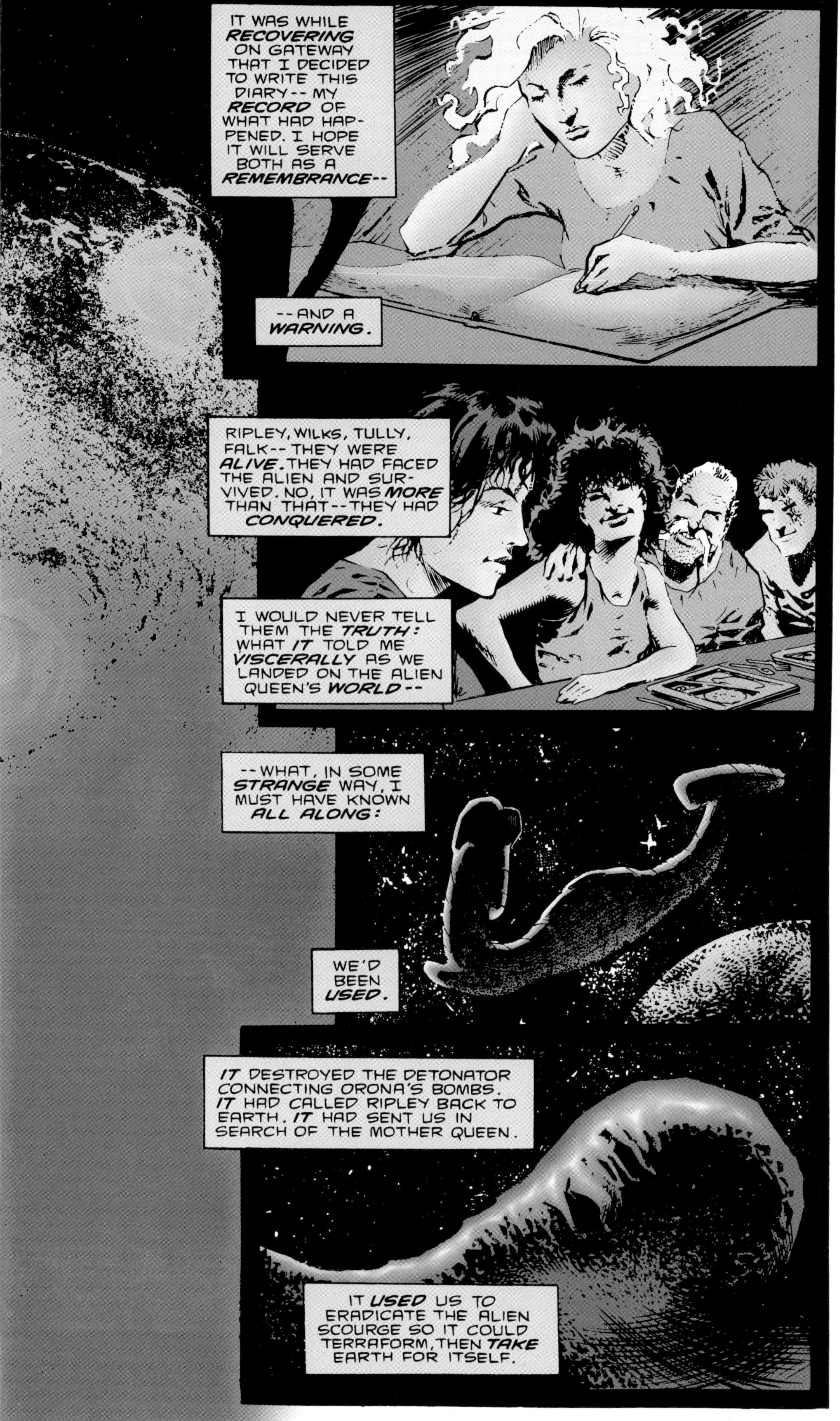
IT WAS WHILE RECOVERING ON GATEWAY THAT I DECIDED TO WRITE THIS DIARY-- MY RECORD OF WHAT HAD HAPPENED. I HOPE IT WILL SERVE BOTH AS A REMEMBRANCE--
--AND A WARNING.
RIPLEY, WILKS, TULLY, FALK-- THEY WERE ALIVE. THEY HAD FACED THE ALIEN AND SURVIVED. NO, IT WAS MORE THAN THAT--THEY HAD CONQUERED.
I WOULD NEVER TELL THEM THE TRUTH: WHAT IT TOLD ME VISCERALLY AS WE LANDED ON THE ALIEN QUEEN'S WORLD--
--WHAT, IN SOME STRANGE WAY, I MUST HAVE KNOWN ALL ALONG:
WE'D BEEN USED.
IT DESTROYED THE DETONATOR CONNECTING ORONA'S BOMBS. IT HAD CALLED RIPLEY BACK TO EARTH. IT HAD SENT US IN SEARCH OF THE MOTHER QUEEN.
IT USED US TO ERADICATE THE ALIEN SCOURGE SO IT COULD TERRAFORM, THEN TAKE EARTH FOR ITSELF.

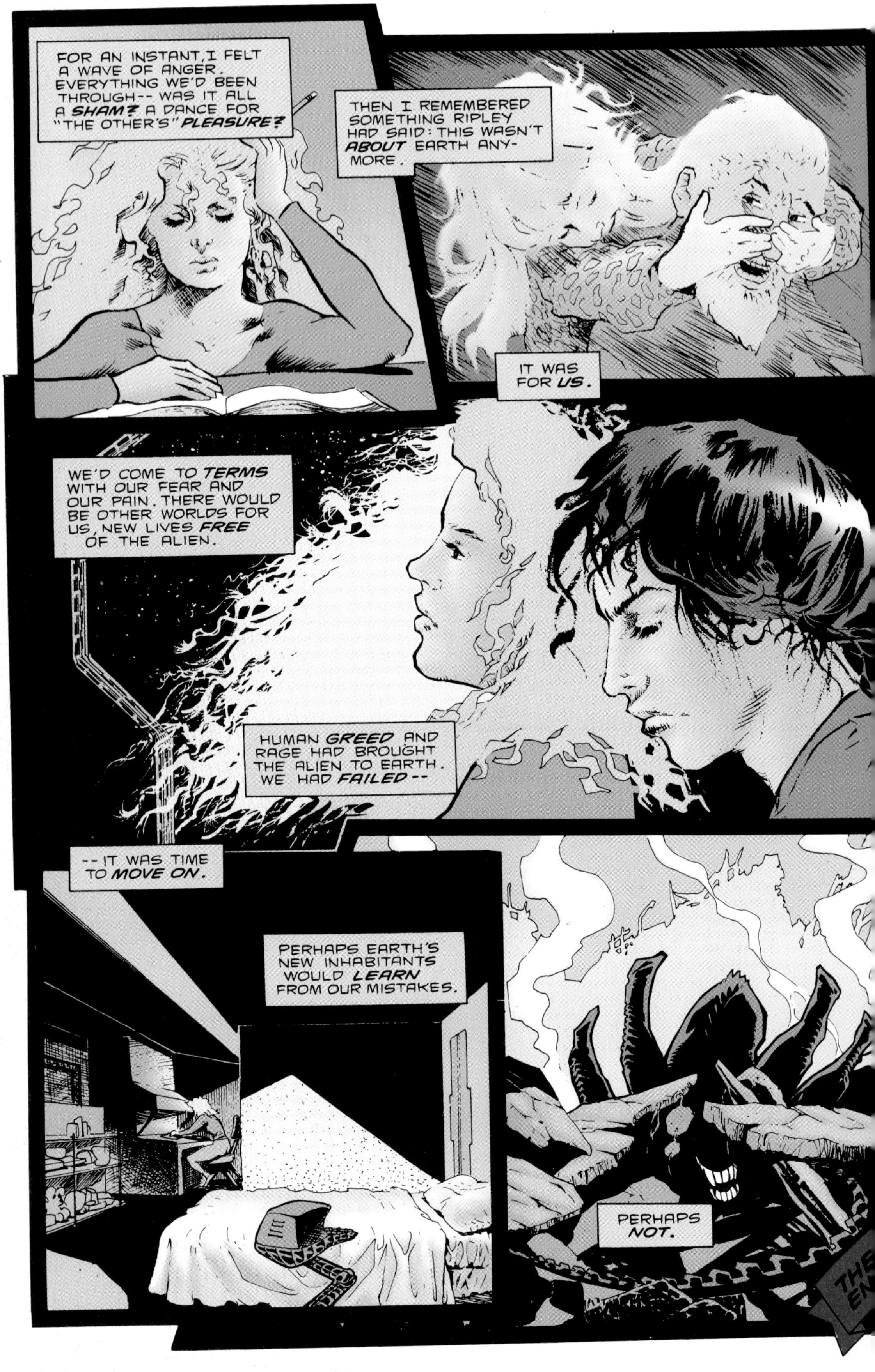
FOR AN INSTANT, I FELT A WAVE OF ANGER. EVERYTHING WE'D BEEN THROUGH-- WAS IT ALL A SHAM? A DANCE FOR "THE OTHER'S" PLEASURE?
THEN I REMEMBERED SOMETHING RIPLEY HAD SAID: THIS WASN'T ABOUT EARTH ANY-MORE.
IT WAS FOR US.
WE'D COME TO TERMS WITH OUR FEAR AND OUR PAIN. THERE WOULD BE OTHER WORLDS FOR US, NEW LIVES FREE OF THE ALIEN.
HUMAN GREED AND RAGE HAD BROUGHT THE ALIEN TO EARTH. WE HAD FAILED--
--IT WAS TIME TO MOVE ON.
PERHAPS EARTH'S NEW INHABITANTS WOULD LEARN FROM OUR MISTAKES.
PERHAPS NOT.

ALIENS ™

Biographies

Mark Verheiden started reading comic books at a very early age — his career dramatic evidence that funny books are ruinous to young minds. Mark's comic-book work includes *The American, Aliens, Predator,* and *Timecop* for Dark Horse, *The Phantom* for DC, and *Stalkers* for Marvel. His feature-film writing credits include *The Mask* and *Timecop,* as well as an episode of the HBO series "Perversions of Science." Mark lives in Pacific Palisades, California with his wife Sonja, son Ben, and an enormous compact-disc collection that threatens to sunder nearby fault lines.

Sam Kieth, a native Californian, worked in comics for ten years getting attention for his illustration of *The Sandman* for DC and for his *Marvel Comics Presents* covers. For Image, in 1993, Sam created *The Maxx,* a story about an ersatz superhero and Julie, his social-worker gal pal. Two years later, Sam was able to twist MTV's arm into adapting the series into a cartoon that went on to win an Annecy award in 1995. Currently, Sam writes and draws *The Maxx* and *Friends of Maxx* while he works on the screenplay for MTV's upcoming movie of *The Maxx.*

John Bolton spends far too much time painting in his eerie, prop-filled studio in North London. An award-winning artist who has worked on books with Chris Claremont, Neil Gaiman, Clive Barker, Sam Raimi, Anne Rice, and many others, and whose ethereal vampire-women and magical creatures have made his work much sought after, John has handled assignments for every major publisher in the comics field. His interest in the stylishly bizarre is evidenced throughout his work, and he currently has his own international fan club and magazine.

ALIENS™

FEMALE WAR

G A L L E R Y

London-born artist John Bolton got his first Aliens gig doing the covers for the *Aliens: Earth War* comic-book series. Following is a mere glimpse into the vast Bolton Alien Archives.

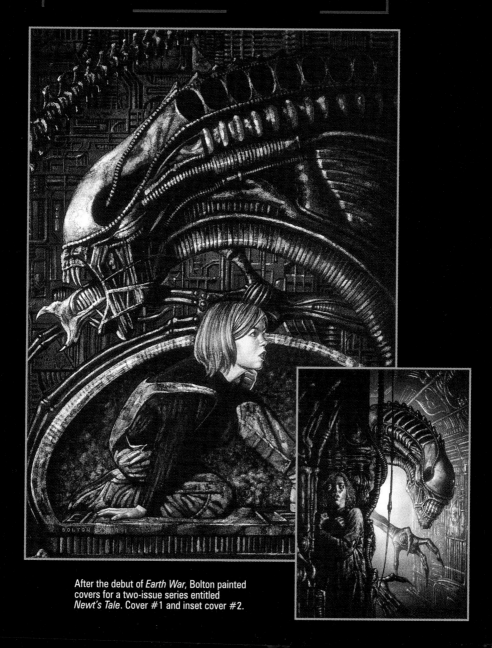

After the debut of *Earth War*, Bolton painted covers for a two-issue series entitled *Newt's Tale*. Cover #1 and inset cover #2.

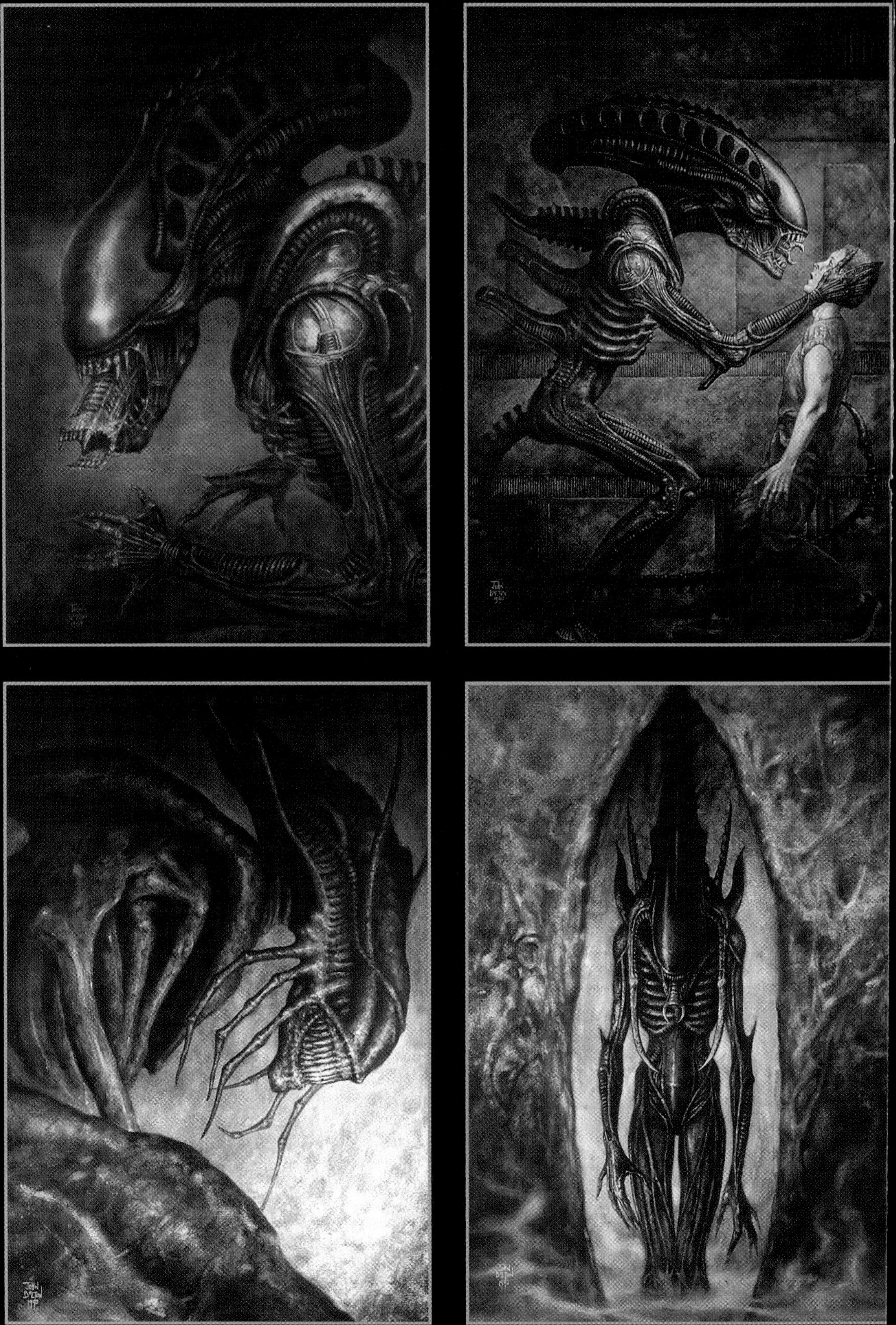

Clockwise from top left: the cover art for the four-issue *Earth War* series.

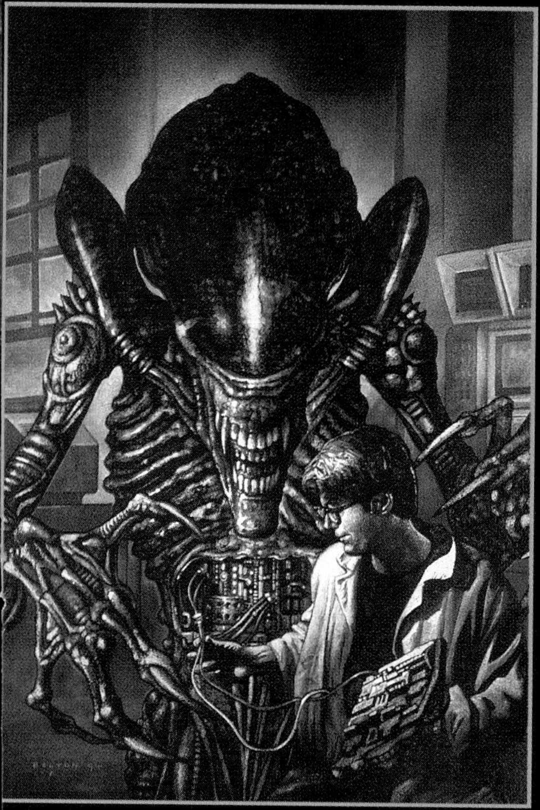

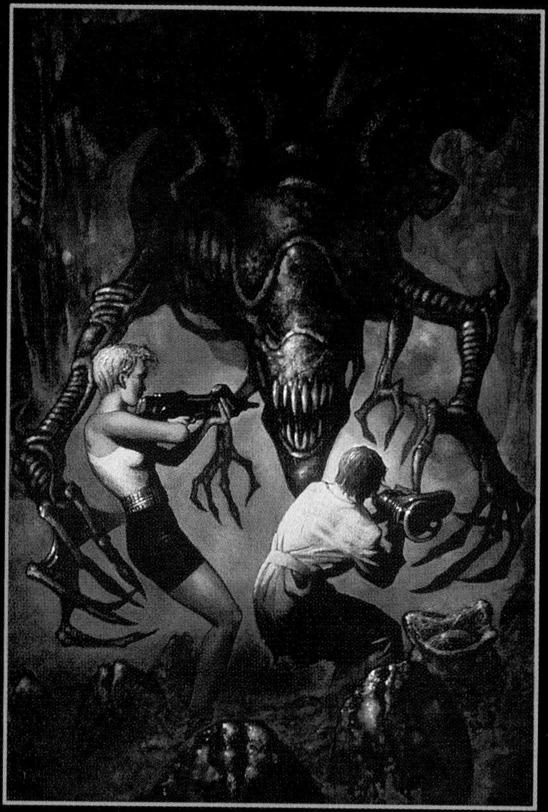

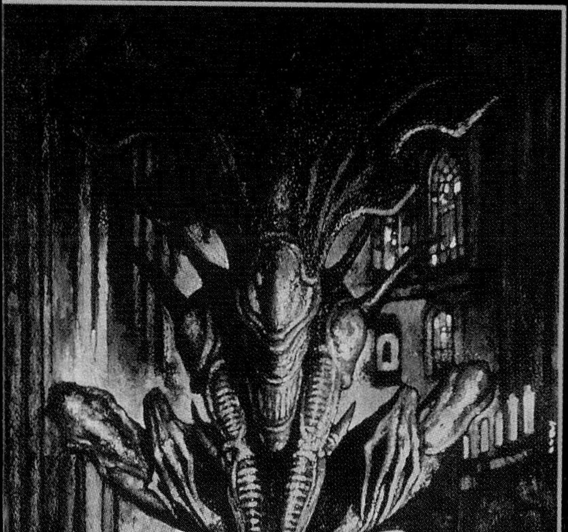

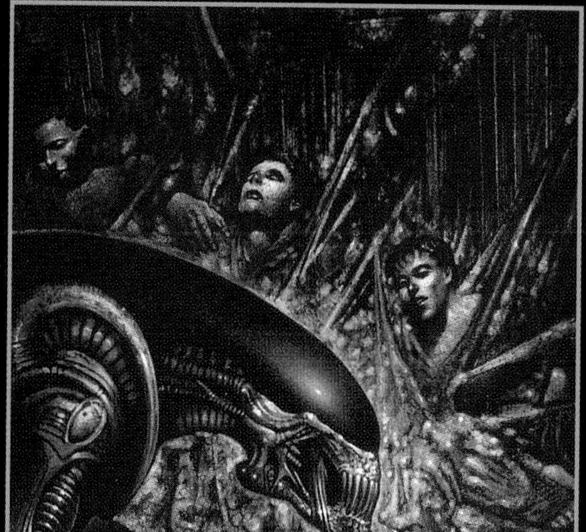

ockwise from top left: the Bantam novelization cover art for *Aliens: Harvest*, *Aliens: Rogue*, *Aliens: Labyrinth*, and *Aliens: Music of the Spears*.

ALIENS

VOLUME ONE
OUTBREAK
Verheiden • Nelson
176-page color paperback
ISBN: 1-56971-174-7 $17.95

VOLUME TWO
NIGHTMARE ASYLUM
Verheiden • Beauvais
112-page color paperback
ISBN: 1-56971-217-4 $16.95

VOLUME THREE
FEMALE WAR
Verheiden • Kieth
112-page color paperback
ISBN: 1-56971-190-9 $16.95

GENOCIDE
Arcudi • Willis • Story
112-page color paperback
ISBN: 1-56971-123-2 $14.95

HIVE
Prosser • Jones
112-page color paperback
ISBN: 1-56971-122-4 $14.95

LABYRINTH
Woodring • Plunkett
136-page color paperback
ISBN: 1-56971-110-0 $17.95

ROGUE
Edginton • Simpson
112-page color paperback
ISBN: 1-56971-023-6 $14.95

TRIBES
Bissette • Dorman
72-page color paperback
ISBN: 1-878574-68-X $11.95

STRONGHOLD
Arcudi • Mahnke • Palmiotti
112-page color paperback
ISBN: 1-56971-154-2 $14.95

ALIENS VS PREDATOR

ALIENS VS PREDATOR
Stradley • Warner
176-page color paperback
ISBN: 1-56971-125-9 $19.95

WAR
Stradley • Warner
200-page color paperback
ISBN: 1-56971-158-5 $19.95

DEADLIEST OF THE SPECIES
Claremont • Barreto
320-page color paperback
ISBN: 1-56971-184-4 $29.95

PREDATOR

BIG GAME
Arcudi • Dorkin • Gil
112-page color paperback
ISBN: 1-56971-166-6 $14.95

CONCRETE JUNGLE
Verheiden • Warner • Randall
112-page color paperback
ISBN: 1-56971-165-8 $14.95

COLD WAR
Verheiden • Randall • Mitchell
112-page color paperback
ISBN: 1-878574-79-5 $13.95

RACE WAR
Vachss • Stradley
144-page color paperback
ISBN: 1-56971-112-7 $17.95

PREDATOR VS MAGNUS ROBOT FIGHTER
Shooter • Ostrander • Weeks
64-page color paperback
ISBN: 1-56971-040-6 $7.95